Woodstock FAQ

Woodstock FAQ

All That's Left to Know About the Fabled Garden

Thomas Edward Harkins

Backbeat
Books

Guilford, Connecticut

Published by Backbeat Books
An imprint of The Rowman & Littlefield Publishing Group, Inc.
4501 Forbes Blvd., Ste. 200, Lanham, MD 20706
www.rowman.com

Distributed by NATIONAL BOOK NETWORK

The FAQ series was conceived by Robert Rodriguez and developed with Stuart Shea.

All images are from the author's collection.

Book design and composition by Snow Creative

Library of Congress Cataloging-in-Publication Data available
ISBN 978-1-61713-666-5 (paperback)

∞™ The paper used in this publication meets the minimum requirements of American National Standard for Information Sciences—Permanence of Paper for Printed Library Materials, ANSI/NISO Z39.48-1992

This book is dedicated to all of the members
of Woodstock Nation, past, present, and future.

You are stardust. You are golden.
Thank you for keeping our garden fertile and growing.

Contents

Acknowledgments

Though writing is by nature a solitary task, no one writes a book alone. The book you are about to read is the culmination of a lifetime spent reading about, listening to, and discussing the performers who played at the Woodstock Music and Art Fair . . . followed by nearly three years of researching, writing, and editing.

Woodstock FAQ: All That's Left to Know About the Fabled Garden began with one of those, "Hey, wouldn't it be cool if . . . " conversations I had with my cousin and agent, author and noted horseracing podcaster Peter Thomas Fornatale. Peter's late father, New York City disc jockey Pete Fornatale, wrote *Back to the Garden: The Story of Woodstock* in 2009, on the occasion of the festival's fortieth anniversary. I said, "Wouldn't it be cool if I wrote a book about Woodstock in time for the fiftieth anniversary in 2019, but take a different approach? You know, make it like a family tradition." Peter was on board.

I pitched the project to Bernadette Malavarca, who was then my editor at Hal Leonard/Backbeat Books, and an excellent musician in her own right. Bernadette is a calm and cool presence, a consummate professional, and always there, whenever I need her. She was into it, too. We went to contract before the end of June 2016, and I've been working on it ever since. I would also like to thank Backbeat Books' Carol Flannery, and Clare Cerullo, who took over as project editor in 2019, when Bernadette moved on to another phase of her career with a new company; and Tom Seabrook, who did such a fantastic job of copyediting.

The source documentation available through the Bethel Woods Center for the Arts and the Museum at Bethel Woods proved invaluable in this endeavor.

I would like to thank those friends and family members who pitched in with ideas, articles, photographs, festival anecdotes, or just plain enthusiasm. My parents, Thomas F. Harkins and Ann Marie Harkins, have financed many of my tools of the trade. My sister, Andrea Harkins, emailed lots of articles. Cousin Pete's better half, Susan Van Metre, executive editorial director at Walker Books, keeps a watchful eye on my career. Perrin Tamar Fornatale, just three when I began, will be nearly seven by the time you read this. USMC Sgt. Walter R. Wolford sent me a set of Woodstock-related photos. Sean Fodera helped me learn the ropes of the publishing business, particularly the ins and outs of understanding contracts!

Thanks to Steven Thompson, formerly of Hal Leonard/Backbeat Books, for Backwing, and for always being so helpful getting the word out.

A special thank you to Bernie Corbett, my co-author on *Pearl Jam FAQ*, who worked on several of Uncle Pete's books and provided me with audio and written transcripts of his many relevant interviews with the likes of Country Joe McDonald, Billy Cox, and Barry "The Fish" Melton.

I learned early on that radio disc jockeys are invaluable resources for projects like this, not only for the uncommon depth of their musical knowledge, but also for interviews and publicity! Thanks to some of my favorites, who have supported my work in various ways: Darren DeVivo and Don McGee of WFUV FM 90.7; Bobby Guthenberg and Tony Traguardo of WCWP FM 88.1; Don Grossinger and Bob O'Donnell, co-hosts of Morning Dew, now at its new radio home at WFDU FM 89.1; Gerry Martire, Ken Dashow, and Maria Malito of Q104.3 FM; Matt Cord of WMMR in Philadelphia; Meltdown from WRIF FM 101; Nick Digilio of WGN Radio; Giles Brown of Talk Radio Europe; and Michael O'Connor, host of Some Good Craic. On the print side, I thank Lynn Saxberg of the Ottawa Citizen (who interviewed Bernie Corbett and me for the *Pearl Jam FAQ*).

Dr. Cormac Sheehan, my fellow Woodstock researcher and scholar, was an encouraging presence via Skype, email, and Facebook, from County Cork, Ireland.

Sue Leventhal, of WHY Hunger, a former music manager and agent, for knowing . . . well, everyone, it seems. See you and all the good WHY folks at Hungerthon!

Brooklyn's own, the Canny Brothers Band: Stephen Canny, Thomas Canny, Michael Canny, Mick Bauer, Kevin Baynes, and last but never least, Keith Fallon. For you and all of your families, I am proud to be your friend, adopted sibling, and, along with Fred "Freddie the Sound Guy"

Pollice, your entire crew! Thanks to our fellow travelers on the local Irish festival scene, especially Shilelagh Law, and the Narrowbacks, for all your continuing support.

Thank you, Dean Russo of Dean Russo Art, and Joann Amitrano of Amitrano Gallery, for all of your support, both moral and material. Brixton Doyle, of Brixton Doyle Studio, another neighborhood artist I have known and admired since childhood, has been an enthusiastic supporter.

Some of the local yokels, the Brooklyn folks who either attended the festival and/or provided me with great material: Chip Cafiero, Pete Tracy (captured in the Woodstock film rocking out to Santana!), Joe D'Urso, Billy Murphy, Tom "T.A." Anthony, Paul DeWolfe of the Groove, and Cliff Goldfarb, who gave me an opportunity to work with Hot Tuna during the Raccoon Lodge's benefit concert for the Guild for Exceptional Children at Grand Prospect Hall on April 14, 2017. Jack Vobis, my former neighbor, whose in-laws, Ira and Maxine Stone, played the festival with Bert Sommer's band.

My old NYU Professor (and member of my abandoned doctoral committee), Salvatore J. Fallica, who attended the festival.

Professor Nancy Nevins, lead singer of Sweetwater, the band that was supposed to open the festival on Friday but was unavoidably detained.

Last but not least, a word on the epigraphs that begin each chapter. They are, unless otherwise indicated, snippets of interviews from the voluminous Pete Fornatale Radio Archives, which will soon be made available to the general public through the New York Public Library for the Performing Arts at Lincoln Center, and the Port Washington Library.

This book belongs to all of you, as much as it does to me.

Introduction

The Woodstock Music and Art Fair, billed as "an Aquarian Exposition at White Lake, New York," is considered by many to have been the definitive sociocultural event of the 1960s. It is also widely considered the most famous concert of all time.

Like a lot of music fans, I have been obsessed with the festival since childhood. But just to clarify: I was not there that weekend. I was merely a toddler, five months shy of my third birthday, and only beginning to discover the joys of music. Even if I had been there, under the watchful eyes of family, odds are good that I wouldn't have remembered much. Had I been older and attended the festival on my own, odds are still pretty good that my memories of the weekend would have been compromised in . . . ahem, other ways.

As I grew, I began to appreciate that we had a locally famous disc jockey in the family, Pete Fornatale. When Pete began his professional radio career at WNEW FM 102.7 on July 27, 1969, the first live commercial he read was a promotional spot for the Woodstock Music and Art Fair. Pete became a valued opinion leader who influenced my taste in, appreciation for, and knowledge of all types of rock and folk music. Thanks in large part to Pete, I managed to meet and have conversations with numerous professional musicians throughout my adolescence and early adulthood. If the musician had performed at Woodstock, invariably I would ask them about the festival. I learned that many of the artists' memories of the festival had become distorted by the passage of time . . . and, in some cases, by other things.

On Thursday, August 15, 2019, the Woodstock Music and Art Fair will celebrate its fiftieth anniversary. As that golden anniversary draws more clearly into focus, I am honored that Backbeat Books has afforded me the opportunity to make a contribution to the great conversation about Woodstock. It is a responsibility I take seriously.

Why Woodstock? What was it about this festival that makes it so important? Was it the first large, outdoor, multi-act, multi-day, rock and pop music festival? No, not exactly. There were already music festivals in the United States, from coast to coast. Ultimately, Woodstock would not even be the largest festival, though it was the largest by far up to that point.

Despite its name, the festival took place more than forty miles away from Woodstock, in the hamlet of White Lake in Bethel, New York. Several of the acts featured on the official poster never showed up, for one reason or another, while several artists who were not originally scheduled to perform wound up onstage. Among the acts that did appear, several held out to be paid cash in advance before performing, and many performances were impacted and pushed back by frequent rain delays, performers' issues, and equipment malfunctions.

The "Three Days of Peace and Music" promised on the festival posters turned out to be four days of relative peace, rain, confusion, and intermittent entertainment. Things got so dicey early on that Governor Nelson Rockefeller considered sending in the National Guard to break the whole thing up. One can only imagine the ugly scene had he done so.

How did this near-disaster of a festival half a century ago become so firmly embedded in our notions of 1960s American popular culture? In a word, film—specifically the movies. Sure, it was a big news story, especially here in the New York metropolitan area, and many remember the festival on that basis. Television, radio, newspapers, and magazines were all over the festival, before, during, and after. But were it not for the fact that filmmaker Michael Wadleigh and his crew documented every aspect of the festival (even the Port-o-Sans!), shooting one hundred and twenty miles of film on a thousand reels over the four days, the world may only dimly remember Woodstock.

Wadleigh edited those miles of raw footage down to just over three hours of material, and *Woodstock*, the Academy Award–winning Warner Bros film ("Best Documentary Feature"), premiered on March 26, 1970, to packed theaters from coast to coast. Make no mistake: this film, more than anything else, cemented the legacy of Woodstock in our collective unconscious.

Woodstock spawned an army of untold legions who convinced themselves that they were there that weekend, romping in the mud and watching history unfold. More than one writer has made the observation that if everyone who claimed to have been at Woodstock was actually there, the crowd would have numbered in the millions.

The film arguably had a greater impact on the artists featured in it, and on those artists left on the cutting-room floor. The measure of that impact must be considered on a case-by-case basis. Inclusion in or exclusion from *Woodstock* affected different performers in different ways, and I like to consider each case in its proper context.

I was not immune to the persuasive power of the film. Rational fellow though I consider myself to be, I went through a phase during high school when, as soon as I was physically able to do so, I grew mutton-chop sideburns in the fashion of Woodstock-era Joe Cocker. I even began crafting my own tie-dye T-shirts . . . though they weren't particularly good. A classmate at my 1985 graduation signed my yearbook, "May your life be a never-ending Woodstock." Sixteen years after the fact, that festival had become a part of our generation's reality. And so it remains today, thirty-four years further on. I suspect that it will always be so.

What is particularly striking to me is that, underneath all the rhetoric about sociocultural relevance and the impact of the festival—beyond the influence of the film, the soundtrack albums, and all the re-releases, director's cuts, and boxed sets over the years—there was one very big rock-and-roll concert.

How is it that the bands and the music always seem to get lost in the shuffle? For some performers, Woodstock was just another gig; it wasn't until later, upon further reflection, that they realized they had been a part of something special. Others recognized the magnitude of the moment immediately.

There were some extraordinary performances that weekend, to be sure, while others failed to meet expectations. Yet in too many descriptions of the festival, the music and the performers have been treated like an afterthought. The film and album version of events, and the performers' recollections in interviews and memoirs, have all served to shape the festival narrative from different—and often contradictory—perspectives.

My goal from the outset has been to correct that, and thereby restore some balance to the conversation.

Woodstock FAQ: All That's Left to Know About the Fabled Garden gives the performers and the music their due consideration. Who were they? Where did they come from? What songs did they play? What happened to them afterward? Those are the questions I wanted to explore. In as much as it was possible to do so, I have restored the chronological arc of the festival from concept to concert, to aftermath and enduring legacy.

The most challenging aspect of this project was conforming to the predetermined scale. I may be a Deadhead, but I am no George R. R. Martin, and this is no *A Song of Ice and Fire*. (Big fan, George; call me!) I had word-count limits and deadlines to contend with. This meant I had to curtail my natural inclination toward thoroughness and painstaking detail. I have never been the type to willingly make a long story short, so I had to constantly remind myself that I was writing one book about the entire Woodstock festival, and not thirty-something different books about every Woodstock-related person and performer simultaneously. It was always a temptation to go down the many "rabbit holes" I came across, but I resigned myself to the fact that not every anecdote or detail would make it to the final cut. I tried to picture someone telling Charles Dickens that he had to write like Ernest Hemingway, and that bizarre, time-warping image helped me find the discipline I needed.

"The garden" is the framing element and underlying metaphor. This serves to highlight not only the agrarian locale but also the illusory sense of Woodstock as some kind of idyllic hippie Eden or Utopia. It also evokes the lyrics of Joni Mitchell's "Woodstock," particularly as manifested in the Crosby, Stills, Nash, and Young version, which became the film's theme song.

The opening chapter considers the vision of Woodstock Ventures, as four very different young men worked together to stage the festival, and the narrowly averted disasters that threatened to derail it. I consider the roles of the major players and unsung heroes. Despite the best efforts of the organizers to control it, the festival took on a life of its own.

Each of the musical acts has a chapter devoted to them, some longer than others, in accordance with their pre-festival history and post-festival longevity. I consider each artist's life and career pre-Woodstock, their performance at the festival, and the impact of the festival on their lives and careers in the years since.

The final chapter considers the mediation of the festival: Michael Wadleigh's groundbreaking 1970 film, *Woodstock*, and how it shaped people's perceptions; the soundtrack albums and subsequent album and film releases of performances from that weekend. I also consider the attempts that have been made over the years to recreate the Woodstock festival, with varying degrees of success.

What is the enduring legacy of Woodstock in the twenty-first century? Many of those who made the festival possible are no longer with us. Even the youngest of the Woodstock performers, commonly thought to be Sha Na Na's Henry Gross (or was it really CSNY's bass player, Greg Reeves?), eighteen years old on that Monday morning, will be sixty-eight by the time of the fiftieth anniversary. The eldest, Ravi Shankar (unless you count fifty-five-year-old Hindu guru Sri Swami Satchidananda, who gave the invocation), forty-nine at the time, would have been ninety-nine, had he not passed away on December 11, 2012, at ninety-two.

Several Woodstock alumni passed away all too young in the years following the festival from the ravages of drug and alcohol abuse, which remains one of the darker legacies of the era. Rock and roll, like life itself, is a war of attrition, and we are losing the members of Woodstock Nation in ever-greater numbers. Who will shape the narrative that preserves their legacies when they are gone? Who will define the importance of the festival for future generations?

Finally, what—if anything—is the significance of the fiftieth anniversary of Woodstock in 2019? From certain perspectives, the world seems to be crying out for a healing of some kind. Is now the right time? And, if so, can we really get ourselves back to the garden?

Well, we can certainly try. And this is as good a place to begin as any. The soil is fertile. The furrows have been plowed. The seeds have been planted and watered. The sun is shining brightly. All one need do is turn the page . . . and let it grow.

—*Thomas Edward Harkins, June 6, 2016–January 21, 2019*

Woodstock Ventures, Inc.

Many Hands Make Light Work

As it happens, the night before these guys came to see us, I'd seen the movie *Monterey Pop*, which had been this fantastic documentary about a rock festival in California in 1967. And, you know, I had just been struck by the energy and the beauty and the music and the excitement of that particular event. And it really spoke to me. I was twenty-three years old at this point. And I said to Michael and Artie, I said, "You mean sort of like a *Monterey Pop*?" and they said, "No, no, no, nothing like that. You know, nothing big like that. Just a little, a little thing, maybe a couple of thousand people."

— John Roberts to WFUV's Darren DeVivo, 1999,
courtesy of the Pete Fornatale Radio Archives

As the Seeds Were Sown: From Dentures to Ventures

The four young men who came together to form Woodstock Ventures, Inc. were each accomplished in their own way, but came from very different worlds.

John Roberts

Roberts, a twenty-four-year-old University of Pennsylvania alumnus, inherited his fortune from the denture products Polident and Poli-Grip, and was eager to begin a lucrative business venture of his own, but he didn't know what, exactly. While golfing in 1966, he met his future business partner, Joel Rosenman, three years his senior.

Joel Rosenman

A twenty-seven-year-old native of Cold Spring Harbor, New York, Rosenman was already an accomplished man. An alumnus of both Princeton and Yale, he had dabbled in the music business as a performer before settling on venture capitalism. When he partnered with Roberts, one of the first major projects they launched was Media Sound Recording Studios. They also placed an ad in the local papers, looking for new ideas. That ad drew the attention of some interesting characters.

Artie Kornfeld

Brooklyn's Artie Kornfeld was twenty-six at the time of the festival. The Adelphi College alumnus had always shown a keen interest in rock and roll. He played the trumpet as a kid, before picking up the guitar at age fourteen. He was also a capable songwriter. The ambitious and talented Kornfeld was barely out of college when he became the youngest ever vice president of Capitol Records, where he shepherded hundreds of albums to the shelves. He met Michael Lang in 1968, and his whole world changed.

Michael Lang

Another Brooklynite, Michael Lang attended NYU, then moved to Florida, where he became the proprietor of a head shop. He attended the Fantasy Fair and Magic Mountain Festival on June 10 and 11, 1967, on Mount Tamalpais in California. Among the acts on the bill were Jefferson Airplane, Canned Heat, and Country Joe and the Fish. Though all but forgotten, this was the world's *first* rock festival.

Inspired, Michael began promoting music festivals in Florida. The Miami Pop Festival, which he co-produced, drew twenty-five thousand fans on May 18, 1968, to hear the Jimi Hendrix Experience, Frank Zappa's Mothers of Invention, Chuck Berry, John Lee Hooker, and Blue Cheer. In a bit of Woodstock foreshadowing, the second day's lineup was canceled on account of rain.

Michael moved back to New York State and settled in the town of Woodstock. He met Artie Kornfeld in New York City, where the two bonded over the dream of opening a recording studio in Woodstock. One day, Michael and Artie were looking through the *New York Times* and the *Wall Street Journal*, when they came across the following ad: "Challenge International, Ltd.: Young men with unlimited capital looking for interesting, legitimate investment opportunities and business propositions."

All Together Now

Artie and Mike went to meet with John and Joel at their apartment on 83rd Street and pitched them the idea of building the upstate recording studio. John and Joel were underwhelmed, and suggested an alternative: how about a small concert featuring some of the local bands? But Mike and Artie had their hearts set on the studio. After some discussion, Roberts and Rosenman proposed a compromise. As Roberts recalled in a conversation with WFUV's Darren DeVivo, "We said, 'Okay, fine, we'll do the rock festival first'—we thought of it then as a party—'we'll do the party, we'll charge admission and we'll use the profits to build a recording studio.' And since they had nowhere else to go, and they had about as much credibility as we did, which is to say none at all, 'Well,' they said, 'Sure, that sounds fine to us.' So that's how Woodstock was born."

Woodstock Ventures, Inc. was off and running. The four men opened an office at 47 West 57th Street and began running ads in *Rolling Stone* and the *Village Voice*. By April, they'd signed Creedence Clearwater Revival for $10,000, which led to a parade of performers signing on.

Not in *My* Backyard

The next order of business was securing a location. The town of Woodstock was the preferred spot, but no logical site presented itself. Joel and John had a meeting about a potential spot in Saugerties, and then laid out $10,000 to lease the three-hundred-acre Mills Industrial Park in Wallkill. Not to worry, they told town officials, there'd only be fifty thousand people. They proceeded with plans and began constructing a stage. But the town board balked, passing a law that required them to have a permit—which they were then *denied*—for any gathering of more than five thousand people.

The *Times Herald Record* reported that the town had "declared war on the proposed rock-folk festival." The Wallkill Zoning Board of Appeals officially banned the festival on July 15. All of this negative press turned out to be great publicity. A solution, albeit a costly one, would present itself thirty miles to the north, in the town of Bethel.

1-2 Original Woodstock Poster.jpg: Wallkill or bust! Somehow the original poster just doesn't capture the spirit of rock 'n' roll . . . or folk music, for that matter.

Partners and Backers

In addition to the four partners of Woodstock Ventures, *hundreds* of people played a role in bringing the festival to fruition, among them Bill Hanley and his sound crew, Chip Monck and his lighting and stage crew, the Joshua Light Show, film crews, photographers, stagehands, roadies, carpenters, plumbers, electricians, food vendors, the US Army, the National Guard, Bill Graham and his Fillmore East staff, local law-enforcement officials, Hugh Romney and the Hog Farm, the townspeople of Bethel . . . even the famous "Port-o-San man" (see: *Woodstock*, the film). Deserving as all of these people are of recognition, the scope of this project will not allow for a full accounting of their contributions, though a few key players bear mentioning.

Eliot Tiber: No Vacancy

The owner of the El Monaco Motel, Eliot Tiber held a permit to host live musical performances, and after reading about the Wallkill ban, he offered to host Woodstock Ventures' "party" on the fifteen-acre grounds of his motel. He also claims to have introduced Michael Lang to Max Yasgur, but Lang recalls that in fact Tiber introduced him to a local real-estate agent, who in turn introduced him to Yasgur. But Tiber made out pretty well for himself when he got the concession to sell tickets for the festival, and he would later parlay his experiences into a book and a film.

Max Yasgur: He's a Farmer

New York University alumnus Max Yasgur (Real Estate Law) ran the largest dairy operation in all of Sullivan County, and he knew a good opportunity when he saw it. On July 20, he sat down at the Lighthouse restaurant in White Lake to talk business. For $75,000, Yasgur would rent Woodstock Ventures a fallow, six-hundred-acre alfalfa field where they could stage the festival. They shelled out another $25,000 to adjoining neighbors for the use of their land as campgrounds and parking lots.

The configuration of Yasgur's field was ideal, as it sloped downward to form a natural amphitheater, with Filippini Pond serving as a border

WOODSTOCK
MUSIC AND ARTS FAIR

JIMI HENDRIX   JANIS JOPLIN

♪ AUGUST 15-16-17 - 1969 ♪
THREE DAY PEACE AND MUSIC FESTIVAL

★ FRIDAY THE 15th - Joan Baez, Arlo Guthrie, Richie
Havens, Sly & The Family Stone, Tim Hardin,
Nick Benes, Sha Na Na

★ SATURDAY THE 16th - Canned Heat, Creedence
Clearwater, Melanie, Grateful Dead, Janis Joplin
Jefferson Airplane, Incredible String Band, Santana
The Who, Paul Butterfield, Keef Hartley

★ SUNDAY THE 17th - The Band, Crosby Stills Nash
and Young, Ten Years After, Blood Sweat & Tears
Joe Cocker, Jimi Hendrix, Mountain, Keef Hartley

AQUARIAN EXPOSITION
WHITE LAKE, NEW YORK

1-1 Woodstock flyer In hindsight, this flyer advertising the festival got the basic idea right, but the actual event turned out to be quite a bit different.

to the north. Woodstock Ventures took out a $3 million insurance policy to cover any damages. But not everyone in Bethel was happy. Someone put up a sign in town that read, "Stop Max's Hippie Music Festival. No 150,000 hippies here. Buy no milk."

David Edward Byrd: Artistic Visions

Finding the right marketing tone for the festival proved to be a challenge. Psychedelic posters were all the rage at concert venues during the late 1960s. David Edward Byrd, resident artist of the Fillmore East, designed the first official poster for Woodstock, when the festival was still scheduled to take place in Wallkill. The poster featured a nude woman surrounded by flowers, hearts, doves, and cherubs, but no mention of any bands. The wording at the top read, "Woodstock Music and Art Fair Presents," and at the bottom, "An Aquarian Exhibition. Wallkill, NY. August 15–16–17." Conservative local shop owners had no idea what an "Aquarian Exhibition" might be, but they wanted no part of it. Most refused to display the poster.

Arnold Skolnick: Designing Man

Next, the partners hired Arnold Skolnick, a slick Madison Avenue ad exec who intuited that the "less is more" approach would work here. It was Skolnick who came up with the iconic image of a white dove resting on a guitar neck, and the slogan "Three Days of Peace and Music." This became the official poster for the festival. It retained the wording and dates from the Byrd original, but changed the locale to "White Lake, NY (a hamlet of

1-3 Woodstock Poster   Brilliant in its simplicity, the classic Woodstock logo, featuring a dove on the neck of a guitar, has long since become iconic. Often imitated, and frequently parodied, it has become a part of American folklore.

Bethel, located on the southeast shore of its namesake lake)," and added the names of the performers, the scheduled start times, and sections labeled "Art Show," "Crafts Bazaar," and "Food." The new poster promised "Hundreds of Acres to Roam On." But even with all of the added verbiage, it was the image of the dove on the neck of the guitar that stood out.

Michael Wadleigh

Artie Kornfeld secured a down payment of $100,000 from Warner Bros executive Fred Weintraub to film the festival. Ohio filmmaker Michael Wadleigh, twenty-six, got the nod, and assembled a crew of a hundred people to handle the task. There would be several camera crews in operation, covering every aspect of the festival. All told, Wadleigh's crews would use one thousand reels of film to cap ture one hundred and twenty miles of raw footage.

Hugh Romney

A native of East Greenbush, New York, Romney was an army veteran and alumnus of Boston University's theater program. While working at the Gaslight Café in Greenwich Village, he had signed a contract with comedian Lenny Bruce, who brought him to Los Angeles in 1962.

Romney fell in with the Merry Pranksters, a group of followers of the author Ken Kesey who lived communally on Kesey's ranch in La Honda, California. They would gain fame—or perhaps notoriety—for their 1964 cross-country journey aboard a fabled Day-Glo-painted school bus named *Further*. When Prankster Ken Babbs absconded for Mexico at the wheel of *Further*, the remaining Pranksters found themselves in a predicament. Romney rented an apartment in the San Fernando Valley, but the landlord disapproved of the Pranksters crashing there, and evicted them.

A nearby hog farm needed help, so Romney and his friends agreed to work the farm in exchange for room and board. The Hog Farm commune was born. By 1966, the Hog Farm had become a professional entertainment organization.

When they got wind of Woodstock, the Hog Farm and the Merry Pranksters answered the call to serve as the Woodstock festival's staff—or what Romney called the "Please Force." (Though he is now better known to the world as "Wavy Gravy," that name did not exist until blues legend B.B. King bestowed it upon him two weeks after Woodstock, at the Texas International Pop Festival.)

John Morris

The straight-laced, thirty-year-old manager of Bill Graham's Fillmore East proved to be a godsend to the inexperienced Woodstock Ventures crew in many ways, and his contributions would fill a book of their own. It was John who figured out how to make Woodstock a "free concert," and he who announced it from the stage. He would also handle most of the master-of-ceremonies duties during Friday's lineup, before recruiting a certain golden-throated lighting director to take over.

Chip Monck

Edward Herbert Beresford "Chip" Monck, a thirty-year-old Massachusetts native with a booming baritone, was a lighting director, and had worked the Monterey Pop Festival and the Newport Folk and Jazz Festivals, among others. Chip spent ten weeks putting together the staging and lighting for a mere $7,000, but due to the last-minute change in venue, the job was still incomplete at showtime. Beginning on Saturday, Chip was deputized as master of ceremonies, making stage announcements and introducing many of the acts.

Hassles

Some Bethel residents remained vehemently opposed to the festival. They filed a lawsuit, forcing the promoters to add more portable toilets. By Wednesday, as the crowds began arriving, some locals linked hands and tried to form a human barricade across Route 17B in an effort to keep them out.

On Thursday morning, it finally occurred to the promoters that there was no infrastructure in place to collect tickets, and there were already fifty thousand people sitting in the field. With people pouring in by the minute, they had no choice but to declare it a free concert from that point forward.

The three hundred New York City Police Officers they'd hired to guide festival attendees toward parking spots in the rented fields got the word from their commissioner that they would be fired for moonlighting at the festival. So nobody parked in the fields, traffic backed up, and people began abandoning their cars along the sides of the road.

As Thursday gave way to Friday, John Morris and Bill Hanley returned from a night out with the crew and decided to test the P.A. When they looked out in the growing light of dawn, they beheld hundreds of thousands of people, far more than the seventy-five thousand they'd been expecting. And so the first words spoken over a live microphone that weekend were Morris's: "Holy shit!"

In the Garden: Showtime, Ready . . . or Not

Determining the lineup for the bands proved to be an adventure, and remained in a constant state of flux. Not every performer that was scheduled would make it to Bethel, and some of those that did make it arrived late. Others, such as the Moody Blues, dropped out when the venue switched from Wallkill to Bethel. A *lot* of acts—or their management—just said no, including Led Zeppelin, the Doors, the Byrds, Raven, Tommy James and the Shondells, Frank Zappa's Mothers of Invention, Love, Free, Spirit, Mind Garage, Lighthouse, Procol Harum, and Jethro Tull. Blues Image had been keen to sign but the group's management balked.

The most bizarre refusal came from "Hollywood Cowboy" Roy Rogers. Michael Lang had a vision of Rogers closing the festival with his signature tune, "Happy Trails." Rogers declined.

And then there were the cancelations.

Chicago Transit Authority

Though originally scheduled to appear, Chicago Transit Authority was also under contract with Bill Graham. In a power play designed to showcase Santana instead, Graham booked Chicago Transit Authority to play a show at his Fillmore West on August 17, forcing the group to withdraw from Woodstock. The band was *not* happy.

Joni Mitchell

The Canadian singer/songwriter was initially scheduled to appear, but because she was promoting her sophomore album, *Clouds*, managers Elliot Roberts and David Geffen decided it would be better for her to remain in New York City, so she could appear on the post-festival episode of *The Dick Cavett Show* on Monday instead.

It's a Beautiful Day

It would not be a beautiful day for the band It's a Beautiful Day. The group was disinvited . . . *supposedly*. Legend has it that while Bill Graham was lobbying for Santana to be put on the bill, Lang flipped a coin to determine whether he would sign Santana or It's a Beautiful Day. Santana evidently won the toss.

The Jeff Beck Group

The Jeff Beck Group featured Ron Wood on bass, Aynsley Dunbar on drums, Rod Stewart on vocals, Nicky Hopkins on keyboards, and Jeff himself on lead guitar. On the eve of Woodstock, after playing several other East Coast dates, including July 4 at the Newport Jazz Festival, Beck disbanded the group. The enterprising Nicky Hopkins would turn up anyway (see chapter 23).

Iron Butterfly

Perhaps the most comical conflict involved Iron Butterfly. The band got stuck at LaGuardia Airport en route to Bethel. The group's manager sent a telegram to John Morris, who asked for time to resolve the issue. In response, the manager demanded that the organizers send a helicopter to pick up the band immediately. Furthermore, he *demanded* that Iron

Butterfly be paid up front, take the stage immediately on arrival, and then be flown straight out afterward. This was one demand too many. Morris got on the phone with a Western Union operator and sent the following cleverly coded telegram:

> For reasons I can't go into
>
> Until you are here
>
> Clarifying your situation
>
> Knowing you are having problems
>
> You will have to find
>
> Other means of transportation
>
> Unless you plan not to come

Translation: "Fuck you." Morris wouldn't be sending any helicopter, and Iron Butterfly would not be performing in Bethel that weekend.

We Want the Show! We Want the Show!

On Friday, August 15, the sun rose at 6:08 a.m. and shone upon a chaotic scene. The field was packed with a sea of humanity. The roads were virtually impassable, so the organizers would have to hire helicopters to shuttle the musicians between their hotels and the festival site.

The 4:00 p.m. start time came and went with nary a chord being struck. The scheduled opening act, Sweetwater, was running late, and the crowd was growing restless. Michel Lang was getting desperate, so he called on Richie Havens. He wasn't scheduled to play until much later in the evening, but he'd take one for the team . . . or *would* he?

2

Richie Havens

Is There a Musician in the House?

When I was flying back in this big, transport helicopter, there were two bands on either side of us . . . the door [was] wide open, and I'm looking out at the trees. I flashed, "This is what Vietnam is like, right now. This is what soldiers see when they look out this door." I imagined tracer bullets coming up out of the trees at us, because you could see no roads . . . just treetops. And it was green, and beautiful, and you're going, "This beauty and all of this stuff could come at you, and that's negative." And I was flashing on that. I then looked up and down the row that I was sitting against, the wall, all of us band members, and I happened to notice that here are all of these tie-dyed people with guitars sitting up in their laps like rifles a soldier might be holding, sitting in the same position. And the basses between their legs on the floor, like soldiers might be sitting in the same position in this Army transport helicopter. I went, "This is the real army, now! They're actually transporting the real army."

— *Richie Havens to Pete Fornatale, 1994*

As the Seeds Were Sown: From Bed-Stuy to Bethel

Richard Pierce Havens was born on January 21, 1941, in Bedford-Stuyvesant, Brooklyn. His mother was of British West Indian descent, and his father was of Blackfoot American Indian descent. Richie's paternal grandfather and great uncle had been performers in

Buffalo Bill's Wild West Show. They came to New York by way of the Shinnecock Reservation, before settling in Brooklyn.

Growing up, Richie displayed a talent for art, and became known for his portraiture. He was enamored with the sounds of doo-wop, and formed a number of street corner a cappella groups. He became involved with church music, and joined the McCrea Gospel Singers during his teens. He then developed a fascination with folk music, and in 1960 he migrated to Greenwich Village. He had been into the beatniks and poetry, so folk music was a natural step in his creative progression.

Encouraged by a neighbor—Noel Paul Stookey of Peter, Paul, and Mary fame—Richie decided to pick up a guitar and get in on the action. His efforts were rewarded. Word spread that Richie was a must-see act, and industry types came calling. He cut two records for Douglas Records before signing a deal with manager Albert Grossman. Under Grossman, Richie released his 1966 debut album, *Mixed Bag*. Douglas Records, looking to cash in, would later release those earlier recordings as a pair of unauthorized albums, *Electric Havens* and *Richie Havens' Record*, in 1968 and 1969, respectively.

Mixed Bag features three of the songs Havens would play at Woodstock, including the opening number, a cover of Billy Edd Wheeler's "High Flyin' Bird"; Gordon Lightfoot's "I Can't Make it Anymore"; and an original, "Handsome Johnny," which he co-wrote with the actor Louis Gossett, Jr. The album is considered by many to be Havens's finest work. *Mixed Bag* revealed that Richie could write a song as well as anyone, but his true gift was for interpreting the songs of others. His next "official" release was 1968's *Something Else Again*, which contains five originals and a cover of Bob Dylan's "Maggie's Farm." But none of those songs would find their way to the Woodstock stage.

In May 1969, Richie released a truly ambitious project, *Richard P. Havens, 1983*, a double album that mixed live recordings with studio recordings, many of them Beatles covers; *too* many, for some critics' taste. Why "1983?" Richie says this was supposed to be a "concept" album, though he never made it clear what the *concept* was, other than that it represented a year in the future. But he must have been doing something right, for a *double* album to hit #80 on *Billboard*'s Pop Albums chart.

Richie Havens's official 1966 debut, *Mixed Bag*, inspired New York City disc jockey Pete Fornatale to adopt the album's name for his groundbreaking WNEW FM 102.7 radio program.

This album allowed Richie to develop his skills in other areas, too. He had a hand in the production, and his overall sound evolved from pure folk into an amalgam of folk, rock, and what is loosely known today as "world music." It had a more complex and exotic sound than his earlier recordings. His cover of the Beatles' "Strawberry Fields Forever" would find its way to Woodstock. All four sides of the album featured Beatles covers, with one Bob Dylan and one Donovan tune thrown in for good measure.

He released several of these songs as singles in the months leading up to the festival, and his performance schedule was fairly light. He played Forest Hills Tennis Stadium on July 19, hit the Mississippi River Festival on the 22nd, and did two dates at Kinetic Playground in Chicago on the 25th and 26th. Then it was on to Bethel a couple of weeks later.

In the Garden: Mr. Havens to the Stage . . . *Please*?

Richie Havens was slated to perform fifth on Friday, and he was operating under that assumption back at the hotel, seven miles from the site, with his bandmates Paul "Deano" Williams and Daniel Ben Zebulon.

Meanwhile, bass player Eric Oxendine had become stuck in traffic and abandoned his car. He grabbed his bass and began to walk the remaining fifteen to twenty miles to the stage. Despite the length of the journey, Oxendine was actually able to make it in time for Havens's *original* starting slot. But because of the last-minute schedule change, his efforts proved to be in vain. He would miss the show.

When the 4:00 p.m. starting time came and went, the festival organizers scrambled to come up with a Plan B. Logic dictated that starting with a solo artist, or an artist with only a few instruments, made more sense than trying to get a full band up there, and nobody was around anyway.

Tim Hardin would have been the logical choice, because he was already on site. But he was also drunk, strung out on heroin, and absolutely terrified at the prospect of opening the festival in front of this enormous audience. So the organizers put in a call to Richie at the hotel, and told him a helicopter was on its way to pick him up.

The concert was only a little over an *hour* late when John Morris grabbed a microphone and said, "Ladies and gentlemen, one of the most beautiful men in the whole world, let's welcome Mr. Richie Havens." It was 5:07 p.m. when Havens (lead guitar and vocals), Williams (rhythm guitar and vocals), and Zebulon (conga drums and vocals) took the stage. Meanwhile, oblivious to the whole thing, Oxendine was hiking down the road.

While re-stringing and tuning his guitar, Richie nervously addressed the audience. "A hundred million songs are gonna be sung tonight. All of them are going to be singing about the same thing, which I hope everybody who came, came to hear, really. And it's all about you—actually—and me, and everybody around the stage and everybody that hasn't gotten here, and the people who are gonna read about *you*, tomorrow. Yes. And how really groovy you were—all over the world, if you can dig where that's at—that's really where it's really at."

And then he began. Among the songs he played were "Minstrel Came Down from Gault," "From the Prison / Let's Get Together / From the Prison" (medley), "I'm a Stranger Here," "High Flyin' Bird," Gordon Lightfoot's "I Can't Make It Anymore," a trio of Beatles tunes ("With a Little Help from My Friends," "Strawberry Fields Forever," and "Hey Jude"), "Handsome Johnny," and "Freedom (Motherless Child)."

This last song was created spontaneously. Richie addressed the crowd: "Freedom isn't what they've made us even think it is, we already have it, all we have to do is exercise it. And that's what we're doing right here." Then he started strumming his guitar, just jamming, and the first word to pop out of his mouth was "freedom." The crowd responded enthusiastically. In a flash of inspiration, he incorporated "Motherless Child" (ironically, a staple of Sweetwater's set), with a snippet of lyrics from his gospel youth, "I've got a telephone in my bosom / And I can call him from my heart." And history was made. The crowd roared its approval. John Morris took the mic for the back-sell. "Mr. Richie Havens. What better way to start than with the beautiful Richie Havens?"

The Harvest Reaped: How Really Groovy We Were

How groovy were we? Probably not *quite* as groovy as Richie would later remember, if his calculations of "grooviness" were anything like his calculations of crowd size, or his recollections about the length of his own set.

Though the best available estimates put the peak crowd size at 450–500,000, Richie was quoted for decades claiming that the actual crowd size was *much* larger: "The number really was 850,000 . . . 850,000 people came together and had a good time," he told Pete Fornatale in 1994.

It remains unclear how he arrived at this figure, but it is nearly *double* most reliable estimates. His recollections about his set were also wildly distorted. While the preponderance of evidence suggests that he played ten or twelve songs (depending on how you keep score) over the course of roughly forty-five minutes to an hour, Richie frequently claimed that he played for much, *much* longer. "Two and a half hours—two hours and forty-five minutes later, as I walked off the eighth time, they said, 'No, no one's here yet, go back.'"

Richie's recollections are a good indication of how the festival grew to mythic proportions in the minds of the American public, whether they had been there or not. Performers were not immune.

Havens's impromptu, take-one-for-the-team performance at Woodstock would define the remainder of his professional life. He would go on to release sixteen more studio albums, up to and including 2008's *Nobody Left to Crown*. He also released two live albums and eight compilations, among an overall total of twenty-nine LPs (counting the unauthorized Douglas releases). He attained his greatest chart success with his seventh album, 1971's *Alarm Clock*, which reached #29 on the *Billboard* Top 200. That album's live cover of the Beatles' "Here Comes the Sun" would later reach #16 on the charts as part of the soundtrack for the 2006 film *The Hoax*.

In 2000, Richie published an autobiography, *They Can't Hide Us Anymore*, co-written with noted horse-racing writer Steve Davidowitz. Three years later, he was awarded the American Eagle Award by the National Music Council. In 2006, he was inducted into the Long Island Music Hall of Fame.

In later years, he appeared in a few films, including 2007's *I'm Not There* and 2009's *Soundtrack for a Revolution*. But age and health-related issues had begun to take a toll. He underwent surgery for kidney disease in 2010, and never fully recovered. By 2012, he had announced that he was retiring from the road. On April 22, 2013, he suffered a fatal heart attack at his home in Jersey City. He was seventy-two years old. On August 18, 2013, his ashes were scattered from an airplane over the festival site in Bethel Woods. As Richie always added, whenever he signed anything, he remains "A Friend Forever."

Richie Havens Two years after the festival, Richie's 1971 album *Alarm Clock* would prove to be his greatest commercial success, "clocking in" at #29 on the *Billboard* 200.

3

Sweetwater

Better Late Than Never

Thank you very, very much. We were supposed to be on first today, but they gave us a police escort here driving, and the man had to stop and bust us all before he could escort us here, so it took a little while. But we're on now, and, as the Maharishi said, in Indian, "Kick out the jams, folks!"

—*Albert Moore*

As the Seeds Were Sown: From the Coffee Houses of Los Angeles

It all began at the Scarab, a coffeehouse near Los Angeles City College. In April 1967, a loose collective of local musicians billed as Jaywalker and the Pedestrians was playing an open-mic set. In walked a seventeen-year-old high-school senior from Glendale High School named Nancy Nevins, who wowed the crowd by belting out an old Negro spiritual called "Sometimes I Feel Like a Motherless Child."

In May, Keyboard player Alex del Zoppo tracked down Nancy and asked her to join the Pedestrians. She bailed out after just one Hollywood gig because there were too many people on the stage—twenty-six, by some counts. But Alex was determined, and he talked some of his fellow Pedestrians into forming a new band with Nancy on lead vocals. Still nameless, this new band's members attended the Monterey Pop Festival as fans. There, Nancy and flute player Albert Moore walked to a nearby stream. When Nancy scolded Albert for drinking from the stream, he

Sweetwater, the band's 1968 debut album, cracked the *Billboard* 200. The opening track, "Motherless Child," was also a staple of Richie Havens's set, and would become one of a handful of songs played by more than one artist that weekend.

replied, "Oh, chicken, this water's good; it's sweet water." That was it. "Sweetwater!" they said, and the others agreed.

Sweetwater, a multicultural octet with a genre-defying sound and an eclectic array of instruments, played its first gig at a July 2 "Love-In" at the Crystal Springs Picnic Area, for a crowd of ten thousand. The band members then honed their chops in the coffeehouses of Los Angeles, playing a heady fusion of folk, blues, jazz, and rock. They would spend much of 1968 and 1969 touring in support of local legends the Doors. They also opened shows for Big Brother and the Holding Company, and Eric Burdon and the Animals. And, along the way, they caught the attention of Warner Bros/Reprise Records.

The group released its 1968 debut, Sweetwater, to somewhat modest acclaim. The album did manage to crack the *Billboard* 200, but this would prove to be the high-water mark of the group's commercial success. Sweetwater released "Motherless Child" b/w "Why Oh Why" as a single, along with "My Crystal Spider" b/w "What's Wrong." Neither of these singles charted, but "Motherless Child" caught some traction on FM radio, mainly in the group's hometown of Los Angeles, where it was soon in heavy rotation.

This local radio exposure, coupled with a solid reputation as an opening act, was enough to keep Sweetwater on the music-business radar and earn the group an invitation to Woodstock. But apart from having a good reputation among industry insiders, the band was largely unknown on the East Coast.

Sri Swami Satchidananda: The Invocation

While waiting for Sweetwater, an unscheduled guest took to the stage to bestow his blessings upon the proceedings: fifty-five-year-old Yogiraj (master yogi) Sri Swami Satchidananda. His invocation, and the resulting segment in the *Woodstock* film, catapulted him into the public consciousness. Here are the words he spoke, while sitting cross-legged atop a large cushion:

My beloved brothers and sisters, I am overwhelmed with joy to see the entire youth of America gathered here in the name of the fine art of music. In fact, through the music, we can work wonders. Music is a celestial sound, and it is the sound that controls the whole universe, not atomic vibrations. Sound energy, sound power, is much, much greater than any other power in this world. And, one thing I would very much wish you all to remember is that with sound, we can make—and at the same time, break. Even in the warfield, to make the tender heart an animal, sound is used. Without that war band, that terrific sound, man will not become animal to kill his own brethren. So, that proves that you can break with sound, and if we care, we can make also.

So I am very happy to see that we are all here gathered to create some sounds—to find that peace and joy through the celestial music. And I am really very much honored for having been given this opportunity of opening this great, great music festival. I should have come a little earlier to do that job, but as you all know, thousands of brothers and sisters are on the way, and it's not that easy to reach here.

America leads the whole world in several ways. Very recently, when I was in the East, the grandson of Mahatma Gandhi met me and asked me what's happening in America. And I said, America is becoming a whole. America is helping everybody in the material field, but the time has come for America to help the whole world with spirituality also. And, that's why from the length and breadth, we see people—thousands of people, yoga-minded, spiritual-minded. The whole of last month I was in Hawaii and I was on the West Coast and witnessed it again.

So, let all our actions, and all our arts, express yoga. Through that sacred art of music, let us find peace that will pervade all over the globe. Often we hear groups of people shouting, "Fight for peace." I still don't understand how they are going to fight and then find peace. Therefore, let us not fight for peace, but let us find peace within ourselves first.

And the future of the whole world is in your hands. You can make or break. But you are really here to make the world and not to break it. I am seeing it. There is a dynamic manpower here. The hearts are meeting. Just yesterday I was in Princeton, at Stony Brook in a monastery, where about two hundred or three hundred Catholic monks and nuns met and they asked me to talk to them under the heading of "East and West—One Heart." Here, I really wonder whether I am in the East or West. If these pictures or the films are going to be shown in India, they would certainly never believe that this is taken in America. For here, the East has come into the West. And, with all my heart, I wish a great, great success in this music festival to pave the way for many more festivals in many other parts of this country.

But the entire success is in your hands, not in the hands of a few organizers. Naturally, they have come forward to do some job. I have met them. I admire them. But still, in your hands, the success lies. The entire world is going to watch this. The entire world is going to know what the American youth can do to the humanity. So, every one of you should be responsible for the success of this festival.

In the Garden: Hey, Sorry We're Late

When Sweetwater hit the stage at around 7:30 p.m., there was still plenty of daylight left. The group offered the crowd a mea culpa, explaining the reason for the delay. Lead vocalist Nancy "Nansi" Nevins, flautist Albert Moore, cellist August Burns, keyboardist Alex Del Zoppo, guitarist Harvey Gerst, bassist Fred Herrera, conga player Elpidio Cobain, and drummer Alan Malarowitz had clearly come to party. Their set, which lasted approximately forty minutes, began with the first repeat song of the festival, "Motherless Child," a version of which had been embedded in Richie Havens's "Freedom" earlier that afternoon. Their other tunes included "Look Out," "For Pete's Sake," "Day Song," "What's Wrong," "My Crystal Spider," "Two Worlds," "Why Oh Why," and a medley of "Oh Happy Day" / "Let the Sunshine In."

It bears mentioning that the finale included a snippet of "Let the Sunshine In," which many will recognize as a classic song from the musical *Hair*. This was a timely selection on Sweetwater's part, considering that the next performer to grace the Woodstock stage, Bert Sommer, had recently starred as "Woof" in the critically acclaimed Broadway production of the play. Sweetwater cleared the stage at 8:10 p.m. to enthusiastic applause, leaving just enough daylight for Sommer to begin his set without the aid of the stage lights.

The Harvest Reaped: Accidents Happen

The band's appearance at the festival was enough to keep them in the public eye through December 1969, when they appeared as musical guests on *The Red Skelton Show*. But tragedy struck on December 8th.

While en route to Silver Lake on the Ventura Freeway, Nancy was involved in a devastating automobile accident. It was raining, and she had narrowly missed a multi-car pileup. When she pulled over to the shoulder, she was violently rear-ended by a speeding drunk driver. Nancy was rendered comatose and suffered brain damage as well as damage to her vocal chords. She would never record with the band again, she would never tour with them again, and she would never fully recover. (She did have a few tracks already recorded, which the band would release subsequently.)

With the waning of the 1960s, Sweetwater began the new decade as a wounded band, but the remaining members were determined to carry on. Their sophomore album, *Just for You*, was released in 1970, with the others taking turns on lead vocals to work around Nancy's absence.

The following year found Sweetwater back in the studio for a final effort, *Melon*. Neither of these albums went anywhere, and the band broke up that summer. But the creative force is strong, and the ties that bind band members together are often as powerful as family relationships. The world had not heard the last of Sweetwater.

After multiple surgeries and years of rehabilitation, Nancy Nevins recovered enough to be able to record an eponymous solo album in 1975, but it barely made a ripple. The Sweetwater story became one of attrition.

Cellist August Burns died in the 1980s, as did drummer Alan Malarowitz, who was involved in a fatal car accident in 1981. His demise was eerie, considering Nancy's accident twelve years earlier. The next decade proved just as cruel, with flautist Albert Moore succumbing to complications from pneumonia in 1994. The eight-member band was now down to four, one of whom, percussionist Elpidio Cobain, had undergone a career change, and was now employed in the film industry. Miraculously, with the Woodstock Music and Arts Fair approaching its silver anniversary, the trio of Nancy Nevins, Fred Herrera, and Alex Del Zoppo reunited as Sweetwater, just in time to perform at Woodstock '94.

The novelty of the group's appearance sparked a renewed interest in Sweetwater. VH1, by this time one of the key arbiters of pop culture in the United States, commissioned a made-for-television film chronicling the ill-fated band's history. The result, *Sweetwater: A True Rock Story*, starring Amy Jo Johnson and Michelle Philips as the younger and older Nancy, respectively, was released to mixed reviews in 1999, in time for the thirtieth anniversary of Woodstock.

In keeping with the old adage that a rising tide lifts all boats, Rhino Records attempted to capitalize on the renewed interest in Sweetwater by releasing a numbered and limited-edition, ten-thousand-copy run of a compilation of the band's early work, *Cycles: The Reprise Collection*.

Six years after the devastating car accident that very nearly killed her, Nancy Nevins released her debut solo album. Little did she know that one day she would be teaching college and known as "Professor Nevins." And you think *your* professor is cool.

Finally, three years later, Sweetwater released a live album, *Live at Last* (2002).

Nancy Nevins is the living embodiment of the word "survivor." The near-fatal automobile accident was but one of the obstacles she had to overcome, yet she persevered, earning a bachelor's degree in American Studies and a master's in English while beginning a new career in education.

Along the way, she endured six throat surgeries, back surgery, foot surgery, traumatic brain injury, and bouts of alcoholism and drug dependence, recovery and sobriety, marriage and divorce. She teaches English at the college level, and continues to tour and perform. She has become a staunch advocate for veterans of the American armed services, and works tirelessly on their behalf. As of this writing, she has been unable to persuade her surviving bandmates to reunite Sweetwater, though she would be very happy to do so.

4

Bert Sommer

Singing for the Setting Sun

Bert Sommer. Just the mention of his name still brings a big smile to my face, and even that has a little bit of irony attached to it, because "Smile" was one of Bert's best songs, and the one he chose to close his Woodstock set with. "Smile, 'cause we all need one another / And it only takes a song to understand." Bert understood—he never gave up on the Woodstock dream. If he were with us here today—years after his hippie hat trick, I could easily imagine him saying, "Yeah. Hair, Woodstock," and, "We're All Playing in the Same Band." That and a Metrocard could get me a New York subway ride!

—*Pete Fornatale,* Back to the Garden: The Story of Woodstock

As the Seeds Were Sown: A *Hair*-Raising Tale

Bert William Sommer was born under on February 7, 1949, in Long Island, New York. During his teenage years he became good friends with Michael Brown, who would go on to form a band called the Left Banke.

During 1967, Sommer briefly joined Brown as the lead vocalist of a renegade offshoot of the Left Banke to record the single "Ivy Ivy" b/w "Suddenly." He also hung around with fellow Long Islander Leslie West, and wrote a total of five songs for West's band, the Vagrants (see chapter 17).

The year 1968 found Sommer pursuing his other love—acting—and he soon replaced Steve Curry, the original "Woof," in the hit musical *Hair*.

That same year, he signed a recording contract with Artie Kornfeld at Capitol Records. His debut album, *The Road to Travel*, was released later that year, but did not sell well. The cover art featured a full headshot of Sommer with a serious, almost somber expression on his angular face. All eleven tracks are relatively short, in keeping with the radio-friendly customs of the day. They include "And When It's Over," "Jennifer," "Things Are Goin' My Way," "She's Just a Girl," "Tonight Together," "The Road to Travel," "She's Gone," "Hold the Light," "A Simple Man," "Brink of Death," and "A Note That Read." The LP, barely more than a half-hour in playing time, was Sommer's only studio release prior to Woodstock.

In the Garden: *"Hair"* Today

In a perfect world, twenty-year-old Bert Sommer would have been the darling of the Woodstock festival. He was the quintessential hippie, with his voluminous afro gracing the cover of a recent *Playbill* (for *Hair*).

The Road to Travel, Bert's 1968 debut album. Woodstock Ventures' Artie Kornfeld, also of Capitol Records, was instrumental in Sommer's early career.

"We're All Playing in the Same Band," a single inspired by Bert Sommer's experiences at Woodstock. Sadly, the quintessential hippie prototype did not enjoy the post-festival career bounce of some of the other acts who appeared that weekend.

Moreover, Sommer was Artie Kornfeld's client, and Kornfeld was banking on the fact that the festival would introduce Sommer to a wider audience.

The singer had a distinctive high, sweet, and melodic voice, and many who were in the audience that evening attest to the fact that Sommer's twilight rendition of Paul Simon's "America" was one of the highlights of the weekend. It seemed in that place and at that moment as though Sommer had everything going for him. And yet his performance has been all but forgotten, and to say that his post-festival career was underwhelming would be putting it kindly.

Bert Sommer and his prodigious "hair" strode to the stage about twenty minutes past eight that Friday evening, with fading light from the 7:58 p.m. sunset still glowing in the western sky. He carried only an acoustic guitar, but he would have some help. Playing in the same band was guitarist Ira Stone, who also played a Hammond B-3 organ and, at times, a harmonica. Stone's wife, Maxine, sang backup vocals, and Charlie Bilello played the bass. The haunting, cathedral-like sound bore more than a passing resemblance to that of the Left Banke. It was perfect for the sunset tableau, and the crowd responded enthusiastically, as the festival seemed to be hitting its stride.

Sommer and his band ran through ten short songs in a set that lasted barely forty minutes. Ira Stone had the presence of mind to make an audio recording of their performance, and in the ensuing decades that tape has become the definitive aural document of it. Apart from the twilight capture of "Jennifer," there is no other publically available footage of Sommer's set. As one would expect, six of the songs he performed were from his Kornfeld-produced debut, *The Road to Travel*.

Sommer had been working on new material, and he played some of it that night. In addition to "Jennifer," he and his band played his debut album's title track, "The Road to Travel"; "I Wondered Where You Be," which would not appear until his eponymous third album; "She's Gone"; "Things Are Goin' My Way"; "And When It's Over"; "Jeanette," which does not appear on any album; the aforementioned cover of "America"; "A Note That Read"; and, finally, the almost anthemic "Smile," which would appear as the opening track on his sophomore album, *Inside Bert Sommer*, the following year.

At one point, the set inspired the crowd to stand and cheer—a gesture that would later prompt the self-deprecating Sommer to joke that the crowd gave him a standing ovation only because they were on their way to the bathrooms. In a possible foreshadowing of Bert's later career misfortunes, John Morris mispronounced his name as he left the stage, appending it with an extra s: "The rather magnificent Bert Sommers."

The Harvest Reaped: Gone Tomorrow

Post-festival, Sommer entered the studio to record his second album, *Inside Bert Sommer*, for Artie Kornfeld's Eleuthera Records. Like many festival alumni, Sommer was inspired to pen a song about that weekend. Sommer's—which he actually wrote while he was still *at* the festival site—was called "We're All Playing in the Same Band." The album also contains a studio version of his Paul Simon cover, "America," which garnered a rave review from Rhymin' Simon himself. Unfortunately for Bert, commercial success continued to elude him.

Sommer's performance was not included on either of the Woodstock soundtrack albums. Michael Wadleigh's team declined to use any of the film footage, shot during the waning of Friday's light, so he would not appear in the movie, either. His omission from *all* of the officially released media about the festival was arguably a factor in his sketchy post-festival career—a circumstance that Sommer bore with good humor and cheer.

He remained undaunted, releasing a *third* album, the eponymous Bert Sommer, on Buddah Records in 1971. The third time, however, was not the charm, and he soon turned his attention back to acting. Television-watching preteens during the 1970s got to see him as "Flatbush," a short-lived character who, for the 1976–1977 season at least, was a member of the fictional band Kaptain Kool and the Kongs on *The Krofft Supershow*.

In essence, Kaptain Kool and the Kongs were the centerpiece of the show, performing as host and house band simultaneously. The goofy role found Sommer sporting a decidedly less impressive coif than the one he wore during his Woodstock days and clad in an outrageous purple suit, with a feather in his hat.

After his "Kaptain Kool" days were over, Sommer returned to making music and performing. He released another self-titled album in 1977, on Capitol Records. It was the last album he would ever record, as he became plagued by health issues. A chronic respiratory condition led to his untimely death at age forty-one on July 23, 1990.

Sommer's festival performance was officially released in 2009 as part of a six-CD boxed set called *Woodstock: 40 Years On: Back to Yasgur's Farm*. The newly released material at last provided music fans with the opportunity to hear what they had been missing all these years, and to ponder what might have been. Smile. And the world smiles with you.

5

Tim Hardin

Troubled Troubadour

He was, rest his soul, gone. He was one of the people who, but for
circumstances which they brought on themselves, could have had
a career that went forever. We didn't know that, but his Woodstock
appearance could have been one of the biggest things that ever happened to him. Everybody loved Hardin. He was a great folk artist. But
he was wasted; those things just mounted up against him. He didn't
do a good performance. He didn't capture the people.

—*John Morris, Pete Fornatale Radio Archives, 2009*

As the Seeds Were Sown: Tim Hardin, United States Marine

Tim Hardin's tale is among the saddest in the annals of music history. He was a gifted songwriter and interpreter of other artists'
work. He had the respect and the good will of his peers. Unfortunately
he also had what was known colloquially at the time as a "monkey on his
back."

Our tale begins in Oregon. James Timothy Hardin was born in Eugene
on December 23, 1941, to Hal and Molly Hardin. Both parents had musical backgrounds, and Molly was classically trained. But Hardin's childhood remains something of a mystery; not much is known about him
during these years, beyond the fact that he enjoyed acting. He was often
noncommittal about his father during interviews, and has been quoted
as comparing his childhood home to a "prison." He managed to make it

most of the way through South Eugene High School before dropping out at eighteen to join the United States Marine Corps.

With a background like this, it isn't surprising that Hardin had an edge to him. He is remembered as being a bit "aggressive" and supremely confident in his musical abilities. His life also reveals some hard truths about one of the less obvious dangers facing American military personnel in Vietnam: the ready access to opiates. His two-year tour of duty was enough to make him a veteran, but it was also enough to make him a junkie. It was a burden he would bear for the rest of his days.

After his discharge, Hardin moved to New York City. He enrolled at the American Academy of Dramatic Arts in 1961, and hung out on the Greenwich Village folk scene with the likes of John Sebastian. But Hardin wasn't really the going-to-school type. A pattern of cutting classes and accumulating unexcused absences ultimately led to his dismissal.

On the Village circuit, Hardin was known as more of a blues guy than a folk guy. A brief move to Boston in 1963 landed him his first recording contract, when a producer named Erik Jacobsen—who would go on to work with John Sebastian and the Lovin' Spoonful—took a liking to Hardin, became his manager, and landed him a deal with Columbia Records.

Upon his return to New York in 1964, Hardin hit the studio and recorded tracks for Columbia. But those tracks were never released, and the prestigious label dropped him. To be fair, this initial misstep may not have been Hardin's fault. Accounts vary, but there is evidence to suggest that the company just got cold feet and pulled the plug on the album.

The following year found the restless spirit headed west, this time to California, where his personal life hit an upswing. He met and fell in love with an actress, Susan Yardley (born Susan Yardley Morss), and, by 1966, the couple had moved back to New York City. His professional life seemed to be on the rise, too. At age twenty-five, thanks to the efforts of Jacobsen and his partners, Charles Koppleman and Don Rubin, Hardin signed a new record deal with Verve Forecast Records, a label related to Folkways, home of the famed recording executive Moe Asch.

A single, "How Can We Hang On to a Dream," was released in February 1966, preceding the album release by five months. And that's how his official July 1966 debut album, *Tim Hardin 1*, came to be. By the

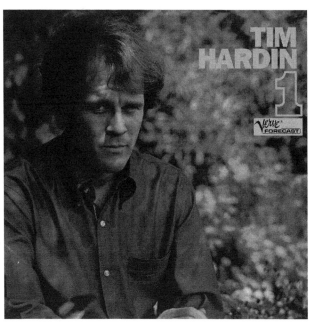

And so it began, with *Tim Hardin 1*, in 1966, the former US Marine's debut album. His facial expression here hints at the burdens he already bore. Soon they would consume him.

time the album was released, Tim and Susan were back living in L.A. On February 28, 1967, the couple welcomed the birth of their son, Damion.

Among the album's gems were the Top 40 hit "Misty Roses" and the infectious "Reason to Believe," which would go on to be covered by more than *thirty* artists, most notably Rod Stewart, who released it as a single. The album's relative success led to the almost predictable appearance of *This Is Tim Hardin* on the Atco label, featuring—you guessed it—the songs he had originally recorded for Columbia Records several years earlier. Hardin and his team were reportedly "furious" at this shameless attempt to cash in on his work by a label that had previously dropped him.

Not to be outdone, Verve Forecast counterpunched in 1968 with a live album, *Tim Hardin 3 Live* in Concert, which showcased a gig at New York City's elegant Town Hall. The label doubled down on its budding star by releasing *Tim Hardin 4*, which emptied the vaults of those remaining unreleased recordings, and fulfilled Hardin's contractual obligation to Verve Forecast. His success there led to Columbia *re*-signing him and promptly releasing a single of him doing a Bobby Darin tune, "Simple Song of Freedom," which cracked the *Billboard* Top 50.

All of this stood Hardin in good stead leading up to the Woodstock festival. But his health was always in question during these years. Not only had he been a stone-cold junkie since returning from Vietnam, he had also been diagnosed with pleurisy in 1967. Pleurisy, an inflammation of the chest cavity surrounding the lungs, is a particular burden for singers, because the condition makes it painful to breathe. And, as if all this wasn't enough, despite his aggressiveness and self-assuredness, Hardin suffered from debilitating stage fright. This confluence of conditions caused him to screw up a *lot* of gigs. He would often be running late, or not show up at all, and he was developing a reputation for being unreliable. It got to the point where no one wanted to book him.

John Morris took a leap of faith and offered Hardin a spot at Woodstock. But one has to wonder whether Hardin would have agreed to play, had he known ahead of time just how large the audience was going to be. Would he have bothered to show up at all? We'll never know for certain. But knowing a little bit more about the man does give one an appreciation for what it took for him to step out onto the stage that night.

In the Garden: See the Man with the Stage Fright

On the night of his Woodstock appearance, Tim Hardin was a mess. He was drunk, paralyzed with fear, overwhelmed by the size of the crowd, and high as a kite by the time he took the stage. He walked on around 9:00 p.m., enveloped in a comforting blanket of darkness, his self-consciousness shielded within the limiting glow of the spotlights.

But he was by no means alone. His band consisted of cellist Richard Buck, Ralph Towner on guitar and piano, Gilles Malkine on guitar, Glen Moore on bass, and Steve "Muruga" Booker on the drums. Hardin opened his set with a rendition of his first single, "(How Can We) Hang On to a Dream," and continued with "Susan." He appeared fragile throughout the performance. At times, there were flashes of his old brilliance. He offered up his signature tune, "If I Were a Carpenter," performed in a spare, solo acoustic arrangement, plus the ever-popular "Reason to Believe," "You

Upset the Grace of Living When You Lie," "Speak Like a Child," "Snow White Lady," "Blue on My Ceiling," a cover of Bobby Darin's "Simple Song of Freedom," and the soft, jazzy ballad "Misty Roses."

As John Morris would later opine, Hardin failed to captivate the audience that night, and none of his performance was included in the film or the soundtrack albums. As he left the stage, the audience was in for an intercultural change of pace, with Ravi Shankar waiting in the wings.

The Harvest Reaped: Of Needles and Damage Done

In spite of his frailty at Woodstock, and his failure to "wow" the crowd, the years 1969 through 1973 were Hardin's most productive. His second signing with Columbia Records yielded three studio albums: 1969's *Suite for Susan Moore and Damion: We Are One, One, All in One*; 1971's *Bird on a Wire*, which features a hauntingly beautiful cover of Leonard Cohen's similarly titled "Bird on the Wire"; and 1972's *Painted Head*, which consists of covers and traditional songs. The next year, 1973, saw the release of Hardin's final completed studio album, *Nine*, on GMA in the UK; it was issued in the United States on the Antilles Label in 1976. *Nine* features a balance of covers and originals, belying the fact that the artist was sinking ever deeper into the depths of heroin addiction. Hardin would not enter a recording studio again for eight years, by which point his addiction had reached the level of an existential threat.

Ever a restless soul, Hardin spent a lot of time shuttling back and forth between the UK—lured, some say, by the prospect of free methadone—and the US, where he moved constantly, from Hawaii, to San Francisco, to Los Angeles, and even to Colorado, where he supposedly intended to raise horses. It never happened. Heroin, not music, had become Hardin's primary focus; it became *the* defining characteristic of his personality. He was a junkie first and a musician second.

On Monday, December 29, 1980, a mere six days after his thirty-ninth birthday, Tim Hardin lost his twenty-year battle with heroin. His good friend Ron Daniles found the singer's lifeless body on the floor of his apartment in Hollywood, California. The official cause of death,

By the time 1971's *Bird on a Wire* hit the shelves, Tim Hardin had begun to cover other artists' material. His version of Leonard Cohen's "Bird on the Wire" is particularly haunting.

according to the L.A. County Coroner's Office report issued on January 26, 1981, was "death from acute heroin-morphine intoxication due to an overdose."

No one who had known Hardin was particularly surprised by the news. In death, his life's journey came full circle when his remains were interred at Twin Oaks Cemetery in Turner, Oregon, slightly more than sixty miles by car from his birthplace in Eugene.

Tim Hardin's incomplete swan song, *Unforgiven*, was patched together in the studio, and the slim, eight-track effort was released in 1981 on the San Francisco Sound label. Fellow Woodstock alumnus Nicky Hopkins appears on the album, playing piano.

In the years since, no fewer than *ten* Tim Hardin albums—a mixture of tribute albums, live recordings, and compilations—have been released, the most recent being 2007's *Through the Years 1964–1966* on the Lilith label.

Hardin is survived by his ex-wife, Susan, and their son, Damion. As Damion later told *Rolling Stone*'s James Sullivan, he still turns to his father's music for comfort and advice: "He always gives me the right answers, right away." Yet another reason to believe.

6

Ravi Shankar

West Meets East, by George

If Monterey was the beginning of a new movement or beautiful happening, I think Woodstock was almost the end. We had to go by helicopter from the motel where we stayed, many miles away, and landed just behind the stage. I performed with Alla Rakha accompanying me on tabla, in front of an audience of half a million—an ocean of people. It was drizzling and very cold, but they were so happy in the mud; they were all stoned, of course, but they were enjoying it. It reminded me of the water buffaloes you see in India, submerged in the mud. Woodstock was like a big picnic party, and the music was incidental.

—*Ravi Shankar,* Raga Mala

As the Seeds Were Sown: From a Bengali Dancer

Rabindra Shankar Chowdhury was born on April 7, 1920, in the town of Varanasi, in what was then British India, to father Shyam Shankar and mother Hemangini Devi. The well-to-do and politically connected family was of Bengali descent, and Rabindra was the youngest of seven brothers (two of whom died in infancy).

One of his older brothers, Uday, was a choreographer, and Rabindra left Varanasi and moved to Paris at age ten to work with Uday's dance troupe, in which he would earn himself a regular spot within three years. He changed his name to the more traditional Sanskrit spelling and shortened it to Ravi, which means "sun." Touring the world with the dance troupe, Ravi gained exposure to different cultures and languages, as well as various cinematic and musical forms. He learned French and became interested in playing music.

By age fourteen, Ravi had found his mentor, master sitarist Allaudin Khan, who was the official court musician for the princely state of Maihar. Khan toured with the dance troupe for a time on a European leg, during which he gave Ravi some introductory lessons. But if Ravi *really* wanted to learn, he discovered, he would have to move to Maihar, devote himself to studying music full time, and leave the world of dance behind. Khan's was a culture that regarded music with a degree of sacrality that seems peculiar to Western sensibilities; one had to be completely devoted.

Ravi was at a crossroads. Both of his parents were now deceased. World War II was rumbling slowly but inevitably to life, and touring had become more difficult as a result. It was time for a change.

When he turned eighteen in 1938, Ravi moved to Maihar to pursue his musical education under the tutelage of Khan. The arrangement was known as a *gurukula* in Sanskrit; the simplest translation of the term is that the student lived in the *kula* or home of their *guru* or master. Think of it like a religious boarding school or seminary—an almost monastic way of life.

Shankar's training lasted six years, during which he mastered the sitar and surbahar (essentially the bass version of the sitar), and all of the classical forms of Indian music. He earned the title of pandit, or master—an honorific that sometimes preceded his name in formal settings. He began to work in professional theater and ballet in Mumbai, composing scores, and eventually got involved in radio. He served as music director for New Delhi's All India Radio—essentially the NPR of India—for seven years, worked in the film industry, and somehow also found the time to found the Indian National Orchestra. His star was clearly in the ascendant, long before he ever met a Beatle.

When one of his colleagues, Ali Akbar Khan, received a positive reception from American audiences during a 1955 recital in New York City, Shankar sensed an opportunity. He left radio and took off on a world tour. He entered the studio for the first time in 1956 to record his debut album, *Three Ragas*, at thirty-six years of age. He was on hand for the United Nations' tenth-anniversary celebrations in 1958, and also played at the UNESCO Music Festival in Paris that same year. He

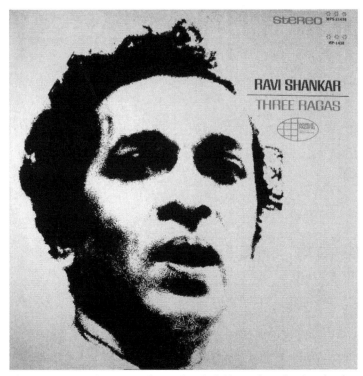

The most seasoned artist on the weekend's bill, Pandit Rabindra Shankar Chowdhury (a.k.a. Ravi Shankar) made his recording debut in 1956, with *Three Ragas*.

was rapidly becoming an international star. In 1962, the indefatigable Shankar founded the Kinnara School of Music in Mumbai.

During the early 1960s, Shankar's work came to the attention of American and British pop stars, largely through Richard Bock, founder of World Pacific Records. Shankar often recorded in Bock's studios. The Byrds (see chapter 30) recorded at World Pacific, and when they encountered Shankar's music they were fascinated. It was the Byrds who introduced George Harrison to Shankar's music, and the guitarist was hooked. Rock stars began dabbling in Indian music. The Byrds, the Beatles, and the Rolling Stones—to name but a few—all began working sitars into their compositions.

Shankar met Harrison in the summer of 1966, when the Beatle traveled to India to take lessons from him. Shankar's association with Harrison forced him into an even brighter spotlight, which proved to be a mixed blessing. One anecdote has the master whacking Harrison on the leg with a stick when the Beatle stepped over his sitar to take a phone call. The lesson Shankar was trying to impart was that, in India, musical instruments are sacred objects, to be revered.

By spring 1967, more than two years before Woodstock, Shankar was making his mark on America. He opened a Los Angeles branch of the Kinnara School, and then played the Monterey Pop Festival. The spotlight shone brighter upon him when the Beatles won the "Album of the Year" Grammy for *Sgt. Pepper's Lonely Hearts Club Band*, on which the song "Within You Without You" attempts to capture the spirit, if not the nuance or technical precision, of traditional Indian music. By 1968, in fact, Shankar was so accomplished that he decided it was a good time to pen his memoirs. His first autobiography, *My Music, My Life*, was released that year. It would not be his last. He headed for Bethel an elder statesman.

In the Garden: The Elder Plays in the Rain

After Tim Hardin, the audience was ready for something different. It was 10:00 p.m., and Ravi Shankar was just what was needed. He wasn't going to allow a little rain to interfere with his performance, or "recital," as he referred to it. Unless one is fluent in Sanskrit, or Hindi, the song titles from Shankar's set list won't hold much meaning, but these linguistic and cultural barriers may help to explain some of the allure. As Sri Swami Satchidananda had suggested during his invocation, music is a visceral, physiological experience.

Sitting cross-legged on the stage, the sitar master was joined by Maya Kulkarni on the tamboura, which resembles a long-necked lute or mandolin, and Ustad Allarakha Qureshi, a.k.a. "Alla Rakha," on the tabla, a percussion instrument bearing an unmistakable resemblance to a bongo drum. Among the selections they played were "Raga Puriya-Dhanashri (Gat in Sawarital)," which Shankar introduced as "an evening raga." For the musically astute, the piece has eleven beats split into four, four, and three. The second piece, "Tabla Solo in Jhaptal," was, for all intents and purposes, akin to a drum solo, its ten-beat rhythmic cycle of Jhaptal serving to showcase the considerable skills of Alla Rakha. "Raga Manj Kmahaj" was also an evening raga—a twenty-plus-minute masterpiece rounded out with selections called "Alap, Jor" (or "sitar solo"), "Dhun in Kaharwa Tal," and "Medium and Fast Gat in Teental."

As difficult as it may be to comprehend these selections on the printed page, audiovisual evidence from the festival reveals Shankar's set to be mesmerizing, the music beautiful and hypnotic. The audience, in spite of the steady rain, responded enthusiastically. In this case, at least, music truly was the universal language.

The Harvest Reaped: Professor Shankar

Shankar's exposure to Western culture was bittersweet. On the one hand, it introduced Indian classical music to a wider audience, but Shankar had his doubts about that audience's cultural sensibilities, and he largely disapproved of their behavior. While he saw his music as being in the same vein as Bach or Mozart, he wasn't performing for classical music audiences in America. Instead, he became a fixture on the rock festival circuit. His interviews over the years reveal his frustration at this. Author Peter Lavezzoli quotes Shankar as saying, "I felt offended and shocked to see India being regarded so superficially and its great culture being exploited. Yoga, Tantra, mantra, kundalini, ganja, hashish, Kama Sutra? They all became part of a cocktail that everyone seemed to be lapping up." He decried the impatient Western expectations for what he termed "Instant Karma."

During the fall of 1970, Shankar became chair of the Department of Indian Music at the California Institute of the Arts. He was a highly sought-after teacher and lecturer, having taught at the City College of New York and lectured all across the United States.

By this point, the Beatles had broken up, and George Harrison was struck by the plight of war-torn Bangladesh. In order to raise public awareness and much-needed funding for the humanitarian relief effort, he turned to Shankar for help. They booked two shows at Madison Square Garden on a single Sunday, August 1, 1971, for an all-star charity concert— the first of its kind.

Harrison and Shankar planned this as a multimedia, multi-revenue-stream affair, with a three-album boxed set and theatrical film to follow. Harrison enlisted the help of fellow Beatle Ringo Starr, Bob Dylan, Eric Clapton, Leon Russell, Billy Preston, and the band Badfinger. With nearly forty thousand tickets sold, the shows generated almost a quarter of a million dollars for the UNICEF-led relief efforts, and made Bangladesh a household name. When the album and film revenues are factored in, the figure rises above $15 million. Today, though Shankar and Harrison are both long gone, the album and film continue to raise funds for the George Harrison Fund for UNICEF.

Shankar continued to work with Harrison for the next couple of years, despite his misgivings about American youth, "hippie culture," and the irreverent attitudes he felt people displayed toward Indian music and culture. His onstage quip at the Bangladesh concert was telling. When the audience burst into applause after Shankar and his fellow musicians finished tuning their instruments, Shankar zinged them with, "If you appreciate the tuning so much, I hope you will enjoy the playing more." *The Concert for Bangladesh* was released at the end of 1971, and won "Album of the Year" at the 1973 Grammy Awards.

That same year, he and Harrison collaborated on the Harrison-produced *Shankar Family and Friends*, released in 1974. That fall, the two embarked on the Ravi Shankar's Music Festival from India tour of the US and Europe, but Shankar was nearing the end of his rope. The master suffered a heart attack in November 1974, followed by a nervous breakdown in 1975, and withdrew from public view.

When he returned to performing, he did so on his own terms, playing in venues where the classical nature of Indian music would be respected. He continued to teach and work on film scores. He wrote an academic book in 1979, titled *Learning Indian Music: A Systematic Approach*. He even garnered a Grammy Award nomination for "Best Original Music Score," for his work on the soundtrack for the hit 1982 film *Gandhi*.

During the late 1980s, Shankar added politics to his ever-expanding resume, serving in the Parliament of India from 1986 through 1992. He continued to suffer heart problems, undergoing an angioplasty near the end of his term.

Sitar master, composer, mentor, professor, and author—Ravi Shankar wore many hats during his (nearly) seventy-five-year musical journey, but he is perhaps best known to modern music fans as the father of artists Norah Jones and Anoushka Shankar.

As he grew older, further awards, accolades, and career retrospectives arrived, fast and furious. *Ravi Shankar: In Celebration*, a four-disc set, hit the shelves in 1996, just as he turned seventy-five. Around this time he began training his youngest daughter, Anoushka Shankar, on sitar. He returned to academia *again* the following year, accepting a position as Regents' Professor at the University of California in San Diego. He penned a second autobiography, *Raga Mala*, in 1997. George Harrison wrote the foreword and served as editor.

Shankar sailed into the new millennium by releasing a live album, *Full Circle: Carnegie Hall 2000*, and touring with daughter Anoushka, just as his *second*-youngest daughter, Norah Jones, was on the cusp of international pop superstardom. That album garnered him the 2002 Grammy Award for "Best World Music Album." But it was also a sad time. Harrison, fifty-eight, had succumbed to lung cancer on November 29, 2001. The subsequent Concert for George featured Anoushka Shankar playing some of her father's music.

Yet Shankar soldiered on. In 2002, Anoushka, also a budding writer and columnist, published her own biographical account of her father's life, *Bapi: Love of My Life*. The tireless master continued to tour into the next decade, even playing with the London Philharmonic Orchestra in 2010. He played his last shows in 2011, when he was ninety-one. On December 6, 2012, he was admitted to the hospital after experiencing difficulty breathing. Despite his advanced age, he underwent heart-valve replacement surgery, but the stress may have been too great. He passed away five days later, at age ninety-two.

While he may be best remembered in the world of rock and roll for his appearances at Monterey, Woodstock, and the Concert for Bangladesh, the pandit lived a long, rich and multifaceted life long before, and after, the Woodstock era. He touched many lives, and he left the world a beautiful, genre-spanning legacy in the form of his music and his musically gifted children.

7

Melanie

Of Candles and Rain

The reason why Woodstock was so special . . . it was just a spontaneous thing. People just didn't know that that many people were going to come; that was a surprise. There was a surprise in Woodstock and there weren't too many surprises after that. It seemed like there was something in the slogan, "Three Days of Peace, Love, and Music," and it wasn't so much in who was going to be performing. It was more like, "Let's go see all of our generation together," or something like that. It seemed like a spiritual call almost. There was no major event that really was calling to our generation in particular or to people who had kindred spirit. It seemed to just click.

—*Melanie to Tony Traguardo, March 3, 1994*

As the Seeds Were Sown: Child Prodigy from Queens

On February 3, 1947, a baby girl was born in Astoria, Queens, to Fred and Polly Safka. They named her Melanie Anne Safka, but the world would know her simply as Melanie. As the surname suggests, Fred was of Ukrainian descent; Polly was Italian American.

Polly had been a jazz singer during her youth, and was very supportive of Melanie pursuing her own musical career. The youngster got her first taste of the performing life in 1951, at age four, when she sang Maceo Pinkard's "Gimme a Little Kiss, Will Ya, Huh?" on a radio program called *Live Like a Millionaire*, after being interviewed by host John Nelson.

It would be the first of many interviews in a career that has spanned a lifetime.

The family moved from Astoria to the artsy enclave of Red Bank, New Jersey, home of the renowned Count Basie Theatre and several other venues. Melanie attended and later graduated from Red Bank High School. As a teenager, she began to sing at local folk-music venues such as the Inkwell, a close approximation of a Greenwich Village coffeehouse located in West End.

Conflict arose when it came time for Melanie to attend college. She didn't really want to go, but she obeyed her parents' wishes, enrolling at the American Academy of Dramatic Arts in New York. There weren't many opportunities for a girl with a guitar, so she went on a lot of auditions for plays, including one for *Fiddler on the Roof*.

One day, she happened upon a role she thought would be perfect for her. It called for a girl who could sing and play the guitar. The role was "Barbara Allen" in a play she knew and loved, *Dark of the Moon*. The audition was in the Brill Building in Manhattan, and in keeping with Murphy's Law, Melanie made it to the building, but she couldn't find the right office. She was worried that she would be late and lose the part, but fate intervened.

While she was on the verge of tears, Hugo Peretti and Luigi Creatore walked in and asked what she did. When they learned she was a singer/songwriter, they set up an appointment for that Thursday.

These men were big-time music writers and publishers, having written, among other things, "I Can't Help Falling in Love" for Elvis Presley. They were also producing a Broadway play. When Melanie played her original songs for them, they were clearly impressed. She got the part, but the play was canceled due to lack of funding while in rehearsal. But that was only the beginning of Melanie's association with Peretti and Creatore, who set up another session for her with a young producer named Peter Schekeryk. She played Schekeryk her songs, and he loved them. He also fell in love with her. For the rest of his life, Schekeryk would be Melanie's only producer.

Melanie began playing the Greenwich Village folk circuit and signed her first recording contracts, with Columbia and then Buddah Records. The signings led to the release of two singles and a debut album, *Born to Be*, in 1968. One single from the album, "Bobo's Party," received some attention and airplay overseas in Europe, particularly in the Netherlands. A third single, "Beautiful People," also became popular in Europe, and by the summer of '69 it had found its way to the airwaves in Melanie's native New York, on WNEW FM 102.7. You couldn't find a copy of the 45 in a store, but the song was becoming popular as what Melanie termed a "turntable song."

Her debut album, considered a promising first effort by *Billboard*, failed to chart. The nine original tracks, including her homage to the world of Winnie the Pooh, "Christopher Robin Is Saying His Prayers," appear alongside her first recorded cover, a version of Bob Dylan's "Mr. Tambourine Man."

In the Garden: Tea and Sympathy

Melanie's Woodstock story was one borne of simple networking genius. Her Manhattan office just happened to be located in the same building as Woodstock Ventures', and she had the wherewithal to ask Michael Lang and Artie Kornfeld if she could play at their upcoming festival. They said yes without giving the matter much thought.

Getting the gig was the easy part; getting to the gig—and *through* the gig—proved a real adventure for the twenty-two-year-old. Afterward, Melanie's life and career would never be the same. The festival not only provided her with the inspiration for her signature song, it also made her a folk icon.

Up until the point she actually got on the stage, however, Melanie's Woodstock experience sounds like something out of a nightmare camping-trip story. Things began smoothly enough on Friday morning, when her mother picked her up at the airport, and the two drove toward Bethel. They found themselves mired in the traffic jam leading to the festival site, but they dismissed it as normal weekend traffic. Surely these people couldn't *all* be driving toward the festival . . . could they?

They decided to pull over, so that Melanie could make a phone call to the festival organizers. They told her that, yes, the heavy traffic was festival-related, and no, don't go directly to the festival site, head for the hotel instead. Armed with these instructions, mother and daughter set out for the hotel. There they beheld a lively scene of press and celebrities milling about the lobby, including Grace Slick and a dazzling Janis Joplin, surrounded by a cadre of reporters. It was then and there they first learned of the festival organizers' ingenious game plan. Because the roads were now virtually impassable, the performers and their managers would be shuttled to the festival site by helicopter.

When Melanie was told that it was her turn to go, she lacked the presence of mind to lie and identify her mother as her manager. Instead, she said, "This is my mom." But there were no moms allowed, only managers, so the pair were separated. Melanie was whisked away onto the waiting helicopter, while Polly was stuck at the hotel. They wouldn't see each other for the rest of the weekend.

It was when the helicopter flew above the festival site that Melanie began to grasp what was happening down below. The largest audience she had performed for numbered around five hundred people. She asked the helicopter pilot, "What is that, down there?" She wasn't expecting him to reply, "People." She was stunned and gripped by a sudden stage fright.

Melanie's fortunes didn't improve much during the hours leading up to her performance. For some reason, she was never given the proper backstage artist credentials. Consequently, any time she wandered too far from the little tent to which she'd been assigned, she ran into hassles with security, who mistook the musical newcomer for some hippie chick trespassing backstage. She was known primarily for her radio hit, "Beautiful People," but few people knew what she looked like, so whenever she was questioned, she had to open up those unique pipes of hers and start singing the song, which seemed to convince them.

Melanie was also fighting a summer cold in the dreary upstate weather, and she had developed a noticeable cough. Among those who noticed her discomfort was Joan Baez. The folk legend and Friday-night headliner was five months pregnant and clearly feeling maternal. She took pity on the younger singer and began sending pots of tea over to her tent—an act of kindness that Melanie would recall fondly in later years.

It should be noted that Baez tried the same approach with Janis Joplin, but the notorious Texas tippler politely declined Baez's offers of tea. Janis was content to avail herself of the free champagne, and whatever other booze may have been floating around backstage (see chapter 20).

Melanie was a devout vegetarian and did not drink alcohol. She would have to look inward for solace until her turn arrived. Fortunately, she was a devotee of Meher Baba, the philosopher and spiritual guru perhaps best known for coining the phrase, "Don't worry, be happy." The festival schedule had been out-of-whack since the fifth act (Richie Havens) played first, and the first act (Sweetwater) played second, so patience was of the essence.

Then Melanie caught an unexpected break. After Ravi Shankar and his band concluded their "recital," playing through the pouring rain, the Incredible String Band decided that they would *not* go on. Why? Because, it was *raining* (see chapter 15). History would reveal this to be a poor decision on the band's part, but in the heat of the moment, it presented an opportunity for Melanie. She jumped at the chance to play—and then immediately found herself paralyzed by stage fright.

Making her way across the wooden bridge toward a metal folding chair in the glare of the spotlight, she could feel her heart pounding. She looked out into the darkness cloaking the huddled, soggy masses and beheld thousands of points of light. Many in the audience were holding aloft candles, cigarette lighters, and lit matches, but to Melanie's eyes they *all* seemed to be candles. In that moment, the seeds were sown for what would prove to be her signature song, "Lay Down (Candles in the Rain)."

This was no Greenwich Village coffeehouse with twenty people. There was a multitude out there. Understandably, the moment weighed upon her. But once she began to strum her guitar, the paralysis subsided, and she was off and running. She played a short but sweet set, featuring "Close to It All," "Momma Momma," "Beautiful People," "Animal Crackers," a cover of Bob Dylan's "Mr. Tambourine Man," "Tuning My Guitar," and "Birthday of the Sun."

Just before she launched into "Birthday of the Sun," some jerk in the audience heckled her, yelling up at her to "Get out of the seat!" But she ignored the boorish oaf and soldiered on to close out her set with all of the Queens, New York, swagger she could muster, even altering the lyrics at certain points, in honor of the present circumstances, from "sun" to "rain."

The Harvest Reaped: Other Worlds to Conquer

Buddah Records sensed an opportunity knocking. The label repackaged and re-released Melanie's *Born to Be* under a new title, *My First Album*. Her sophomore effort, *Affectionately Melanie*, released in December '69, contained twelve originals, including "Beautiful People" and "Tuning My Guitar." The album only reached #196 on *Billboard*, but better days lay ahead.

The third time really was the charm for Melanie. Her 1970 release, *Candles in the Rain*, became her career-defining album, reaching #17 on the US Charts and rising even higher abroad. The single "Lay Down (Candles in the Rain)" hit #3, the gospel tones of the Edwin Hawkins Singers helping to give the song its signature feel.

But the album features other treasures, too. A cover of the Rolling Stones' "Ruby Tuesday" tore up the UK charts and hit #9. Another treasure is a heartfelt rendition of James Taylor's "Carolina in My Mind."

Melanie's 1968 debut, *Born to Be*. She certainly seems to have been—who could argue the point with a girl who gave her first public performance on a live radio show at age *four*?

With imagery inspired by her set at Woodstock, Melanie's third album, 1970's *Candles in the Rain*, cemented her place in the pantheon of American folk artists.

"Alexander Beetle" continued Melanie's Winnie the Pooh fixation, and A. A. Milne even got a co-songwriting credit for the use of his words. Other favorites include "What Have They Done to My Song, Ma?"—a bit of cabaret-like fun—and the haunting "Leftover Wine."

Now that Woodstock had broken the ice in the public's consciousness, many more festivals lay ahead. Melanie played the Isle of Wight festival, where she was introduced by Keith Moon. (*Forty* years later, in 2010, she would return to the Isle of Wight stage, still going strong.) She defied a court order to play the Power Ridge Rock Festival in Connecticut. She appeared at the three-day Strawberry Fields Festival in Ontario, Canada. In 1971, she appeared at the Glastonbury Fayre, the precursor to the Glastonbury Festival, which continues in England to this day. Here, again, she would reappear forty years later, gracing the stage in 2011.

On the personal front, she moved in with and eventually married Peter Schekeryk. The couple had three children: daughters Leilah, born in 1973, and Jeordie, born in 1975, who would go on to serve as her backup singers; and a son, Beau Jarred, born in 1980, who also inherited his famous mom's vocal gifts, and tours with her to this day on guitar.

In a career that already spans more than half a century, Melanie has released more than thirty studio albums, three live albums, and three compilations. Her 1971 single "Brand New Key" was her first and only #1 on *Billboard*. All told, she has released twenty-eight singles, up to and including 1983's "Every Breath of the Way."

Peter Schekeryk passed away suddenly in 2010, just as Beau Jarred was beginning to work as his co-producer on the album *Ever Since You Never Heard of Me*. In 2011, Melanie was the subject of a John Lambo biography, *Melanie: The First Lady of Woodstock*. Her most recent album (as of this writing) was a live album, 1984. She has not produced an album of original material since Schekeryk's passing, but she remains active.

Recently, Melanie partnered with twenty-four-year-old vocal powerhouse Miley Cyrus and her Happy Hippie Foundation, a charity for homeless LGBTQ teens. During a backyard session, the cross-generational stars performed duets of "Look What They've Done to My Song, Ma," "Peace Will Come (According to Plan)," and "Yaw Baby (Break My Heart)," all of which appear on Cyrus's 2017 album *Happy Hippie Presents: Backyard Sessions.*

Melanie continues to tour and perform with her children. Her live act remains every bit as riveting and vibrant as it was on that long-ago Friday night when candles shone through the rain.

8

Arlo Guthrie

Champagne Dreams

We had some hesitation about going there, 'cause—people don't remember, but back in 1969, every time over fifty people got together, there was riots, and cops would come and hit ya and everything, and it was disaster time. So, we weren't sure when we heard that there were gonna be a hundred thousand people at a festival that was supposed to have maybe sixty-seventy; we thought, ah, it's gonna get out of hand and, ya know, the cops are gonna come—it's gonna be a big drag. But, we decided to go anyway, and, of course, by the time before the gate even opened there were eighty thousand people before they'd had time to even collect any tickets. So, we didn't have any idea how big it was gonna be.

—Arlo Guthrie to Pete Fornatale, 1987

As the Seeds Were Sown: Woody's Children

Arlo Davy Guthrie arrived in this world on July 10, 1947. He was the second of four children born to folk singer Woody Guthrie and dancer Marjorie Mazia Guthrie (née Greenblatt). Their first child, Cathy Ann, died tragically in a fire at age four, five months before Arlo was born.

Though raised in Coney Island, Arlo attended the Woodward School in Clinton Hill, around ten miles away. Arlo and his siblings, Joady Ben and Nora, were raised in the traditions of Judaism. Arlo's Bar Mitzvah party has been described as evolving into a full-blown, old-fashioned folk-music hootenanny.

Arlo began to play the guitar and show an interest in music . . . mainly *other* people's music; he had no plans of becoming a professional musician. He was coping with the paradox of growing up with a father who became more famous with each passing day, even as he wasted away in the hospital from Huntington's chorea. Arlo and his siblings also had to cope with the possibility that they might have inherited Huntington's, and they wouldn't know one way or another until they hit middle age. It was a lot to process.

Marjorie would take Arlo to Greenwich Village on the weekends, to places like Gerde's Folk City, where they would watch family friends like Ramblin' Jack Elliott and Cisco Houston perform. It was at Folk City, back in 1961, that Cisco called Arlo up to the stage to perform a few of his father's songs. This was his first performance in front of a live audience. The crowd was supportive, but the teen was just glad to get it over with. He always figured he'd be a forest ranger, and go live off in the woods somewhere, chopping wood with an axe. But life had other plans.

Around this time, Bob Dylan began hanging around the Guthries, and would frequently visit Woody in the hospital. The future Rock and Roll Hall of Famer was a Woody devotee who spent the first few years of his career as a virtual Woody clone. Woody was incapacitated, so Marjorie was running the household. One time, as Arlo tells it, Marjorie allowed Dylan to babysit him on a trip to the Newport Folk Festival, where the older singer delighted in introducing the boy to others. As Arlo put it, "And he just kept walking me around saying, 'Hey this is Woody's kid,' or something."

After graduating from the Woodward School, Arlo was sent to Massachusetts, to attend high school at the Stockbridge School, an eclectic boarding school with a heavy focus on music, globalism, and human rights. The school librarian there was a woman named Alice Brock, and her husband, Ray Brock, was the shop teacher. The couple would become dear friends of Arlo's, and would go on to play a role in arguably the most significant event in his life.

Upon graduation from the Stockbridge School, Arlo headed west and enrolled at Rocky Mountain College in Billings, Montana. But this foray into higher education had more to do with a desire to avoid the draft than it did with any academic ambitions. During the fall semester of 1965, he returned to Massachusetts to celebrate Thanksgiving with Alice and Ray at their Great Barrington home. Alice and Ray's place was a deconsecrated church, so it was unusually roomy. The story that follows may seem oddly familiar.

Arlo noticed that the couple had amassed a great deal of garbage, which was clearly in need of disposal. So he volunteered his services, and took off with a friend, Richard Robbins, toward the town dump, to get rid of it. When they arrived at the dump, the teens discovered, much to their dismay, that it was closed, on account of the holiday.

Undaunted, they drove over to Stockbridge, where they disposed of the garbage over the side of a cliff. But that cliff was located on private property, and the owner reported the incident to local sheriff, William J. Obanhein, who begrudgingly picked through the trash until he found an envelope with Ray Brock's address. This clue led to Arlo and Richard being arrested for the crime of "littering." They were fined $25 apiece by Special Justice James E. Hannon, who also ordered the boys to spend their Saturday cleaning up the mess they had made. But the story doesn't end there.

Leaving the world of higher education behind, Arlo became eligible for the draft, which—along with Vietnam—he still hoped to avoid. On the appointed day, after a night of drinking, he went down to 39 Whitehall Street in Manhattan to appear before the draft board, to try to convince them he wasn't army material. When his hangover ploy didn't work, he tried to fail the psychological exam by feigning a desire to kill. That didn't work, either. But when the draft board asked if he'd ever been convicted of a *crime*, Arlo hit his stride. He dutifully recounted the story of his arrest for littering.

Incredibly, due to some bureaucratic phenomenon, littering was morally indistinguishable in the eyes of the draft board from rape, robbery, or murder. Anyone convicted of any crime needed to be granted a "moral waiver" before they could serve. The long-haired Guthrie was rejected.

Back on the home front, Alice Brock opened a restaurant on Main Street in Stockbridge called the Back Room. She enlisted Arlo to pen a little jingle to advertise the place on local radio. That jingle, of course, would go on to become the refrain of "Alice's Restaurant Massacree," a satirical, eighteen-minute-and-thirty-four-second "talking blues" that would take up the entire first side of Arlo's 1967 debut album.

The album, *Alice's Restaurant*, hit the shelves in September 1967. Just two months earlier, Arlo had made his debut performance at the Newport Folk Festival, where he premiered "Alice's Restaurant Massacree." Judy Collins, Joan Baez, and Pete Seeger all joined him onstage to sing along.

Alice's Restaurant reached #17 on the Billboard charts. Arlo's career was gaining momentum. He released his sophomore effort, *Arlo*, in October of 1968, and a third offering, *Running Down the Road*, in 1969. By the time he arrived in Bethel for the Woodstock festival, he was not only a folk-music legacy; he was a veteran performer and recording artist in his own right.

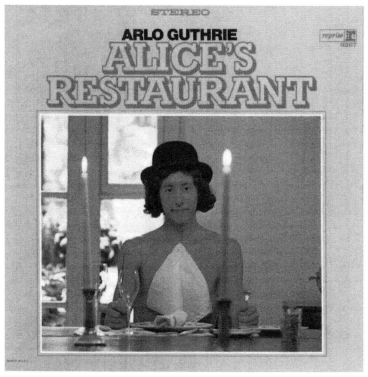

You can get *anything* you want . . . "excepting Alice." The 1967 debut that inspired a Thanksgiving tradition that continues to this day!

In the Garden: Watch Your *Step*, Kid

As it turned out, a number of adventures awaited the Brooklyn native and folk music scion at the festival site. Arlo's experiences at Woodstock have provided him with a seemingly endless supply of humorous anecdotes. He was, and remains, one of the best storytellers in the business.

> I remember being there. And I remember there was nothing to eat or drink, it had all been ate or drunk. And I was thirsty. But there were a hundred or somethin' cases of champagne in the back that they had saved for the end of the third day or somethin' . . . well, we started attacking that—I think I drank about a case or two before we went out, and I was totally gone. But I walked out there and they had a big hole in the middle of the stage cause they were gonna turn the stage around and set up the guys in the back while the guys in the front was playing. Well, the hole never worked and they never turned the stage around. But they didn't tell me about the hole—so, I walked out there and fell right into a six-foot hole. But, just—you know how it is sometimes when you're feeling like that—I just like walked right through the wood and came out the other side; I kept going, and uh, walked out and played, and, uh, I forget what I sang.

At 11:55 p.m., after surviving the ample backstage champagne and other temptations, and after narrowly escaping serious injury from falling through the hole in the stage, Arlo and his band began their set. The band consisted of multi-talented musician, producer, and photographer John Pilla on guitar; Bob Arkin—younger brother of the actor Alan—on upright bass; and veteran jazz drummer Paul Motian. They opened with "Coming into Los Angeles," a song from the new album that would become inextricably linked to the Woodstock experience. Arlo's vocals were barely audible for the first seventy seconds, and the recording proved unusable for the proposed film and soundtrack album.

Afterward, amid chuckles, the addled Arlo addressed the crowd. "I don't know if you can . . . I don't know . . . uh, like, how many of you can dig how many people there are, man? Like, I was rappin' to the fuzz, right? Can you dig it? Man, there's supposed to be a million and a half people here by tonight. Can you dig that? The New York State Thruway is *closed*, man! Yeah, it's far out, man. . . . Lotta freaks!"

For the record, the New York State Thruway was *never* closed, though the state police did close the Harriman and Newburgh exits to try to stem the flow of traffic to the area. As to where he got the idea that "a million and a half" people were en route, who can say? Arlo was well known for his quirky sense of humor. Or it may have just been the champagne talking. Either way, he was just getting warmed up.

"Wheel of Fortune," another new song, followed. And then they launched into a particularly raucous cover of Bob Dylan's "Walking Down the Line," during which the heavy-lidded Guthrie stopped the song and offered up one of his patented comical stoner raps, much to the delight of the audience.

He followed this with a wacky story about Moses and the Exodus. In Arlo's version of the ancient tale, Moses and the freed Israeli slaves were able to escape their Egyptian captors by consuming the "manna" from heaven, which was really a "special" type of brownies, laced with LSD. After consuming the acid brownies, Moses and the Israelites were able to walk across the *surface* of the Red Sea to their freedom; there was no need for Moses to part the waters.

Arlo gamely continued with the pre–Civil War Negro spiritual, "Mary Don't You Weep," a slave song he'd learned from Pete Seeger. Then it was back to the new album for "Every Hand in the Land." Arlo finished his set with a traditional song that remains a concert staple to this day, "Amazing Grace." And then, with a simple, "Thank you, man. Good night," he took off his guitar and walked off the stage.

The Harvest Reaped: Still Walkin' Down the Line

As Arlo tells it, his Woodstock festival legacy has been somewhat distorted by the film and album versions of events, and during interviews and stage banter, he often attempts to set the record straight, with varying degrees of success.

I know I did "Coming into LA," but the one on the record, the one that you see in the movie, is not the "Coming into LA" that we did.

That's the one that they took from another recording somewhere and snuck it on there; which is why you never see us playing in Woodstock, 'cause they couldn't synch it up. They always have pictures of people smoking dope or something like that, you know. That was a shame, too, because they took the worst possible recording of some terrible night we did somewhere, you know, in the city, and stuck it on there and I was always horrified at that.

Nobody remembers the music. They all come up and say to me something about, "The New York State Thruway is closed," and there's "alotta freaks" or whatever. You know, people, young kids, that's a big deal for them somehow or other; I don't know.

The day after Woodstock ended, Arlo Guthrie added "actor" to his already impressive resume. Arthur Penn's film adaptation of *Alice's Restaurant*, featuring Arlo as himself, Pat Quinn as Alice, and James Broderick as Ray, debuted on August 19, and featured cameos from several of the real people involved. The soundtrack album appeared on record-store shelves the same day. The film would go on to garner a "Best Director" Academy Award nomination for Penn.

Arlo would continue to dabble in television, appearing on shows as diverse as *The Muppet Show* (1979) and Bill Maher's *Politically Incorrect* (1998). He filmed a pilot for a variety show, *Arlo Guthrie and Friends*, in February 1987. The pilot aired, but the show was never picked up. In 1992, he had a cameo in the film, *Roadside Prophets*. Later, in 1994, he would play a small role on the short-lived ABC drama *Byrds of Paradise*.

He went on to release another twenty-five albums over the next forty years, including 2009's *Tales of '69*. At least two of these albums were live recordings of duo shows with Pete Seeger, and many of them were independent releases, or re-releases, on Arlo's own Rising Sun Records label. As for critical acclaim, Arlo's 1976 album *Amigo* garnered the most praise, earning a perfect five-star rating from *Rolling Stone* magazine. But his most successful *single* would be a cover song.

One night after a show, a young man approached Arlo and told him he wanted to play a song for him. Arlo told the guy he would have to buy him a beer first, and that he would only give him until he finished the beer to play his song. He agreed, and Arlo listened. That young man's name was Steve Goodman, and the song he'd written was "City of New Orleans."

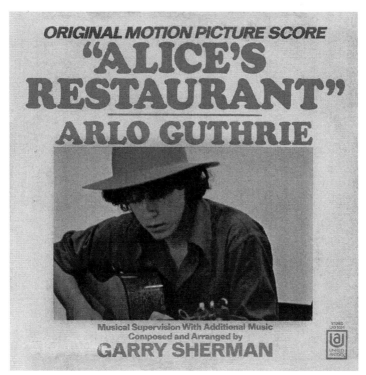

The year 1969 was a busy one for Brooklyn's own Arlo Guthrie, with the release of his third album, *Running Down the Road*, his appearance at Woodstock, and, of course, the debut of the movie version of *Alice's Restaurant*. Here's the soundtrack album cover.

Arlo liked what he heard, befriended Goodman, and went on to record the song for his 1972 album *Hobo's Lullaby*. "City of New Orleans" hit #4 on *Billboard*'s Easy Listening chart and #18 on the Hot 100. It would prove to be Arlo's highest-charting song, and many other artists—among them David Allan Coe and the great Willie Nelson—went on to record and have success with the song. Goodman passed away from leukemia in 1984, and Guthrie continues to play the song in honor of his friend.

New York Daily News crossword puzzle editors may persist in using Arlo's name as the answer to the frequently recurring clue, "The younger Guthrie," but patriarch Woody has been deceased since 1967. Arlo turned seventy in 2017, the threat of inheriting Huntington's disease long past. He has four grownup children and seven grandchildren, several of whom have musical careers of their own. At press time, Arlo was booked through June 2019 on the Alice's Restaurant Back by Popular Demand

Tour with Sarah Lee Guthrie, with a series of dates across the continental US, Hawaii, and Australia.

"The younger Guthrie's" life path and career may have turned out quite differently from that of his legendary father, but it has been every bit as special. Nearly sixty years after Cisco Houston called that nervous thirteen-year-old boy to the stage at a Greenwich Village folk club, he is still "Walkin' Down the Line."

9

Joan Baez

Singing for Two

Woodstock was drugs and sex and rock 'n' roll. Woodstock was Janis "coitus interruptus" Joplin and Jimi "genius" Hendrix, and the gorgeous sweating chest of Roger Daltrey . . . Woodstock was Country Joe McDonald and Dirty Sly and the Family Stone gettin' HIGH-YUH! . . . Woodstock was Wavy Gravy and his Hog Farm. . . . Woodstock was a city. Yes, it was three extraordinary days of rain and music. No, it was not a revolution. It was a Technicolor mud-splattered reflection of the 1960s. Woodstock was also me, Joan Baez, the square, six months pregnant, the wife of a draft resister, endlessly proselytizing about the war. I had my place there. I was of the '60s, and I was already a survivor. I sang in the middle of the night, I just stood up there in front of the residents of the golden city who were sleeping in the mud and each other's arms, and I gave them what I could at the time. They accepted my songs. It was a humbling moment, in spite of everything. I'd never sung to a city before.

—*Joan Baez,* And a Voice to Sing With

As the Seeds Were Sown: From Staten Island, Before the Bridge

Joan's father, Albert Baez, the son of a Methodist minister, was just two years old when the family arrived in the US and settled in Brooklyn. Albert grew up and worked as a scientist and inventor. He left the Methodist Church and became a Quaker, before moving his young family to Staten Island. It was there that Joan Chandos Baez was born, on January 9, 1941.

Joan's mother, Joan (Bridge) Baez, was also the child of a clergy member, an Anglican priest. "Big Joan" or "Joan, Sr." as they often called her, hailed from Baton Rouge, Louisiana, which may account for that faint Southern twang you hear in her famous daughter's speaking voice.

Joan and her siblings were raised in the Quaker tradition. The values the children learned in the faith helped to inform their budding social consciousness, particularly their ideas about pacifism and nonviolence. Joan was the middle child, with one older sister, Pauline, and one younger sister, Margarita Mimi, better known, later on, as the singer/songwriter Mimi Fariña.

By the time Mimi was born, the family was living in Palo Alto, California, but rarely dwelt in one place for long. Albert's work required him to move around a lot, so the Baez family led an almost nomadic existence, living in states all across the country, up in Canada, all over Europe, and even in Iraq for a brief period of time.

It was a ukulele that first sparked Joan's interest in playing music. Her aunt took her to a Pete Seeger concert in 1954, when she was just thirteen—the same age Arlo Guthrie was when he first performed for an audience—and there she found her role model. She began to emulate him, singing his songs with her naturally beautiful voice and strumming along on the ukulele. Then, as now, she was much more concerned with the sociopolitical aspects of the folk scene than she was with the techniques of musicianship or the craft of songwriting. Joan considers her legendary vocal prowess to be a "gift," something that was always there for her; she never dwells on it.

The half-Mexican Baez sisters experienced racial discrimination first-hand while growing up, which further helped to inform their social consciousness and empathy for others, and those experiences strengthened their resolve to fight for the rights of all people, everywhere.

Her parents' Quaker sensibilities made it difficult for them to accept that Joan seemed determined to become a professional performer, and they were wary when she bought herself a guitar in 1957. They didn't want to see their daughter get caught up in the drugs and the illicit behaviors that often accompany that lifestyle. They needn't have worried.

When Joan's dad landed a position at the prestigious Massachusetts Institute of Technology, it seemed as if the fates were conspiring to help launch Joan's career. Boston was a college town with a built-in audience and ample opportunities for young folk singers to ply their craft. Joan wasn't cut out for the student lifestyle, lasting less than half a semester at Boston University, but she could certainly *sing* for them.

Her first official "concert," a gig at Club 47 in Cambridge, quickly evolved into a biweekly residency. At age seventeen, she was pulling in over $200 a month. Soon enough, the studio beckoned. Joan collaborated with local folkies Bill Wood and Ted Alevizos to record an album called *Folksingers 'Round Harvard Square* in the spring of 1959. The album was a modest production, recorded in a friend's basement studio, but it was a start.

Joan then came to the attention of the legendary Odetta, and folk singer Bob Gibson, who engineered her debut at the Newport Folk Festival in 1959, where she joined him on two spiritual songs, "We Are Crossing Jordan River" and "Virgin Mary Had One Son." That brief appearance was enough to capture the attention of some record executives, and it landed Joan her first deal with Vanguard Records, which signed the nineteen-year-old in 1960.

Her eponymous debut, *Joan Baez*, was released that same year. The 1961 follow-up was the similarly titled *Joan Baez, Vol.2*. Both albums consist solely of covers, traditional folk songs, hymns, and several of Francis James Child's English and Scottish ballads, which date back to the 1800s.

Joan released two consecutive live albums over the next two years, *Joan Baez in Concert, Part 1* (1962) and *Joan Baez in Concert, Part 2* (1963). She made the cover of Time magazine on November 23, 1962, and her albums began to go gold. Her recording schedule was relentless. Joan *Baez/5*, released in 1964, yielded the hit Phil Ochs cover, "There but for Fortune," as well as covers of songs by Bob Dylan and Johnny Cash. *Farewell Angelina* (1965) features four Dylan tunes, alongside covers of Donovan, Pete Seeger, and Woody Guthrie.

Dylan is the eight-hundred-pound gorilla in the room for anyone writing about Baez, but a full treatment of their tumultuous relationship would take us beyond the scope of our narrative. Suffice it to say that Baez was a star *before* Dylan. She took him under her wing professionally, and they became lovers. She introduced him to her audiences and shared her stage with him—sometimes to the chagrin of her own fans. Dylan absorbed it all and kept on going. It became apparent that he was a once-in-a-lifetime talent, and his star began to eclipse her own. They parted ways. Dylan never looked back, but he left Baez hurting by the sidelines, trying to figure the whole thing out. His presence would loom large in her life and work for many years.

The now-obligatory Christmas album, *Noël*, appeared in 1966, and paired Baez with a full orchestra and conductor. She continued in the orchestral vein in 1967, albeit with more secular fare, on *Joan*, which features her late brother-in-law Richard Fariña's "Children of Darkness," as well as a musical arrangement of the poet Edgar Allen Poe's "Annabelle Lee." The poetry experiment proved so successful that Joan continued that theme throughout 1968's *Baptism: A Journey Through Our Time*. That album features Joan reciting and/or singing poems by the likes of Walt Whitman, William Blake, John Donne, Henry Treece, Arthur Rimbaud, and James Joyce over classical orchestral arrangements.

These three years demonstrated Joan's willingness to experiment with musical forms beyond the traditional acoustic guitar and vocals of the typical folk singer. When she returned to the form later in 1968, it was with *Any Day Now*, an album comprised solely of Dylan songs, several of them previously unreleased. Those same marathon studio sessions in Nashville also provided the material for 1969's *David's Album*. *Any Day Now* went gold and received critical acclaim. *David's Album*, released in May, was filled with traditional folk and country tunes, and, as the title suggests, was intended as a present for her husband, David Harris, just prior to his imprisonment for draft resistance.

By the time Joan landed in Bethel that Friday afternoon, she was a seasoned veteran. She had eleven albums to her credit—more than *any* other performer on the weekend's schedule—and, to top it all off, she was visibly pregnant.

In the Garden: Methinks Ye Don't Protest *Enough*

When the Friday-night headliner took to the stage, it no longer *was* Friday; it was 12:55 a.m. on Saturday, August 16. The Woodstock audience was beginning to wind down after an eventful first day, and Joan was the perfect person to sing them a lullaby.

Joan was joined onstage by guitarist Richard Festinger, and, at times, vocalist and guitarist Jeffrey Shurtleff. Her thirteen-song set was a veritable history lesson—a joyful lecture on American folk, country, rock, and gospel. Naturally, she also managed to discuss the draft-resistance movement and the anti-Vietnam scene.

She began with "Oh Happy Day," a cover of the Edwin Hawkins Singers' gospel-flavored interpretation of a Christian hymn that dates back to the eighteenth century. (You may recall that Sweetwater covered this tune earlier on, pairing it with "Let the Sunshine In" from the musical *Hair*.) Next up was "The Last Thing on My Mind," a popular cover written and recorded by respected folk-music veteran Tom Paxton. Then things got personal, as Joan dipped into her past for "I Shall Be Released," a song written by Dylan and first recorded by the Band, a quintet of local veterans who were scheduled to perform on this same stage two nights later (see chapter 27). The self-described "square" then got hip with a cover of the Rolling Stones' 1968 classic "No Expectations," a song Joan liked so much that she would go on to record it for her 1970 album *One Day at a Time*.

Now it was time to get *political*. Joan acknowledged her pregnancy, and then regaled the audience with the tale of her husband's arrest and experiences in prison as a leader of the draft resistance movement. This was Joan's way of introducing "one of my husband David's favorite songs," "Joe Hill," Earl Robinson's 1936 ode to Joel Emmanuel Hägglund, a Swedish immigrant labor activist in Utah who was executed after being wrongly convicted of murder. Hill became a *cause célèbre*, immortalized in books, poetry, and song. The lyrics were based on Alfred Hayes's 1930 poem "I Dreamed I S aw Joe Hill Last Night."

She continued with her first original, "Sweet Sir Galahad," prefacing it with the self-deprecating message, "It's the only song that I've ever written that I sing anywhere outside of the bathtub, 'cause I'm just smart enough to know that my writing is very mediocre." She told the crowd she'd written the song in honor of her long-haired brother-in-law, Milan Melvin (Mimi's *second* husband, after Richard Fariña passed away), who, during courtship, used to crawl, feet first, through Mimi's window in the middle of the night.

Then it was back to covers, including "Hickory Wind," a beautiful tune co-written by the godfather of country-rock, Gram Parsons, during his brief tenure as a member of the Byrds. This provided her with the perfect segue to introduce Jeffrey Shurtleff, who up until this point had been kneeling reverently toward the rear of the stage, over Baez's right shoulder. Shurtleff had been a friend of Joan's husband, David, since their Stanford University days, and was a vocal member of the draft-resistance movement.

"Hello to all friends of the draft resistance revolution in America," Shurtleff began, before commenting that he hoped it would stop raining, and then making the questionable assertion that the draft resistance had "no enemies." Even Baez did a visible double take at *that* one.

The Byrds theme continued with the Gram Parsons–Roger McGuinn tune "Drug Store Truck Drivin' Man," which Shurtleff cheekily dedicated to the "governor of California, Ronald 'Ray Guns,' ZAP!" They continued with Willie Nelson's "I Live One Day at a Time" and the traditional "Take Me Back to the Sweet Sunny South," before finishing their duet with Percy Sledge's "Let Me Wrap You in My Warm and Tender Love."

As her set drew toward a close, Baez removed her guitar for an explosive a cappella rendition of "Swing Low, Sweet Chariot." John Morris stepped up to the mic and announced, "The very beautiful Joan Baez," at which point she picked up her guitar for a solo encore, "We Shall Overcome." And then, with a simple, "Thank you very much, bye-bye," the legendary folk Madonna walked off the stage, bringing Friday's proceedings to an end. But, to paraphrase Bob Dylan, she wasn't a-goin' nowhere. Joan hung out for the rest of the festival, taking in as many of the bands as she could.

The Harvest Reaped: Of *Diamonds and Rust*

Joan Baez's career was already firmly established by the time of Woodstock, and while her appearance there, and in the subsequent 1970 film, may have introduced her to a wider audience, it did little to alter her artistic trajectory. But first came motherhood. Gabriel, her son with David Harris, was born on December 2, 1969.

Her first post-festival album, 1970's *One Day at a Time*, contains several of the songs she sang in Bethel. She followed up the next year with a *double*, 1971's *Blessed Are . . .* , her thirteenth and final album for Vanguard Records. A highlight of that album is her cover of the Band's "The Night They Drove Old Dixie Down," which landed her in the Top 5 on the *Billboard* charts.

"Well, I'll be damned." The Staten Island native's 1975 album *Diamonds and Rust* is but one gem in a discography full of treasures.

The following year, she changed record labels for the first time, signing with A&M Records, but her basic approach remained the same: offer up a mix of carefully selected covers, traditional tunes, and a few originals; showcase those famous pipes; and then take the show out on the road.

Her album-a-year pace continued unabated from 1972 through 1977, a period when she released *Come from the Shadows*, *Where Are You Now, My Son?*, *Gracias a la Vida*, *Diamonds and Rust*, *Gulf Winds*, and, finally, *Blowin' Away*, which marked her transition from A&M to Portrait Records, an imprint of CBS. After an unprecedented one-year gap, she returned in 1979 with *Honest Lullaby*, her second and final album for Portrait, and her last album for *any* label for the next eight years.

While her Spanish language cover of Violeta Parra's "Gracias a la Vida" ("Here's to Life") from the 1974 album of the same title remains a standout from this prolific period, it was an original composition, the title track from 1975's *Diamonds and Rust*, that proved to be her masterpiece. A wistful ode to Bob Dylan, "Diamonds and Rust" would be one of her only songs to inspire cover versions. The most intriguing of these was arguably the one by British heavy-metal band Judas Priest, who released the song as a single from the Roger Glover–produced 1977 album *Sin After Sin*. The song proved to be a big radio hit for Priest, and a concert favorite—much to the delight of Baez, who was unaccustomed to such cross-genre recognition.

The title of 1979's *Honest Lullaby* proved oddly prophetic, as Baez's recording career suddenly seemed to fall asleep, though she continued to tour. During her recording hiatus, she serenaded a new generation of fans on July 13, 1985, as the official opening act for the Philadelphia portion of the Live Aid Concert for African Famine Relief. "Good morning, children of the '80s, and others," she said. "This is your Woodstock, and it's long overdue." After trying to impress upon the crowd the significance of the event, she offered to "say grace" in the form of an a cappella "Amazing Grace," which segued into "We Are the World," the unofficial theme song of the event.

The following June, in 1986, Baez participated in the six-date A Conspiracy of Hope tour, which had been assembled to raise awareness for the human rights organization Amnesty International, which was marking its twenty-fifth anniversary. In the middle of an all-star lineup, Baez sang solo and with both Nigerian star Fela Kuti and the Neville Brothers.

Baez's experiences at these large outdoor events, plus her exposure to younger audiences and a new generation of artists, ultimately led her back into the recording studio to cover some of their material. Her 1987 return on the Gold Castle label, *Recently*, featured covers of songs by new friends—Mark Knopfler, U2, and Peter Gabriel—along with her usual eclectic mix of traditional and original material. That same year saw the release of her autobiography, *And a Voice to Sing With*, published by Simon and Schuster.

While Baez never quite resumed the breakneck pace of her youth, she did have more to offer. She returned on Gold Castle in late 1989 with *Speaking of Dreams*, which features duets with Paul Simon and Jackson Browne, and a George Michael cover. She switched to Virgin Records for 1992's *Play Me Backwards*, which features covers of John Hiatt and Mary Chapin Carpenter. And then the gaps between album releases began to grow once more.

Five years passed before 1997's *Gone from Danger*, on the Guardian label. The album features Baez's takes on material by younger folk singers like Dar Williams, Sinéad Lohan, and Richard Shindell. She began to muse publicly that her own songwriting days might be behind her. Six years later—three years into the first decade of the new millennium, and two years after the untimely death, from cancer, of Mimi Fariña—Baez returned with 2003's *Dark Chords on a Big Guitar*, which found her interpreting the works of artists like Steve Earle, Ryan Adams, and Natalie Merchant. The album was critically well received but not a great commercial success. She wouldn't make another studio album until 2008, but she bridged that gap with a live album, 2005's *Bowery Songs*. Those fourteen career-spanning tracks were all recorded during a show at the Bowery Ballroom in Manhattan on November 6, 2004.

Baez's 2008 offering on the Proper label, *Day After Tomorrow*, produced by Steve Earle, garnered her a Grammy nomination for "Best Contemporary Folk Album." The album features a mix of tunes by the likes of Earle, Tom Waits, and Elvis Costello. On March 2, 2018, Joan released her first studio album in a decade, *Whistle Down the Wind*, a collection of cover songs that garnered her a Grammy nomination.

Baez was the subject of the 2009 American Masters documentary *Joan Baez: How Sweet the Sound*, filmed during her 2008–2009 Day After Tomorrow tour. Joan bid farewell to her mother and namesake, "Big Joan," who passed away in California in 2013, aged one hundred.

On January 9, 2016, Baez passed yet another personal milestone when she turned seventy-five. To mark the occasion, she appeared alongside an all-star lineup at New York's Beacon Theater on January 27 for an evening of duets. Joining her onstage were contemporaries like Judy Collins and Mavis Staples, Paul Simon and David Crosby; "next generation" stars like Emmylou Harris, Jackson Browne, David Bromberg, and Fairport Convention's Richard Thompson; and comparative youngsters like Mary Chapin Carpenter, the Indigo Girls' Amy Ray and Emily Saliers, Damien Rice, and the baby of the bunch, Chilean Nano Stern, then just thirty.

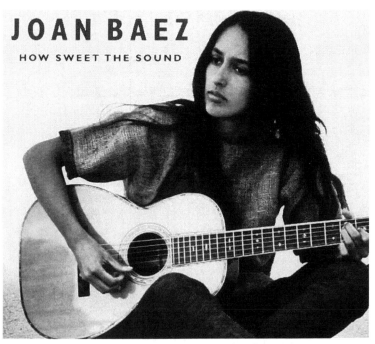

How sweet it was . . . and remains. This 2009 soundtrack compilation spans over half a century of Joan Baez's remarkable career. She was already a seasoned veteran with eleven albums under her belt when she headlined the Friday-night festivities in Bethel.

That birthday bash served as the kickoff for Baez's ambitious three-month 2016 tour. That June, PBS aired the birthday concert as *Great Performances: Joan Baez's 75th Birthday Celebration.* Though Baez has lamented in recent years that she's lost a bit of her vocal range, audiences at her sold-out concerts don't seem to notice or to mind. Then, in April 2017, Jackson Browne did the honors at the podium as Baez was inducted into the Rock and Roll Hall of Fame. It was an honor long overdue.

Although the draft is no longer an issue, Joan's political activism continues. She has taking up the cause of the Standing Rock Sioux in opposition to the Dakota Access Pipeline. In September 2018, Baez hit the road for what she has said will be her last international tour, but I doubt we have heard the last of her. She's still got it. With twenty-seven albums and more than six decades of live performances to her credit, Joan Baez remains as vibrant a force as ever, bringing the spirit of Woodstock Nation to new audiences wherever she roams.

10

Quill

Michael Lang's House Band

Quill was one of the bands that were booked by Mike Lang's company,
Amphion. That's why Quill was there. They were the opening band
on Saturday. They are probably the only band of the whole weekend
that was not a nationally known band. They were a Boston band—
they never really got their due. I roadie'd with them for about a week
after college. They were kind of jazzy blues-based. They had some
pop songs. They sounded like a lot of the . . . you know that bluesy,
psychedelic, stretched-out, jazzy, sometimes modal sound. They were
a great band.

— *Arthur Levy (rock historian), Pete Fornatale Radio Archives, 2009*

As the Seeds Were Sown: The Brothers Cole, from Boston

Quill was a humble East Coast band, a Boston quintet playing
mostly small clubs and bars. From 1967 through 1969, the group
became a staple on the New England scene in Boston and Providence,
occasionally dipping down into New York City. The odd one-off occasionally found them in places like Aspen, Colorado, where they once
performed for the ski set.

Quill built a solid reputation as a fun live act, routinely switching
up a variety of musical instruments, with members sharing lead vocal
duties, and getting audiences involved in the act by making them into

extended parts of the rhythm section. Audiences *loved* it, and provided the group with a small but loyal following.

Quill's star seemed ascendant as the band caught the attention of others in the "big leagues." Like fellow West Coast act Sweetwater, Quill wound up opening for a series of big-name headliners. Several of these acts were slated to perform at Woodstock, including the Jeff Beck Group, Janis Joplin, Sly and the Family Stone, the Who, and the Grateful Dead. But Quill also went out on the road in support of monster acts like the Kinks, Deep Purple, and legendary blues guitarist Buddy Guy.

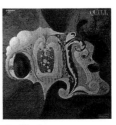

Quill, the eponymous 1970 debut . . . and swansong. Though brimming with talent, Woodstock Ventures' deputized goodwill ambassador band never made it to that next level of success.

Quill was such an exceptional live act, in fact, that at times the group came close to upstaging the headliners. A timely appearance at a Manhattan rock club called the Scene in early 1969 found Quill on the same bill as another Woodstock-bound newcomer, Johnny Winter. That New York appearance caught the attention of Artie Kornfeld and Michael Lang, which led to the band's "residency" in and around the site of the Woodstock Music and Arts Fair.

Michael Lang, an associate of Amphion Management, was also a friend of Quill's managers, dating back to his head-shop days in Florida. He had big plans for Quill, future stardom being just one of them. He also intended to deputize the group for a little "public relations" work.

In the Garden: We've Been Here All Week, Folks

While the majority of the acts slated to perform at Woodstock arrived on the day they were scheduled to perform and then beat it out of town, Quill was in it for the long haul. Lang had the group arrive a full *week* before the festival was scheduled to begin, and put the band members up in the motel with the festival crew.

In essence, Quill served as the house band, performing for festival staff, the Hog Farm crew, and whoever else was around in the days leading up to the Friday opener. Woodstock Ventures had been under a tremendous amount of pressure and public scrutiny, with many local people and businesses still grumbling about the event as it drew near, so Lang deputized Quill as musical goodwill ambassadors. He sent the musicians all over the area to play in prisons, halfway houses, and even mental institutions, all in the name of good community relations.

Legendary Atlantic Records mogul Ahmet Ertegün was paying close attention to the developments in Bethel. Sensing a business opportunity, he rolled the dice and signed Quill to a recording contract with his Cotillion label. Ertegün calculated that the timing for the group's prospective debut album would be perfect. If all went according to plan, and Quill was featured in Michael Wadleigh's film, the album's marketing campaign would essentially pay for itself.

Quill got Saturday's festivities off to a lively start at about a quarter past noon, and the cameras were loaded and rolling. The brothers Cole—Dan on vocals, Jon on bass and backing vocals—took to the stage, joined by guitarist and backing vocalist Norman Rogers, Roger North on the drums, and the multi-instrumentalist Phil Thayer on keyboards, saxophone, and flute. Their set was brief, consisting of just four tunes and lasting only half an hour.

Quill's opening number, "They Live the Life" had the band members using scraps of two-by-fours from the stage as percussion instruments, several of which they chucked over the plywood fencing into the crowd. While such shenanigans would be a lawsuit waiting to happen in our modern era, 1969 was a much more permissive and tolerant time when it came to the eccentricities and indulgences of rock-and-roll bands.

Quill had become such a familiar part of the scenery at the festival site during the preceding week that John Morris even felt comfortable enough to interrupt the group's set. It seemed that Hugh Romney of the Hog Farm had something he just *had* to say, and it could not wait.

Just after the band finished the unusual song "That's How I Eat," Morris addressed the assembled. "I apologize to all of you for doing this, but Hugh has something he's got to talk to us about. So let Hugh talk."

Romney, true to form, did not disappoint. While the musicians stood by, patiently waiting to resume their set, he took the mic. "Listen. We are all different parts of the same revolution. But if somebody's got an attitude and they're looking for some kind of violence, if this is love and peace, let's all jump up and kiss 'em . . . and *lick* 'em! And then I think everybody will feel real good, 'cause this is love, peace, and music. And I got one announcement that's important. Mark, Sandy, or Heady, please bring Patty's asthma medicine to the Information Booth. She is having an attack. Okay. So, kiss those guys if they start punching somebody."

If you are wondering why the presumably urgent matter of "Patty's" asthma attack had to wait until *after* Hugh's advice on defusing violence by kissing and licking the perpetrators, you are not alone. Romney, a.k.a. Wavy Gravy, is alive and well at the time of this writing, but he has never been the most coherent of interview subjects, so the world may never know.

Quill picked up where they left off with the song, "Drifting," before closing out with the raucous and tribally percussive "Waitin' for You," which got the crowd revved up, clapping, stomping and chanting along. It was a short and sweet set that got the crowd in the spirit for the music still to come. But it was not what one could call "career defining."

The Harvest Reaped: Plucked into Obscurity

When Michael Wadleigh and his crew checked the recordings from Quill's set, they discovered that the film footage would be unusable in the movie, because the audio tracks were out of sync with the video. Now you may recall that essentially the same problem occurred during Arlo Guthrie's set on Friday night (see chapter 8). In Guthrie's case, they found a workaround, but poor Quill's performance wound up on the cutting room floor. The group would not be appearing in *Woodstock*, after all.

Ertegün was bummed, to say the least. He was savvy enough to understand the business implications of Quill's omission from the film, as the band would learn soon enough. But there was still a contract to fulfill. The recording of Quill's self-titled debut album proceeded according to plan at Natural Sounds Studios, but sales expectations were lowered. Weighing in at seven tracks and just under forty minutes of playing time, *Quill* was in the can before year's end, and was officially released on New Year's Day, 1970, to mixed reviews. Ertegün held the purse strings tight on promotions, and the album went nowhere commercially.

Jon Cole was the first band member to see the writing on the wall. He bailed out on his brother and bandmates after a few months of watching the album languish. He dabbled in the music business for a while, but he was also innovative and really good with his hands. He became a businessman, first by teaching people the fine art of auto mechanics, and later by getting in on the ground floor of the solar energy craze.

Brother Dan, Roger, Norm, and Phil rallied to record a second album for Cotillion, but this was more in fulfillment of their contractual obligation than anything else. The label never even bothered to *release* it. And that was all she wrote. Before the summer of 1970 rolled around, Quill was officially disbanded, and the members went their separate ways.

Dan opened his own business, Intermedia Sound Studio, the first 16-track recording studio in Boston. He produced a number of albums, and also became a pioneer of laser light shows, which became a late-night fad at planetariums and a staple activity among the stoner rock set during the '70s and '80s. He also started his own production company, Dan Cole Productions, and collaborated on projects with his early backer, Michael Lang. In the mid-'70s, Lang took over management of Joe Cocker (see chapter 24), who ditched the Grease Band and embarked on the Mad Dogs and Englishmen tour. After that tour, Joe needed a new touring band, and wound up employing Cole's clients, Boston's own American Standard Band (ASB).

But Dan, like his brother, was a restless spirit. When the digital revolution began to take shape in the early '80s, he bailed out on the music industry and tried to get in on the action in the computer industry. He worked for Sony for more than a decade, before the winds of change led him to set up a business and investment consultancy. In the middle of all of this, he still maintains a recording studio, and has been dabbling with music in recent years.

Norm Rogers returned to New England, and settled down in Brattleboro, Vermont. Sadly, he went off to join that great rock-and-roll band in the sky on July 9, 2011. Phil Thayer is "alive and well," according to an email I received from him in November 2016, and "still playing music."

And, last but not least, Roger North got his patent for North Drums in 1970. The innovative and unusual-looking instruments hit the market in 1972, and by 1976, they were being manufactured by Music Technology Incorporated (MTI). The drums developed a following among marquee names like Yes's Alan White and Doug "Cosmo" Clifford of Creedence Clearwater Revival, but they never became the mainstream, standard-issue instruments that Roger had hoped. By the early 1980s, production of North Drums had come to a halt, and they are now considered collector's items.

North Drums: the shape of things to come? Roger North thought so, and though they have been out of production since the early 1980s, his signature instruments remain a collector's item among drum aficionados.

On the music front, North wound up manning the skins for one of Joan Baez's mentors, Odetta, and later joined a wacky band called the Holy Modal Rounders, with whom he enjoyed a solid eight-year run. Most recently, he was a member of the locally popular Oregon-based jam band the Freak Mountain Ramblers, and is still using his signature drums. The beat goes on.

11

Country Joe McDonald

Friday on My Mind

People always ask me what Woodstock was like, and I always say, like a family picnic. They always say that they are sorry that they were not there, and I always say don't be. I have played hundreds of Woodstocks before and after. In places all over the world. Small ones and big ones. All it is, in my opinion, is good vibes, nice music, outdoors, and some snacks. It doesn't get any better than that.

—*Country Joe McDonald, foreword to* Back to the Garden

As the Seeds Were Sown: In the Navy

Joseph Allen McDonald was born in Washington, D.C., on New Year's Day, 1942, and named by his parents—both former members of the Communist Party—after the infamous Soviet Union dictator Joseph Stalin. Stalin was nicknamed "Uncle Joe" by the American press, and McDonald's "Country Joe" may have been a riff on that.

McDonald began life as more of an *average* Joe. He became a California kid when his family—parents Worden and Florence, brother Billy, and sister Nancy—relocated to El Monte, a suburb of Los Angeles. Joe shared something in common with fellow Woodstock alumnus Joan Baez (see chapter 9). Like Joan, Joe was the grandchild of a clergyman, in this case a Presbyterian minister.

Young Joe was musically inclined, taking up the trombone during grade school. He would later trade in his trombone for a guitar. The teenage Joe was a real go-getter. He led his high school's marching band, serving as president *and* conductor, and later led the school orchestra. But his musical direction was rapidly evolving. He began playing the guitar during his senior year of high school, and tried his hand at songwriting.

It seemed almost fitting that he joined the United States Navy in 1959, at age seventeen, and was deployed to Japan, guitar in tow. But his views on the military soon changed. Following his discharge, he enrolled at Los Angeles City College, but the student life was not for Joe, who dropped out after three semesters. He settled in Berkeley and married his first wife, Kathe Werum, in 1963.

During this period, he busked for passersby on Telegraph Avenue, worked in a local guitar store, and began to form bands, such as the Instant Action Jug Band, and the Berkeley String Quartet. Joe was a folkie at heart, and obsessed with Woody Guthrie, but he loved *all* sorts of music, dabbling in jazz, gospel, and bluegrass, before moving into psychedelic rock and roll. Joe's road manager and friend, Bill Belmont, mentions Dolphin's Record store, the radio station KFWB, and the time Joe spent hanging out at the Lighthouse Club in Hermosa Beach as being significant factors in Joe's musical development.

In 1964, at age twenty-two, Joe entered a recording studio for the first time, in a collaborative effort with fellow musician Blair Hardman. The result was a recording called *A Collection of Songs with Blair Hardman*. It would not be released to the public for thirteen years, when it was issued on First American Records in 1977 as *The Early Years*.

Joe's marriage to Werum lasted barely three years before the young couple divorced in 1966. At some point during 1965, Joe had formed his first rock-and-roll band, Country Joe and the Fish (see chapter 25), and by now was living in the San Francisco Bay Area.

Undaunted by his first foray into matrimony, and a period of time as the boyfriend of Janis Joplin, Joe wed Robin Menken in 1967. By the following year, the twenty-six-year-old became a father, as the couple welcomed daughter Seven Anne to the world.

In the years leading up to the Woodstock festival, Joe was known primarily as the lead singer for Country Joe and the Fish, and the band was getting some serious recognition. At the same time there were growing tensions within the band, and there was a part of Joe that was a solo artist just aching to strike out on his own. The audience in Bethel got to see *both* sides of "Country Joe": the psychedelic, freak-out rock singer and the protest folk singer. The way things worked out that weekend, it was the folk-singer side of Joe who took to the stage first.

In the Garden: A Two-Timer

Navy veteran "Country" Joe McDonald has maintained—for *years*—that he was standing around the Woodstock stage after Richie Havens's performance when the festival organizers coaxed him onto the stage to play an unscheduled solo acoustic set. But the preponderance of evidence suggests that he is mistaken. Not mistaken about being coaxed up onto to the stage to play, mind you; just about the timing.

The most credible evidence reveals that Joe did play a solo acoustic set, but that set took place on *Saturday*, after Quill's set and before Santana's. (Carlos Santana even mentions in his autobiography that he heard McDonald singing right before he was asked to perform; in fact, he writes that it was "Country Joe and the Fish," but at least he was *partially* right—see chapter 12.) But a solo Country Joe McDonald set is a treat *any* day of the week, and any time of the day. This set was no exception. Using a rope in place of a guitar strap, Joe and his borrowed Yamaha FG-150 acoustic guitar wowed the crowd with a spirited mix of originals and covers.

His opener, "Janis," was an ode to his fellow Woodstock performer and former lover, Janis Joplin. He continued with his own "Donovan's Reef," followed by the 1959 country classic "Heartaches by the Number," Johnny Cash's "Ring of Fire," Driftwood's "Tennessee Stud," "Rockin' 'Round the World," "Flying High," and "I Seen a Rocket," before launching into the infamous "Fuck Cheer," which led into the poignant and timely "I-Feel-Like-I'm-Fixin'-to-Die Rag."

"I-Feel-Like-I'm-Fixin'-to-Die Rag" is a *tough* song to follow, so when Joe returned to the front of the stage for the obligatory encore, he broke out one more verse and chorus of the same song. He may have been just one man, wielding a borrowed guitar, but he must have done *something* right that day; the crowd was electrified, and primed for Santana.

By 1970, Country Joe had branched out into doing soundtrack work, which included music for the racy Danish film *Quiet Days in Clichy*.

The Harvest Reaped: From Fish to Folk

Woodstock, the film, showcases Joe's musical versatility for an infinite and timeless audience. One moment, there he is, fronting Country Joe and the Fish, extolling the virtues of "Marijuana!" The next moment, there he is, the prototypical long-haired hippie folk singer, wearing a green army field jacket and a headband, strumming an acoustic guitar and delivering protest songs.

The fact that the order of these performances was in reality the opposite matters little in the context of the film. Wadleigh's decision to use onscreen graphics—a follow-the-bouncing-ball-over-the-lyrics effect during the "I-Feel-Like-I'm-Fixin'-to-Die Rag"—instantly made Joe's solo acoustic turn one of the most noteworthy and beloved moments of the film.

In December 1969, Joe released his debut solo album, *Thinking of Woody Guthrie*, on Vanguard Records. The album, filled with Guthrie covers, preceded *Tonight I'm Singing Just for You*, an album of country standards recorded during the same studio sessions. Even though there was still one more Country Joe and the Fish album due for release in 1970, *CJ Fish*, Joe was now, in his heart of hearts, a solo artist, and so he remains to this day.

Leaving his fellow "Fish" behind, Joe packed his guitar and headed for Europe during the summer of 1970, performing at a series of festivals and in halls throughout the land. He paused in London long enough to record an album for Vanguard Records, *Hold On, I'm Coming*, which would be released in 1971. During the European tour, Joe found himself wrapped up in another project, composing five songs for the soundtrack

Thinking of Woody Guthrie, Joe McDonald's 1969 solo debut. Always a folkie at heart, he released this album four months after the Woodstock festival.

of *Quiet Days in Clichy*, a comedic film adaptation of the classic 1956 Henry Miller novel. Joe's title track became the center of a controversy. The song, deemed "obscene" because of its connection to Miller's work, was banned from the radio, and the filmmakers also had to fight "obscenity" charges in court in order to distribute the film in the United States.

Joe went on later in 1970 to score original music for a Chilean film, Saul Landau's *¡Que Hacer!* Joe appears in the film as, essentially, *himself*, a character called "Country." That same year, Joe appeared in a brief clip as "AM Radio" in a film called *Gas-s-s-s!* (or, alternately, by the more convoluted title *Gas! Or It Became Necessary to Destroy the World in Order to Save It*).

With folk, country, film soundtrack albums, and even a little *acting* to his credit, Joe was demonstrating his artistic versatility to the world. It would be difficult for *any* artist to maintain the pace that Joe managed from 1969–1971, but he still managed to release at least one album per year through the end of the 1970s.

Joe didn't really *pursue* film or TV projects, though he did pop up with his Country Joe and the Fish bandmates as "The Cracker Band" in the 1971 B-Western flop *Zachariah*. Country Joe and the Fish also pop up in 1979's mid-'60s-themed *More American Graffiti*. Finally, Joe appears as "Joaquin" in the 1993 TV series *Tales of the City*, based on the Armistead Maupin novels.

On the home front, Joe's marriage to Janice Taylor yielded fruit in the form of two daughters, Devin in 1976, and Tara in 1980. Later, while married to Kathy Wright, Joe welcomed Emily in 1988, and Ryan in 1991.

Joe has released thirty-five solo albums to date, most recently 2017's *50*. With tracks like "Blackfish," chronicling the plight of captive orcas, and the pro–gun control "Era of Guns," it is clear that, long after Vietnam, Joe continues to fight for causes he believes in. He walks the line between folk and rock, performing solo shows and others with a full band.

12

Santana . . . and Bill Graham

An Offer You Can't Refuse

I remember the sound before it came out of my fingers, then I heard it come out of my fingers into the guitar strings. From the guitar strings to the amplifier. From the amplifier to the P.A. From the P.A. to a whole ocean of people—a mountain—a whole ocean of people, and then it comes back to you. You never forget that. That's where I discovered my first mantra. Most people know by now that I was totally peaking on mescaline, because they told me I didn't have to play until two o'clock in the morning or something. They lied to us. As soon as I took it and started totally flashing, it was two o'clock in the afternoon. So that was the first time I repeated my first mantra, which was, "God! Please help me stay in time and in tune!" I just repeated that mantra.

— *Carlos Santana, Pete Fornatale Radio Archives, 2009*

As the Seeds Were Sown: Don't Quit Your Day Job

Carlos Santana was born July 20, 1947, in Autlán de Navarro, Jalisco, Mexico, to Josefina Barragán and José Santana. José was a popular local musician who played the violin and spent a good deal of his time traveling to support his extended family. Carlos's paternal grandfather, Antonino, was also a professional musician, as was *his* father before him. Carlos began taking violin lessons at age five, and soon added acoustic guitar.

Things began to happen for him when the family relocated to the festive border city of Tijuana in 1955, just after his eighth birthday. There, at José's urging, Carlos began busking in the street for tips. Before long, he was entering music contests and playing alongside his father. But the convergence of Carlos's adolescence with the emergence of American rock and roll, and Tijuana's proximity to the California border, led to some musical conflicts between father and son. When José took his act north of the border to San Francisco, in search of more lucrative gigs, Carlos put his violin aside and turned his attention to rock and roll. He found himself following a local musician, Javier Batíz, and his group, Los TJs, who turned the teen on to the American sounds of B.B. King, Jimmy Reed, Ray Charles, James Brown, and Little Richard.

José didn't care for Carlos's new music, but he was supportive enough to buy him his first electric guitar, a Gibson. Carlos began sitting in with the TJs, often on bass, before joining a band called the Strangers that had a regular gig at a place called El Convoy.

When the Santana family decided to join José in San Francisco in 1962, Carlos was so busy playing at El Convoy that he insisted on staying behind. He wouldn't make his *final* move to California until his mother and brother Tony returned to Tijuana in 1963 and "kidnapped" him from the El Convoy in the middle of a set. The only possessions he had with him were his guitar, his amp, and the clothes on his back.

After a period of adjustment to a new language and a new environment, Carlos settled down and formed an unnamed trio with school-mates Sergio "Gus" Rodriguez on bass and Danny Haro on the drums. He considered this new ensemble to be a step below the bands he had played with in Tijuana, but he persisted. During the fall of 1965, conga player Michael Carabello joined the nameless band, and Babatunde Olatunji's "Jingo" became a part of their regular set.

Even though Carlos was held back two grade levels, he stayed in school, never realizing that this was the only thing keeping him from the draft. He worked as a dishwasher at the Tic Tock Drive In, and fed a good portion of his earnings into the jukebox.

He became a regular at the Fillmore Auditorium, where, in 1966, he joined a hastily assembled group of guitarists asked to fill in for a wasted Paul Butterfield, and in doing so caught the attention of Bill Graham.

Butterfield was tripping on acid, clearly in no state to play, so the other guitarists were getting together for a jam, among them Jerry Garcia, Mike Bloomfield, and Jorma Kaukonen. Stan Marcum, Carlos's manager, asked if Carlos could join them. The ensemble launched into the blues standard "Good Morning, Little Schoolgirl." Jerry Garcia took the first solo, and then, when they gave Carlos the nod, he just closed his eyes and let it fly. Everyone was impressed with his skills, most importantly Graham, who agreed to start booking Carlos's band for opening slots.

Rodriguez and Haro grew jealous when Carlos began jamming with singer and guitarist Tom Fraser and keyboardist Gregg Rolie during 1967. This would prove to be a transitional year for Carlos. He was *finally* scheduled to graduate from high school, when a positive result on a tuberculosis test landed him in medical quarantine for three months. With the aid of a tutor, he was able to earn his diploma just a month shy of his twentieth birthday, and he went AWOL from his quarantine soon thereafter.

Carlos and his band had *just* started breaking into playing at Bill Graham's Fillmore Auditorium when they opened for the Who on a Friday night in June. The first incarnation of the Santana Blues Band was a four-piece featuring Carlos, Gus Rodriguez, Danny Haro, and Michael Carabello. It was Carabello who decided on using Carlos's last name, mostly based on the way it *sounded*.

The Friday night show went off without a hitch, but the next night they committed the cardinal sin of being late . . . *very* late. Bill Graham didn't like it when bands were late, and he promptly banned them from the premises . . . *indefinitely*. He didn't even want them there as audience members, but they kept sneaking in to see bands anyway.

After much soul-searching, Carlos decided to part ways with his school friends and move forward. He joined forces with Tom Fraser on vocals and guitar, "The Magnificent" Marcus Malone on percussion, Seattle native Greg Rolie on lead vocals and Hammond B-3, Rod Harper on drums, and David Brown on bass, to form the next incarnation of the band. According to popular legend, when the lineup of Santana, Rolie, Harper, Malone, and Brown auditioned for Chet Helms at the Avalon Ballroom, Helms lacked the foresight to realize that the band's blend of Latin-jazz-African fusion had potential. He dismissively suggested that Carlos ought to keep his dishwashing job.

Helms's loss would turn out to be Bill Graham's gain. By the summer of 1968, the band had worked its way back into Graham's good graces enough to be booked to open a series of shows at his newest venue, the Fillmore West. Before long, the band had begun headlining, its name now just Santana.

Knowing that Santana needed shorter, more structured songs if the group were ever going to land a record deal, Bill introduced the musicians to Willie Bobo's version of Sonny Henry's "Evil Ways." It became an audience favorite. The group inked a recording deal with CBS's Clive Davis and Columbia Records in October 1968. Those first recording sessions did not go very well.

The low point came when Marcus Malone wound up in jail . . . for *murder*. Apparently Marcus had been fooling around with another man's wife; when the man caught them together, a fight ensued, and Marcus stabbed the man, who later died. Marcus wound up doing a stretch in San Quentin, and his time with Santana was over.

The recording sessions were put on hold while the band returned to San Francisco to regroup. There, Carabello stumbled upon the solution to one of their problems in the diminutive person of José "Chepito" Areas, a Nicaraguan multi-instrumentalist who played congas, timbales, and even trumpet. Chepito may have been small in stature, but he was a musical giant.

Carabello and Rolie were unhappy with Livingston's drumming, so they let him go. They employed a few fill-in drummers for live shows, but they needed a permanent replacement. By this point, they were back in the studio, preparing to record their first album. In walked Michael Shrieve, a local drummer and friend of the Jefferson Airplane. When Santana invited Shrieve to jam, something just clicked. They asked him to join almost immediately. With Shrieve in the fold, the recording sessions fell into place. The drummer would have a profound influence on Carlos's musical taste when he introduced him to the likes of Miles Davis and John Coltrane.

One day, Bill Graham got a call from Michael Lang, who was looking for help organizing the Woodstock festival, *and* for permission to use Bill's name as leverage in some of his artist negotiations. Bill agreed to help, and Lang agreed to book Santana for $750, along with the more established Grateful Dead for $2,500.

Graham booked Santana for pre-Woodstock gigs at his Fillmore East on August 1 and 2, the Atlantic City Pop Festival on the 3rd, the Pavilion at Flushing Meadows Park in Queens on the 8th and 9th, and Central Park on the 10th, before heading upstate play at SUNY Stony Brook on the 11th. After Stony Brook, Bill rented a house in Woodstock for the band while he worked behind the scenes on behalf of Lang and company.

In the Garden: Riding the Snake

Santana's wakeup call came at 5:00 a.m. Saturday. The group piled into vans to drive to the helicopter pickup point, and then waited for liftoff. The aerial view revealed just how big an event Woodstock had become. In his memoir, Carlos writes, "A few minutes later we were swooping over a field, looking down in the morning light at a carpet made of people—flesh and hair and teeth—stretched out across the hills."

The chopper set down in the field behind the stage just after noon. Quill was onstage, playing the first set of the day. In addition to the overwhelming sight, the festival held surprises for the rest of the human sensorium, particularly the olfactory. Humid summer air on a farm is fragrant under ordinary circumstances, but when you factor in all of those sweaty, unwashed bodies, overwhelmed Port-o-Sans, incense, patchouli oil, warm, stale beer, and vast clouds of marijuana smoke, the atmosphere was pungent indeed. Carlos took note of the smell.

Carlos thought he wasn't going to play until three bands *after* the Grateful Dead, and the first familiar face he spotted was Jerry Garcia's. The Dead wasn't playing until late that night, so Carlos had no qualms about accepting a hit of mescaline from Jerry. He was sure he would come down from his trip long before he was scheduled to play. The sounds of Country Joe McDonald filled the air, and Carlos began *tripping*. Just then, a festival staffer Carlos did not recognize told the band to grab their gear and start setting up. They were on *next*. Carlos prayed silently and found his mantra.

Carlos Santana (lead guitar), Jose "Chepito" Areas and Michael Carabello (timbales, congas, and percussion), Gregg Rolie (lead vocals and Hammond B-3), David Brown (bass), and Michael Shrieve (drums) took to the stage and launched into "Waiting," the instrumental opener from the group's first album . . . which hadn't been released yet. This was a band of unknowns, playing before the biggest audience in history, and the lead guitarist was hallucinating that his red Gibson SG had turned into an "electric snake" in his hands; what could possibly go wrong? Not much, as it turned out.

The scrappy San Francisco sextet killed it during a funky forty-five-minute set. "Waiting" led into "Evil Ways," followed by "You Just Don't Care," "Savor," and "Jingo." They continued with "Persuasion" and the finale, "Soul Sacrifice," highlighted by the baby-faced Shrieve's blistering drum solo. They played "Fried Neckbones and Some Home Fries" as an encore, and then they were done.

Suddenly, like a proud uncle, Bill Graham was there, clapping Rolie on the back and urging the band to turn around, look out at the crowd, and savor the moment. Unbeknown to his bandmates, Carlos had made a silent vow as he left the stage to never trip again . . . at least not before an important gig like this.

They left the festival on the next available helicopter, and were back on the road the next day, their memories of Saturday afternoon already beginning to fade. In the years ahead, they would each come to understand just how important their Woodstock appearance had been.

The Harvest Reaped: Seeking *The Universal Tone*

Santana hit the shelves days later and soared to #4 on the *Billboard* charts. "Evil Ways" cracked the Top 10 at #9. Graham knew what he was doing. In spite of tepid reviews in *Rolling Stone* and the *Village Voice*, *Santana* was a hit; one that would attain RIAA-certified double-platinum status. There would be no sophomore slump.

Woodstock premiered at movie theaters on March 26, 1970, and Santana's "Soul Sacrifice" was a highlight. In the wake of the film's release,

Santana's 1969 debut album came roaring out of the gate two weeks after the band's remarkable Saturday-afternoon performance at the festival.

Santana entered Wally Heider Studios in San Francisco to begin work on a follow-up. The group's masterpiece, *Abraxas*, arrived in September 1970. The album was certified five times platinum, selling in excess of five million units in the US alone. The first single, a cover of Peter Green's "Black Magic Woman" interlaced with Gábor Szabó's "Gypsy Queen," hit #4. The second, a cover of Tito Puente's "Oye Como Va," hit #13 on *Billboard*'s Hot 100 the following year. The third, Gregg Rolie's "Hope You're Feeling Better," failed to chart, but it foreshadowed later Santana lineups with its guest appearance by seventeen-year-old guitarist Neal Schon, a friend of Shrieve and Rolie's who added a solo.

The same lineup entered Columbia Studios in San Francisco on the 4th of July, 1971, and *Santana III*, or *Man with an Outstretched Hand*, was released in September, and became the group's second #1 album in a row. It was certified double platinum in the US but made less of an impact overseas. Neal Schon was brought in to help out on a few tracks, including "Everybody's Everything."

The ever-evolving Santana deftly avoided the "sophomore jinx" with the 1970 masterpiece *Abraxas*.

When Chepito was sidelined due to health issues, Joseph Thomas "Coke" Escovedo was brought in on percussion. He co-wrote the hit single "No One to Depend On"—which also features a Schon guitar solo—with Rolie and Carabello. But cracks in the band's facade were beginning to show. This would be the last album by the Woodstock-era lineup, and Santana's last #1 album . . . for twenty-eight years.

Part of the band's troubles owed to typical excesses of the rock-and-roll lifestyle: money, cocaine, booze, and a parade of readily available women. The gritty band members who thought of themselves as "street" and "real" found their heads becoming swelled by success. But their musical tastes were evolving in different directions, too. Shrieve had gotten Carlos heavily into jazz by this point, and the guitarist had also begun a spiritual journey, meditating and delving into Eastern philosophy. Rolie, meanwhile, wanted to run off with Schon and play more mainstream, commercial rock and roll, which is what they did when they split off from Santana after recording *Caravanserai* (1972) to form Journey, a band that went on to enjoy enormous commercial success.

Santana mutated into an ever-changing array of musicians orbiting around Carlos, the group's musical and spiritual center. Over the next twenty years, Santana released thirteen studio albums, only one of which, 1981's *Zebop!*, cracked the Top 10 and was certified platinum, fueled in part by the hit single "Winning."

Santana appeared at Live Aid with Pat Metheny on July 13, 1985, and continued to tour, but commercial success remained elusive. In 1992, *Milagro*, a "goodbye" letter to Bill Graham, who had been killed in a helicopter crash in October 1991, and Miles Davis, who died a month earlier of complications from stroke and pneumonia, bottomed out at #102.

Santana had released one live album, *Lotus*, in 1974, and a second, the critically acclaimed *Sacred Fire*, in 1993. The group was on a seven-year recording hiatus and would not return to the studio until early 1999. In the interim, the band was inducted into the Rock and Roll Hall of Fame in 1998, and was poised for a return to action. *Supernatural*, released on June 15, 1999, proved to be the biggest album of Santana's career. Carlos's career had come full circle, back to Clive Davis, the man who first signed his band in 1968.

Davis's concept was simple: match the guitar god with modern music stars for a series of collaborative duets. Fueled in part by the #1 singles "Smooth," featuring vocals by Matchbox Twenty's Rob Thomas, and "Maria Maria," featuring R&B duo the Product G&B, *Supernatural* hit #1 in ten countries, sold more than thirty million copies worldwide, and was RIAA-certified *diamond*—fifteen times platinum. *Supernatural* cleaned up at the Grammy Awards, winning in eight categories, including "Album of the Year," and did much the same at the Latin Grammy Awards.

The album also features performances by fellow grizzled veteran Eric Clapton, Swedish jazz legacy Eagle-Eye Cherry (son of trumpeter Don), hip-hop goddess Lauryn Hill (formerly of the Fugees), Dave Matthews, the critically acclaimed Mexican rock band Maña, and hip-hop singer Cee-Lo Green.

Supernatural proved so successful that the same production team assembled for the 2002 follow-up, *Shaman*, and employed a similar approach in terms of guest stars. The most famous of these was Spanish tenor Plácido Domingo. Others included Nickelback's Chad Kroeger, singer/songwriter Michelle Branch—who features on the Top 10 single "The Game of Love"—and Alex Band of the Calling. Clocking in at a whopping seventy-six minutes, the album debuted at #1 on *Billboard* and was certified double platinum.

All of Santana's subsequent releases have comfortably cracked the Top 20, and most continue the trend of featuring guest vocalists and musicians: *All That I Am* (2005), *Guitar Heaven* (2010), *Shape Shifter* (2012), *Corazón* (2014), and, most recently, 2016's *Santana IV*. Carlos reassembled as much of the old gang as possible for that one, including Michael Carabello, Gregg Rolie, and Michael Shrieve, along with Neal Schon, Benny Rietveld, and Karl Perazzo. Ronald Isley of the Isley Brothers performs guest vocals on two tracks. Carlos tackled a new medium in 2014 when he released his bestselling autobiography, *The Universal Tone: Bringing My Story to Light*.

In hindsight, it is clear that evolution and change have always been the hallmarks of Santana's career. The ever-expanding solar system of bandmates who have orbited Carlos over the years now numbers almost seventy. He has released twenty-four studio albums, seven live albums, and appeared on thirteen collaborative albums. Somehow or other, there are also twenty-two Santana compilation albums; the sheer volume of this body of work is a testament to the man's work ethic. Carlos Santana's quest for the universal tone continues, and the light of the band that bears his name continues to shine.

13

John Sebastian

Summer, but *Not* in the City

Personally speaking, I feel like I ended up doing myself a great disser-
vice in retrospect, because I was very much a member of the audience
that weekend. I was not scheduled to perform; I had no . . . instruments or special performing gear. I'd been living in the mud for two
days participating liberally in the psychedelics of the era and, by the
time I got onstage I was just about as stoned as I'd ever been. And,
uh—the fact is that, although it was very much in keeping with the
mood of the weekend, I have sung and played better almost anytime
including when you wake me up in the middle of the night. So, uh—so
in a lot of ways I'm sorry that that performance had to go that way. I
wish I'd had a little more warning.

—*John Sebastian, Pete Fornatale Radio Archives, 2009*

As the Seeds Were Sown: It Took a Village

John Benson Sebastian was born March 17, 1944, under the sign of
Pisces, and raised in Greenwich Village during the height of the folk-
music revolution. His father, also named John Sebastian, was a classically
trained harmonica player. The Sebastians were financially well off and
friendly with many stars of television, literature, and music. They were
able to offer young John the benefits of a private boarding-school education at New Jersey's Blair Academy, which led to his acceptance at NYU.
But like many of his fellow Woodstock alumni, John wasn't cut out for the
collegiate lifestyle. He left school after one year to concentrate on music.

With his father's connections, his proximity to some of the nation's greatest folk, jazz, and blues clubs, and his growing skills on blues harmonica, autoharp, and guitar, John found himself caught up in the local music scene. By age twenty, he was appearing on professional recordings, such as banjo player Billy Faier's 1964 album *The Beast of Billy Faier*. That same year, he also got a taste of what it was like to be part of a group when he joined the Even Dozen Jug Band for the recording of its one and only self-titled album. By the time *Even Dozen Jug Band* was released, the band had already broken up. Among his fellow "dozen" was the brilliant mandolin player David Grisman, who went on to play with the likes of Jerry Garcia in Old and in the Way; and Steve Katz, who went on to play in the Blues Project, and later appeared at Woodstock as a member of Blood, Sweat, and Tears.

The following year found John back in the studio, playing harp alongside bassist and fellow Woodstock alumnus Felix Pappalardi on Fred Neil's album *Bleecker and MacDougal*. He also appeared on folk singer Tom Rush's eponymous 1965 album. Then came the Mugwumps, a band that would split, amoeba-like, into two of the biggest bands of the 1960s, both of them future Rock and Roll Hall of Fame Inductees. Cass Elliot and Denny Doherty left to join John Philips and Michele Philips in the Mamas and the Papas in Los Angeles; John Sebastian and guitarist Zal Yanovsky split to form the Lovin' Spoonful with bassist Steve Boone and drummer Jan Carl (promptly replaced by Joe Butler) in New York City.

After a shaky debut at the Night Owl in Greenwich Village, the Lovin' Spoonful, at the suggestion of the club owner, devoted themselves to rehearsal time, honing their chops to the point where they began drawing respectable crowds. The group's newfound popularity led to a deal with Elektra Records, which promptly found itself outflanked by rival Kama Sutra Records. Before the ink was dry on the contract, the group had recorded four tracks for Elektra, but those would not see the light of day until after the band's debut on Kama Sutra.

Perhaps there *was* a bit of "magic" at work here, for the Lovin' Spoonful's debut single, 1965's "Do You Believe in Magic," was a bona-fide Top 10 hit. But this was just the beginning of the hit parade. The group's next six singles—"You Didn't Have to Be So Nice," "Daydream," "Did You

The Lovin' Spoonful's 1965 debut album. The title track, "Do You Believe in Magic," cracked the Top 10. By the time of the Woodstock festival, lead singer John Sebastian was flying solo.

Ever Make Up Your Mind," "Summer in the City," "Rain on the Roof," and "Nashville Cats"—would *all* crack the Top 10.

John also found time to compose original music for two films in 1966: Francis Ford Coppola's *You're a Big Boy Now,* and Woody Allen's comedic feature-length directorial debut, *What's Up, Tiger Lily?* The latter features a cameo by the members of the Lovin' Spoonful as themselves.

Draconian drug and immigration laws threw the band a curveball when Yanovsky was busted and charged with possession of marijuana—a much more serious crime in 1967 San Francisco than it is in modern times. Yanovsky, a Canadian citizen, decided to "narc." Fearing deportation, he cooperated with the authorities and identified his suppliers—an act of betrayal in the eyes of the counterculture. Neither he, nor the band, would ever fully recover from the incident. Yanovsky left the band in disgrace, and the Lovin' Spoonful suddenly found itself boycotted by many former fans. The group also parted ways with original producer Erik Jacobsen, and would never again reach those early commercial heights.

John Sebastian must have seen the writing on the wall, for he struck out on his own in 1968 to become a full-time solo artist, while also continuing to write music for film and stage. Yes, that was his work (music and lyrics) in 1968's *Jimmy Shine*, Murray Schisgal's Broadway play starring fellow icon, Dustin Hoffman. Though the play only enjoyed a short run, from December of '68 through April of '69, it gave John the experience and the confidence he needed to tackle similar projects in the years to come. Then, one weekend in August, he decided to attend a little music festival in upstate New York.

In the Garden: What a Lovely Dream It Was

As noted above, when John Sebastian arrived in Bethel for the Woodstock festival, it was with the intention of enjoying himself as a member of the audience. Then he got the tap on the shoulder, and a hastily arranged deal was struck. Chip Monck announced, "Ladies and gentlemen, please welcome with us, John Sebastian."

Clad in perhaps *the* finest homemade tie-dye outfit of any festival performer, John somehow found himself onstage. "Thank you," he began. "I don't know if you can tell how amazing you look. But you're truly amazing; you're a whole city."

Appearing solo, with just an acoustic guitar borrowed from Tim Hardin, John delivered an impromptu five-song set. He opened with "How Have You Been" and continued with "Rainbows All Over Your Blues" and "I Had a Dream," before ending with the Lovin' Spoonful's "Darlin' Be Home Soon." Between each song, the delightfully stoned legend rapped cheerfully to the audience about a variety of topics, including marijuana, living in a tent,

John Sebastian's 1970 solo debut. The Woodstock audience got a preview performance of several of these songs on the Saturday afternoon.

and learning how to make tie-dyes. The crowd was enraptured and roared in approval.

On his way back to the stage for an encore, John misinterpreted something Chip had said about a birth, and incorporated it into his stage banter:

> Oh, boy. This is really a mind-fucker of all times, man. I've never seen anything like this, man. I mean, like, you know, there was Newport, right? But they *owned* it! It was something else. Wow! Just love everybody all around you and clean up a little garbage on your way out and everything gonna be all right. Yeah, man, and Chip—my man, Chip—he's just . . . oh, you're doing so well, man. He says to look out for the fence, too, man. You have to look after the fence. You know, like the press can only say bad things unless there ain't no fuck-ups, and its lookin' like there *ain't* gonna be no fuck-ups. This is gonna work! Yay! Yay, for you. Yay for the Diggers, and everybody, wow. Hey, I don't know, you know. I don't know how I can come much harder, but . . . right now, but I'll . . . I'd like to sing you one little song. I'd like to sing you a song. Actually I'd like to dedicate it to . . . there's a cat and I really don't even know his name, but I remember that Chip said that, uh . . . that his old lady just had a baby. And that made me think, wow, it really is a city here. But this is for you and your old lady, man. And, uh . . . whew! That kid's gonna be far out.

And, with that, John went into his encore, "Younger Generation." But in spite of his birth announcement, there is no evidence that anyone gave birth *at* the festival site (though it is certainly likely that a few pregnancies *began* there). In reality, a woman in labor had been airlifted from the festival site to give birth at a nearby hospital.

After he sang the final line, "Could it be that you can't live up to your dreams?" John answered his own question: "No, it's not true, because we're doing it! I love you. Goodbye!" And, with that, he took off Tim Hardin's guitar and walked off the stage.

The Harvest Reaped: Welcome Back, John

Whatever misgivings John may have felt about his Woodstock set, he essentially recreated it for the sixth annual Big Sur Folk Festival the following month in California. He was much better prepared this time, and the following summer at the 1970 Isle of Wight Festival. During his post-Woodstock years, he continued to write, record, and perform, but he also branched out into other creative endeavors.

His long-delayed solo debut, *John Sebastian*, recorded in 1968 and produced by Paul Rothchild, dropped on January 19, 1970. The album features appearances by David Crosby, Stephen Stills, and Graham Nash—before there ever was a Crosby, Stills, and Nash, or a Crosby, Stills, Nash, and Young. It was released amid a lot of legal drama, with two record labels, Reprise and MGM, claiming distribution rights. *Both* companies released the album simultaneously, with different covers. Eventually, the legal issues were resolved, with Reprise besting MGM to claim the prize. *John Sebastian* hit #20 on the *Billboard* charts, making it a bona-fide hit record, but not a "monster" by any means. It would prove to be John's solo commercial peak.

When *Woodstock: Music from the Original Soundtrack and More* hit record-store shelves in May 1970, John's voice was the first thing listeners heard when they dropped the needle. "I Had a Dream" is the haunting opening track, and "Rainbows All Over Your Blues" finishes up the penultimate fifth side.

Because MGM had also been forced to withdraw the 1970 album *John Sebastian Live*, there was a void, so instead of a studio follow-up, 1971 saw the release of *Cheapo Cheapo Productions Presents Real Live John Sebastian*. The studio follow-up, *The Four of Us*, released later that same year, hit only #93 on the charts, and 1974's *Tarzana Kid* failed to chart at all, despite guest appearances by the Pointer Sisters, Phil Everly, Emmylou Harris, Little Feat's Lowell George, and old friend David Grisman. But 1976 brought a most welcome change. The album *Welcome Back* only charted at #79, but its title track became the theme song for ABC's sitcom hit *Welcome Back, Kotter*, which aired from 1975 to 1979.

"Welcome Back" would be John's first and only post–Lovin' Spoonful #1 single. He hasn't released a full studio album of *new* original material since, but he has tried his hand at other creative projects. His godfather was the artist Garth Williams, who did the illustrations for E. B. White's timeless children's classic *Charlotte's Web*. That connection prompted John to compose a stage musical based on the beloved book, but he never managed to bring the project to fruition.

In 1989, Rhino Records released a compilation, *The Best of John Sebastian*. John's next studio effort was a collection of previously unreleased originals, 1992's *Tar Beach*, on yet *another* label, Shanachie Records. In 1993, he would call upon his godfather once more, this time to illustrate his own children's book, *JB's Harmonica*, which tells the tale of a musically inclined bear living in the shadow of a father who is already a respected and accomplished musician . . . a circumstance endured by many a musical legacy over the years.

During the '90s, John found a renewed passion for jug-band music, touring with the J-Band—Jimmy Vivino, Fritz Richmond, and James Wormworth—and releasing two albums, 1996's *John Sebastian and the J-Band: I Want My Roots*, and 1999's *John Sebastian and the J-Band: Chasin' Gus' Ghost*, which features a slightly different lineup, adding Annie Raines to the mix, and relegating Jimmy Vivino to the role of guest musician.

In 2000, the Lovin' Spoonful was inducted into the Rock and Roll Hall of Fame. The band's induction was followed by a career-spanning John Sebastian boxed set, *Faithful Virtue: The Reprise Recordings* (2001), and *One Guy, One Guitar* (2001), a live album cobbled together from his appearances at the Cambridge Folk Festival in 1981 and 1984. That same year, the Hal Leonard Corporation published *The John Sebastian Songbook*.

Six years later, another compilation, *John Sebastian, Life and Times 1964–1999*, hit the shelves. The year 2007 was also noteworthy for John's collaboration with old Even Dozen Jug Band friend David Grisman, *John Sebastian and David Grisman: Satisfied*. Sales were tepid, but good enough for #8 on *Billboard*'s Top Bluegrass Albums chart.

John's contributions to rock and roll can't be summed up by looking at his solo career. From the late '60s on, he was a formidable session musician, and his work is immortalized on some of the greatest albums of all time. That's John, billed under the pseudonym "G. Pugliese," on the Doors' classic "Roadhouse Blues," from *Morrison Hotel*. He also blows harp on

"Little Red Rooster," as featured on the live Doors album *Alive, She Cried*, and is prominently featured on seven tracks of the group's *Live in Detroit*.

John's mighty harmonica is also featured on the title track of Crosby, Stills, Nash, and Young's 1970 debut album, *Déjà Vu*. In fact, Crosby, Stills, and Nash, who each performed on 1970's *John Sebastian*, had asked *him* to be the fourth member of their band before getting together with Neil Young (see chapter 30).

Morrison Hotel and *Déjà Vu* may have been the most famous albums John guested on, but they were far from the only ones. He and fellow Woodstock veterans Stephen Stills, Jimi Hendrix, and Buddy Miles all appeared on LSD guru Timothy Leary's freaky three-track 1970 album *You Can Be Anyone This Time Around*. That same year found him (and Hendrix) on Stills's own solo debut, *Stephen Stills*, providing backing vocals on four tracks, including the ever popular "Love the One You're With."

Later, he appeared on Keith Moon's one and only solo album, 1975's *Two Sides of the Moon*, as a guest guitarist. He also appeared with folk duo Happy and Artie Traum on "Woodstock Mountains," from the 1977 album *More Music from Mud Acres*, which also features contributions from folk singer Eric Andersen and Paul Butterfield.

John worked with Happy Traum's company, Homespun Tapes, as a music instructor to produce a series of educational materials across several media—audio, video, and print—offering the benefits of his talent and experience to generations of would-be singers, songwriters, guitarists, auto-harpists, and harmonica players.

In 2008, John was inducted into the Songwriter's Hall of Fame, arguably an even greater honor than being inducted into the Rock and Roll Hall of Fame. Even the United States Armed Forces showed its appreciation for the legend, awarding him the 2012 Silver Eagle Patriot Award.

To date, John's music has been covered by more than a dozen prominent artists, including Joe Cocker, who recorded a beautiful rendition of "Darlin', Be Home Soon." His music is ubiquitous in television and radio advertisements. The last time we had any studio work from John it was yet another compilation, a repackaging of his four Reprise albums—*John B. Sebastian*, *The Four of Us*, *Tarzana Kid*, and *Welcome Back*—bundled with a fancy booklet and a DVD of a 1970 BBC concert appearance, released in 2014.

In spite of dealing with throat issues and vocal problems over the past twenty years, John continues to perform. John is one Woodstock veteran who has no need to get back to the garden, because he carries it with him wherever he goes.

14

The Keef Hartley Band

Ringo's "Replacement" Was a Real Bluesbreaker

Decca/Deram Records got us onto the Woodstock festival. It all happened so fast. It was a new lineup of the Keef Hartley Band, and we were very under-rehearsed . . . We did not play well, as we could not use our own equipment. We used Santana's gear. It was a missed chance for the band. . . . Woodstock was not as romantic as it has later been suggested. It has become quite historic, I know, and I am proud in a way to say I was a little part of it, but at the time it was a mess, mass confusion.

— *Miller Anderson (the Keef Hartley Band) to Dmitry M. Epstein, 2008*

As the Seeds Were Sown: Like a Hurricane

Keef Hartley was born in Preston, Lancashire, England, on April 8, 1944, and not much has been written about his formative years. The drummer's chief claim to fame was that he was the guy who replaced Ringo Starr as the drummer for Rory Storm and the Hurricanes when Ringo went off to join a little band called the Beatles. That oft-cited origin story is misleading, though, because Hartley wasn't the *first* replacement for Starr.

Original Beatles drummer Pete Best had been offered the job initially, in what would have been a one-for-one trade between the Beatles and Rory Storm: *You give us Ringo, and we'll give you Pete.* But Pete put the kibosh on that idea. A succession of drummers manned the skins for Rory Storm and the Hurricanes, including Gibson Kemp, Brian Johnson, and John Morrison, before Hartley became the group's *fifth* drummer in August 1963.

Hartley would not stay long. Drummers Ian Broad and Trevor Morais became the Hurricanes' sixth and seventh drummers, respectively, while Hartley moved on to other opportunities. "Moving on to other opportunities" would become his career *modus operandi*. Hartley's approach to music arose from the world of big band jazz, where the expectation was that musicians would come and go, and never become permanently attached to any one band.

Keef's next project was with a promising band called the Artwoods, fronted by Arthur Wood, eldest brother of future Faces and Rolling Stones guitarist Ronnie Wood. Art Wood had previously sung lead for Alexis Korner's band Blues Incorporated, while also dabbling with a side project called the Art Wood Combo. When Wood joined forces with future Deep Purple keyboardist Jon Lord and guitarist Derek Griffiths, the Artwoods were born. And when Hartley and bass player Malcolm Pool joined their ranks, the lineup was complete.

The Artwoods took their act on the road at the end of 1964, inking a deal with Decca Records and landing a residency at London's prestigious 100 Club. They were a terrific live act, but they could never capture that magic in the studio. Their first single was a cover of Leadbelly's "Sweet Mary," and the band performed it on the first live broadcast of the BBC's *Ready Steady Go!* on April 2, 1965. More singles featuring blues covers followed, but chart success proved elusive, and Decca grew impatient. Likewise, the group's lone studio album, 1966's *Art Gallery*, went nowhere.

When Decca dropped the group at the end of 1966, the Artwoods went on to release singles with a couple of other small labels, but nothing ever caught on with the music-buying public. Art Wood went into the graphic arts business with his brother Ted, but he kept one foot in the world of music. Jon Lord went on to fame and fortune with Deep Purple, and Keef Hartley continued his musical journey, next joining John Mayall and the Bluesbreakers.

Replacing the likes of Aynsley Dunbar and Hughie Flint, Hartley played drums on the Bluesbreakers' 1967 album *Crusade*—alongside eighteen-year-old future Rolling Stones guitarist Mick Taylor and future Fleetwood Mac founders John McVie, Mick Fleetwood, and Peter Green— and was the only other musician featured on John Mayall's May 1967 solo album, *The Blues Alone*. But Mayall became disenchanted with Hartley, and fired the drummer by telephone.

That sacking by Mayall inspired Hartley to form his own band. Though called the Keef Hartley Band, the band could just as easily have been named for the multi-talented Miller Anderson. The guitarist and lead vocalist was born on April 12, 1945, in Renfrewshire, Scotland. He began his career playing alongside Ian Hunter, who would go on to glam-rock fame as the leader of Mott the Hoople. The young Hunter and Anderson teamed up in London during 1966 to form a band called the Scenery, which Anderson left in 1968.

Anderson returned to join Hunter's *next* band, the oddly named At Last the 1958 Rock and Roll Show, which eventually changed its name to Charlie Woolfe. Anderson then *briefly* played with future King Crimson/ Yes/Genesis drummer Bill Bruford in an obscure underground band called Paper Blitz Tissue. Thereafter, Anderson joined forces with Hartley to form the original incarnation of the Keef Hartley Band.

Bass player Gary Thain was born in Christchurch, New Zealand, on May 15, 1948. He began his career in an Australian band called the Secrets, and then worked with a trio called the New Nadir before joining Hartley's band. Hartley has remarked on more than one occasion that Thain was the best musician of the bunch.

Violinist and trumpeter Henry Lowther, born on July 11, 1941, in Leicester, England, was a journeyman musician who worked with too many other musicians to list, among them Manfred Mann, Jack Bruce, and—like Hartley—John Mayall and the Bluesbreakers. Rounding out the Woodstock-era lineup of the Keef Hartley Band was veteran British saxophonist Jimmy Jewell, who began his career in 1962, with Kris Ryan and the Questions, and went on to play with soul band Mack's Sound, the Paramounts, the Magics, Screaming Lord Sutch, and the Stewart James Inspiration, before joining the Keef Hartley Band in 1969.

Jewell was the only member of the group who did not take part in the recording sessions for the Keef Hartley Band's debut album, *Halfbreed*, released early in 1969. Hartley demonstrated a keen sense of humor by

For reasons known only to himself, British citizen Keef Hartley displayed an unusual affectation for dressing up in Native American garb, as seen here on the cover of his band's 1969 debut, *Halfbreed*.

incorporating a reenactment of the telephone conversation where John Mayall informed him that he was fired into the opening track, "Sacked (Introducing Hearts and Flowers)," as a sad violin plays in the background. As if to further emphasize the point, the second half of the conversation is tacked onto the end of the album as "Too Much to Take." Rather than get into a big argument with Mayall, Hartley says, "Just a minute, I'll put the kettle on; I can't take much more of this."

The album cover features Hartley clad head-to-toe in Native American garb, chief's headdress and all. He had a fascination with the iconography of what would have been called, at the time, the "American Indian," and those motifs and Hartley's odd affectation continued throughout his career.

In the Garden: The British Are Here

At approximately 4:45 p.m., drummer Hartley hit the stage with Miller Anderson on guitar and lead vocals, Jimmy Jewell on the saxophone, Henry Lowther on trumpet and violin, and Gary Thain on bass.

As Miller alluded to in the opening quote, he and his fellow musicians were not at all comfortable onstage that day. Even though they were all industry veterans, the lineup was new and had not properly rehearsed. Compounding their woes—and typical of the odd situations that arose during the festival—they were using Santana's equipment instead of their own. So their five-song, forty-five minute set was not particularly noteworthy. They played "Spanish Fly," "She's Gone," "Too Much Thinkin'," and "Believe in You," before finishing with a medley of "Sinnin' for You"/ "Leaving Trunk"/ "Just to Cry"/ "Sinnin' for You."

No official film or audio of the Keef Hartley Band's set has ever been released. There *is* an audio recording of the opening number, "Spanish Fly," taken from an audience member's bootleg tape, but the best anecdotal evidence suggests that the group just did not have it that day, and did not go over well with the crowd.

The Keef Hartley Band would not be the only act that failed to reach its true potential that weekend; the Incredible String Band was waiting in the wings.

The Harvest Reaped: Success Proves Elusive

The Keef Hartley Band followed up its underwhelming Woodstock appearance with the October 1969 release of a sophomore album, *The Battle of North West Six*, which featured an extended lineup, sometimes called the Keef Hartley (Big) Band, that included a second guitarist, Spit James, plus percussion, organ, piano, and a robust brass section featuring two tenor saxophones, a baritone sax, three flutes, two flugelhorns, and a trumpet. The album also features a guest guitar solo by Mick Taylor.

The band continued its prolific pace in August 1970 with a third album, *The Time Is Near*, for which Anderson penned six of the seven tracks. During the sessions, Jimmy Jewell and Henry Lowther left to seek their fortunes elsewhere. The group's fourth and final studio album with Anderson—*Overdog*, for which he penned five of the seven tracks—hit the shelves in April 1971. That year also saw the release of *Little Big Band (Live at the Marquee Club)*, after which Anderson struck out on his own with the Miller Anderson Band.

The group's October 1969 sophomore album, *Battle of North West Six*, features a horn section known as the Keef Hartley Big Band.

Hartley, his "Indian" fixation intact, forged ahead with Junior Kerr on guitar to release 1972's *Seventy-Second Brave*. And *that* was the end of the Keef Hartley Band. The following year, Hartley released *Lancashire Hustler* as a "solo" album, though it features an eleven-member band. He and Anderson would reunite briefly to form Dog Soldier, a collaboration that yielded one self-titled album in 1975. But neither felt the new band measured up to their standards, so they moved on.

They may not have made much of a splash on that rain-soaked stage in Bethel, but all of the members of the Keef Hartley Band carved impressive paths through the world of music before and after the festival. Suffice it to say that Woodstock neither made nor broke them; they were merely passing through on their way to a veritable kaleidoscope of other musical projects.

15

The Incredible String Band

Out of Order

What happened then was, I said, "You don't know what's going to happen—you may never get onstage," but they wanted to wait for the rain to stop and so someone else went on—Melanie—who triumphed in that time slot and wrote "Candles in the Rain" about that exact moment [see chapter 7]! We talked to John Morris . . . who was a friend of mine, about the logistics of where we could pick up the following day . . . and it sort of haunted me, that moment, because I should have pushed—just dragged them bodily to the stage and said, "Forget the amps, just play acoustically." It might have been wonderful, it might have been a great triumph—we might have been in the film and on the record, the whole thing! We ended up going on the following after-noon . . . in the baking sun. People were ready for something heavy and loud and they came on and just—died!

—*Joe Boyd (manager, the Incredible String Band), as quoted in* Be Glad

As the Seeds Were Sown: Psychedelic Scotsmen

Robin Williamson was born Robin Duncan Harry Williamson in Edinburgh, Scotland, on November 24, 1943. He dropped out of school at age fifteen to pursue the life of a professional musician. Though he started out playing in jazz bands, he turned his attention toward tra-ditional folk music and learned to sing and play a wide variety of instru-ments, including guitar, banjo, harp, flute, fiddle and the penny whistle.

Williamson threw in his fortunes with fellow musician, Glasgow native Herbert "Bert" Jansch, who would go on to achieve critical acclaim and some commercial success with his band Pentangle. Williamson and Jansch shared an apartment. In 1963, when Williamson was nineteen going on twenty, the two set out to seek fame and fortune on the London club circuit.

Williamson next began performing at the Crown Bar as a folk duo with future ISB co-founder Clive Palmer on the banjo. One day in August 1965, a talent scout walked into the bar and "discovered" them. The scout, Joe Boyd, of Elektra Records, took note of the duo, and would later return upon his promotion to head of Elektra's London offices. Meanwhile, Palmer and Williamson were toying with the idea of expanding their sound, so they added a local rock musician, Mike Heron, on rhythm guitar, and started calling themselves the Incredible String Band.

Palmer, in addition to being a skilled musician, had good business instincts. He began running his own folk music club in Glasgow, Clive's Incredible Folk Club, making the Incredible String Band the *de facto* house band. In early 1966, Boyd returned to the area and offered the new trio a record deal, which led to the release of an eponymous debut, *The Incredible String Band*, in June of that year. Though it garnered good reviews from folk music publications like *Sing Out!* and more mainstream music press like *Melody Maker*, the album was a slow starter. The trio proved to be short-lived.

Palmer left the band, deciding that he wanted to travel the world. Williamson took up with future band member Christina "Licorice" McKechnie, and the pair split for Morocco. Heron stuck around the club scene in Edinburgh and continued to play music with local bands. When Williamson returned to Scotland, he was flat broke; judging by the baggage he

This June 1966 debut album, *The Incredible String Band*, features an all-boys club in the trio of Mike Heron, Clive Palmer, and Robin Williamson.

was carrying, he'd spent most of his money in Morocco on exotic musical instruments.

They decided it was time to get the band back together and start making a few bucks. Williamson and Heron reunited as a duo. Under Boyd's guidance, they began opening shows for the likes of Judy Collins and Tom Paxton, and found themselves with a coveted slot at the 1967 Newport Folk Festival, along with Joni Mitchell and Leonard Cohen.

But the Williamson–Heron duo was a marriage of convenience; they were only friends through Clive Palmer, and, with Clive out of the picture, they functioned mainly as rivals. The duo's pretentiously titled July 1967 album *The 5,000 Spirits or the Layers of the Onion* features guest appearances by Bert Jansch's Pentangle bandmate Danny Thompson on the upright bass, and Christina "Licorice" McKechnie on background vocals and percussion.

In keeping with the spirit of the times, the Incredible String Band's sound began to evolve from pure, traditional folk to something more psychedelic. This sophomore effort gained the group peer recognition (Paul McCartney was an early fan), radio play, and increased fan support. It didn't hurt, either, that Boyd was part owner of the prestigious UFO club, famous for launching the career of Pink Floyd. The band played the UFO, and all the other clubs on the circuit, until *5,000 Spirits* hit the top slot on the UK Folk Chart.

Poised for greater commercial success and critical acclaim in 1968, the Incredible String Band made the most of the opportunity, resulting in a one-two punch of studio releases, *The Hangman's Beautiful Daughter* and *Wee Tam and the Big Huge*. Like Pink Floyd and other psychedelic pioneers, the Incredible String Band's signature sound required the layering of multiple tracks and overdubbing. As the technology of the recording studio grew more and more complex, the musicians utilized that technology to take their sound into uncharted territory. The only downside to this approach was that it was difficult to capture that multilayered sound in a live concert context. You needed more personnel to pull it off, and it was during this year that Simpson and McKechnie were officially added to the lineup.

Released in March, and bolstered by heavy rotation on local radio, *The Hangman's Beautiful Daughter* hit #5 on the UK charts. Robert Plant, of the fledgling Led Zeppelin, joined Paul McCartney among the ranks of the band's musician fans. Things were different on the American side of the pond, where the album only reached #161 on *Billboard*, though it did earn a Grammy nomination in the "Best Folk Performance" category.

The next album, *Wee Tam and the Big Huge*, lived up to its name; it was a double album. Or *was* it? Elektra Records took the unusual approach of releasing it in the UK as both a double album and two single albums. American audiences were offered no such choice; they got two separate single LPs: *Wee Tam* was one, *The Big Huge* the other. The split-in-two American versions fared even worse on *Billboard* than *The Hangman's Beautiful Daughter*, with *Wee Tam* stalling at #174 and *The Big Huge* at #180.

The Incredible String Band was now officially a quartet. Heron and Williamson still did most of the heavy lifting in terms of instrumentation,

By the time of the band's March 1968 release, *The Hangman's Beautiful Daughter*, the lineup had changed, expanded, and gone co-ed. If not for their reluctance to play in the rain on Friday night, they may have been better received at Woodstock.

but Simpson and McKechnie pitched in on backing vocals and percussion, with McKechnie also demonstrating some skill on the Irish harp.

The group's success continued in the UK, where a growing reputation as a live act catapulted the band into larger venues like the Royal Albert Hall, and they toured regularly when they weren't in the studio. Stateside, the band was on Bill Graham's radar, and played at his Fillmores on both coasts.

Around this time, the band got caught up in the controversial world of Scientology, a development that some argue had a negative impact. Perhaps 1968 would have marked the group's commercial and creative peak either way; at this point, one can only speculate. But the band's reputation was strong enough to earn an invitation to play at Woodstock. The phone rang on May 28, 1969. It was Michael Lang calling.

In the Garden: A Self-Imposed Rain Delay

Whatever else it may have been, in terms of a musical or cultural event, Woodstock was no place for weather wimps. The Incredible String Band *refused* to play during its initial scheduled time slot on Friday night. Why? Because, it was *raining*.

Rescheduled for Saturday, and sandwiched in between the muscular blues of the Keef Hartley Band and the raucously fun boogie tunes of Canned Heat, the Incredible String Band, with its gentle, psychedelic weirdness, kind of got lost in the shuffle. The group just didn't go over very well with the crowd.

The band's sketchy post-festival career makes one wonder if there isn't a lesson to be learned here, a cautionary tale: when someone tells you your band is up next, you had better be ready to walk onto that stage and *perform*. You may not get another chance. Rose Simpson knew it. To paraphrase Frank Sinatra: regrets, she's had a few. "He [Boyd] should have just said, 'Get on that blessed stage and you play, shut up moaning about getting wet, and get up there,' and we should have done it, we were silly not to, he regrets it now I know," she told *Be Glad*, the Incredible String Band fanzine. "The String Band would have had a different history if we had. One of our big mistakes really. I can see why we did it. We were a bit miffed really, it was just unpleasant, it wasn't very nice being in the wet and cold, hungry and not knowing how the hell we were going to go anywhere next."

At about 6:30 p.m., partially obscured by the noise from the helicopters and the restless chatter of the audience, the Incredible String Band took the stage. Robin Williams began the proceedings with an "Invocation"—just a few lines of poetry, the refrain of which was "I make a pact with you," and thereafter some variations on the theme.

Between the size of the crowd and his rapid, almost nervous delivery, those words had little impact on those around him. This was a hot, sweaty audience, all psyched up and ready to rock. Before a single note had been struck, it was already abundantly clear that the Incredible String Band was simply the wrong band in the wrong place at exactly the wrong time. The group had missed its golden opportunity by refusing to take the stage the night before.

The group's set list included "The Letter," which sounded for all the world like a performance piece from a renaissance fair, plus "Gather Round," "This Moment," "Come With Me," and "When You Find Out What You Are." The twenty-five minute set went largely unnoticed. When Chip Monck took the microphone to deliver the back-sell, his own lack of enthusiasm was evident as he said, "Ladies and gentlemen, the Incredible String Band. Please thank them."

Whatever gratitude the audience members may have been feeling at the time, it is a safe bet that most of it was reserved for the fact that the band was *leaving* the stage and making room for Canned Heat. No one clamored for an encore, and none was forthcoming. The musicians left the stage to a smattering of polite applause.

The Harvest Reaped: The String Unravels

The ISB remained stateside post-Woodstock, appearing just two weeks later at the Texas International Pop Festival, joined there by many Woodstock alumni, including the Merry Pranksters, Hugh Romney and the Hog Farm, John Sebastian, Canned Heat, Janis Joplin, Sweetwater, Ten Years After, Johnny Winter, Santana, and Sly and the Family Stone.

Afterward, the communal-living quartet returned to the studio, releasing *Changing Horses* in November 1969. The album, highlighted by Mike Heron's nearly fifteen-minute "White Bird" and Robin Williamson's sixteen-minute-plus "Creation," featured the addition of electric guitar, with Rose Simpson now credited as bass player, and marked another step toward the world of progressive rock.

The release of *Changing Horses* coincided with the band members' official conversion to the Church of Scientology, so the title is really quite clever. The album hit #166 on *Billboard* and #30 in the UK, and made more money than *Wee Tam and the Big Huge*. Many in the industry regarded the album as a disappointment, however, because they thought the band would have gotten a bigger boost out of its Woodstock appearance. But with the Incredible String Band nowhere to be found in either the film or soundtrack albums, the group's ill-timed appearance there was all but forgotten. Nevertheless, the band forged ahead at a prolific pace, releasing two more records during 1970, *I Looked Up* and the double album *U*, its last set of studio originals for Elektra.

Its contract with Elektra Records fulfilled, the group inked a deal with Island Records and released a pair of albums during 1971: *Be Glad for the Song Has No Ending* and *Liquid Acrobat as Regards the Air*. Meanwhile, Elektra repackaged some of the band's leftovers and released the compilation *Relics of the Incredible String Band*. Rose Simpson left the band that same year.

That lineup change was just the first of the foundational cracks that would lead the group to disband a few years later. Malcolm Le Maistre took Simpson's place, and would remain with the band through its 1974 breakup. Forging ahead with Island Records, the remaining members released *Earthspan* in 1972—a year that also saw the release of the group's first official live album, *First Girl I Loved: Live in Canada*, and the departure of Christina "Licorice" McKechnie.

Without Rose and Licorice, the Incredible String Band became an all-boys club, and a *bloated* one at that. Gerard Dott took McKechnie's place, and Jack Ingram and former Fillmore employee Stan Schnier were added to the mix. The sextet released *No Ruinous Feud* in 1973, and, finally, *Hard Rope and Silken Twine* in 1974. That album ends with Mike Heron's nearly twenty-minute opus, "Ithkos," a musical salad that seems to indicate a band with an identity crisis.

As far as Island Records was concerned, the band had become hopelessly unraveled, and rather than find itself entangled in yet another dead-end studio project, the label dropped the band in 1974. The timing was right, for the Williamson–Heron "marriage of convenience" had finally soured to its breaking point. In October of that year, citing irreconcilable musical differences, they called it quits and left to work on solo projects. Island Records released a posthumous compilation, *Seasons They Change*, in November 1976.

As the 1990s dawned, the BBC released its Incredible String Band recordings as *BBC Radio 1 Live on Air* in 1991, followed in 1992 by *BBC Radio 1 Live in Concert*. Twelve years would pass before the 2004 release of the live *Nebulous Nearness*, which was followed by a collection of unreleased demos, *The Chelsea Sessions 1967*, in 2005. *Across the Airwaves: BBC Radio Recordings 1969–74* followed in 2007, and then *Tricks of the Senses: Rare and Unreleased Recordings 1966–1972* in 2008.

Heron and Williamson shared a stage again in 1997, and began flirting with the idea of putting the band back together. Two years later, with Clive Palmer back in the fold, they gave it a go. Lawson Dando and Robin's new wife, Bina, appended the original trio, so the band bore only a passing resemblance to the two-couple quartet that played Woodstock.

This new era hit a snag after four years, when the Williamsons pulled out to focus on other projects. Heron and Palmer carried on as Incrediblestringband2003, adding Claire "Fluff" Smith to the lineup. After a UK festival gig in September 2006, the remaining fibers of what had once been the Incredible String Band frayed once more.

Apart from Palmer and Heron organizing an Incredible String Band tribute concert with special guests (and no Williamson) in 2009, there has been no activity since. Clive Palmer passed away in 2014. Mike Heron continues to perform, collaborating with other artists. Robin Williamson doubled down on his prolific solo career, with nearly fifty albums to his credit, most recently 2014's *Trusting in the Rising Light*.

Rose Simpson left the music business the day she left the band. Though she briefly entertained the idea of opening a recording studio, she settled down and raised a family. She lived in Wales, married Bob

Griffin, and became Lady Mayoress of Aberystwyth in 1994. As recently as 2003, she was said to still live there, no longer in politics but pursuing an interest in anthropology.

There is a mystery surrounding the fate of Christina "Licorice" McKechnie. She was last seen hitchhiking in the Arizona desert back in 1987, and no one—not even her family—has heard from her since; her whereabouts remain unknown. Some, including former bandmate Rose Simpson, have speculated that she may no longer be among the living.

The Incredible String Band was immortalized in print in 2003 with the publication of *Be Glad: An Incredible String Band Compendium*, authored by a team from *Be Glad* magazine, led by editor Adrian Whittaker. The lovingly detailed book, still in print, would later return in a *New Revised and Updated 2013 Edition.*

A resurgence of interest in the psychedelic era led the BBC to release *Across the Airwaves*, a 2007 compilation of Incredible String Band material from 1969 through 1974, much of it previously released. The fortieth anniversary of Woodstock led to the 2009 release of a double-CD compilation, *Tricks of the Senses*, a sixteen-track collection of studio outtakes, live tracks, and rarities. While interest in the Incredible String Band remains strong, particularly in the UK, it is safe to say there are no longer any loose threads remaining.

16

Canned Heat

Students of the Blues Game

Canned Heat is just one of my favorites . . . I loved that group. They were musicians' musicians. They were known as the best good-time-boogie band ever. Very, very much a part of the Woodstock generation. They were loved by everybody. Everybody's favorite people. [Bob] Hite is just so friendly. And then the fan comes onstage and he gives him a cigarette and a hug. It was really in the spirit of Woodstock. They were friendly and really a part of the audience.

—*Michael Wadleigh (director, Woodstock),*
Pete Fornatale Radio Archives, 2009

As the Seeds Were Sown: The Los Angeles Blues

When considering the origins of Canned Heat, the phrase "students of the game" comes to mind. Founding members Bob Hite and Alan Wilson were avid record collectors and blues historians, and that knowledge spilled over into their careers. The name of the band is a history lesson unto itself. "Canned Heat" references the title of a 1928 song, "Canned Heat Blues," by Delta bluesman Tommy Johnson, *and* the Sterno brand of cooking fuel, colloquially known as "canned heat."

In Johnson's heyday, during the height of prohibition, impoverished alcoholics were known to drink methanol harvested from Sterno cans, squeezed through cheesecloth and mixed with fruit juice. Unfortunately for practitioners of this primitive, labor-intensive form of mixology, the jellied, denatured alcohol found in this "squeeze" or "jungle juice" was *poisonous*, and drinking it resulted in multiple deaths over the years, including, ultimately, Johnson's.

Canned Heat's roots can be traced back to the Topanga Canyon area, where, one day in 1965, Hite and Wilson decided to form a jug band with their friends Mike Perlowin, Stu Brotman, and Keith Sawyer. That lasted all of two days before Sawyer and Perlowin were out, and drummer Ron Holmes and future Stone Poneys guitarist Kenny Edwards were in. But they weren't long for the band, either. The arrival of guitarist Henry Vestine, an original member of Frank Zappa's Mothers of Invention, prompted Edwards to move on. Holmes then ceded his drum stool in deference to the more seasoned jazzman Frank Cook.

Veteran musician and producer Johnny Otis recorded an album's worth of material with the band in 1966, but those recordings were shelved—which was just as well, because the lineup was still evolving. Original bass player Stu Brotman bailed out, and was temporarily replaced by future Spirit bassist Mark Andes. The band made great strides during 1967, hiring managers Skip Taylor and John Hartman, and finally finding its man in bass player Larry Taylor, whose career went back to his days working with Jerry Lee Lewis and the Monkees, who joined in March.

The group then inked a contract with Liberty Records, and entered the studio in April. With an album in production, Canned Heat appeared on Saturday, June 17, at the Monterey Pop Festival. The band's spirited renditions of blues classics like "Rollin' and Tumblin'," "Dust My Broom," and "Bullfrog Blues" had the orderly Monterey crowd dancing in their metal folding chairs.

The following month, *Canned Heat* hit the shelves. Even though all of the tracks were old blues standards, the album managed to crack the *Billboard* charts at #76. The group then released "Rollin' and Tumblin'" b/w "Bullfrog Blues" as its one and only single.

When the band members got busted in Denver on trumped-up marijuana possession charges, the incident earned them street cred with the counterculture; it also led to the departure of Frank Cook and wound up causing a series of financial problems. Replacement drummer Adolfo de la Parra brought a Latin music perspective from his days with Los

Released more than two years before the festival, Canned Heat's
self-titled 1967 debut features a band of blues purists determined
to showcase this quintessentially American music in the best way
possible.

Hooligans and Los Sinners. With the addition of de la Parra, what is
widely considered the "classic" lineup of Canned Heat was in place.

Taylor and Hartmann had the idea that, in honor of the time-honored
blues tradition, the band members ought to adopt nicknames. Alan "Blind
Owl" Wilson joined a long list that included Blind Lemon Jefferson and
Blind Willie McTell. (Bolstering his credibility, Wilson *was* actually visu-
ally impaired.) Bob "The Bear" Hite may not have been the first to use his
nickname, but it suited the burly, black-bearded three-hundred-pounder
just fine. The others became Henry "The Sunflower" Vestine, Larry "The
Mole" Taylor, and Adolfo "Fito" de la Parra. ("Fito" is simply the Spanish
diminutive for Adolfo; less clear are the meanings behind the Mole and
the Sunflower.)

All the band needed now was a breakout hit. During 1968, with the
release of *Boogie With Canned Heat*, the group got one, "On the Road

Again." Wilson adopted a falsetto in homage to his blues idols, Tommy Johnson and Skip James, and the song cracked the *Billboard* Top 10.

From that point forward, 1968 was a whirlwind that included a residency at the Kaleidoscope Club, TV appearances at home and abroad, an appearance at the first Newport Pop Festival, and a return to the recording studio. Released in November, *Living the Blues* featured the song that would become an unofficial anthem of Woodstock, "Going Up the Country." The nine-part, twenty-minute opus "Parthenogenesis" reveals the band expanding its sound into the realms of psychedelia. But for sheer indulgence, few songs can match the live, forty-one-minute, two-album-side rendition of "Refried Boogie."

On New Year's Eve, Canned Heat took a page out of the Bill Graham playbook, with the Bear perched atop a purple-painted elephant to kick off a show at the Shrine Auditorium. And 1969 was shaping up to be just as eventful. Canned Heat returned to the studio early in the year. *Hallelujah* hit the shelves on July 8, but cracks in the band's foundations were beginning to show. During a show at the Fillmore West, Taylor and Vestine nearly came to blows, and Vestine quit afterward. With little time to spare, the band offered his slot to Mike Bloomfield, who declined. Enter young guitar whiz Harvey "The Snake" Mandel.

Mandel played just two Fillmore shows with the band before the festival. Fito de la Parra was upset that the new lineup hadn't had enough time to rehearse. In a huff, he announced that *he*, too, was quitting, and locked himself in his motel room. Skip Taylor broke into the drummer's room, ushered all of them onto the helicopter, and got them to the festival site in the nick of time. He was just one of many unsung heroes that weekend.

In the Garden: Unwitting Anthem

The quintet strode onstage at 7:30 p.m. as the sun sank low in the overcast sky. There's a bit of comic irony in the idea that Michael Wadleigh's favorite band took to the stage at the worst possible time of day for filming.

The hour-long set kicked off with a raucous version of "I'm Her Man," featuring some nasty harmonica stylings from Blind Owl, the tasteful, finessed drumming of Fito de la Parra, and the frenzied, nearly manic bass of Mole Taylor. Fito's drum kit featured double bass drums—a setup that would soon become commonplace among the emerging heavy-metal genre, although his own style was more like a funky, rat-a-tat marching band.

Harvey "The Snake" Mandel, a silent assassin in the spirit of Mick Taylor, handled the bulk of guitar duties on the opener, and was pretty composed for a guy playing in front of an audience this size at his third ever gig. The Bear stalked the stage, smoking an occasional cigarette, the fierceness of his black beard offset by a bright yellow T-shirt.

The next number, to paraphrase Joe Cocker, had one of those titles that just about put the whole thing into focus. "Going Up the Country" was *precisely* what the bulk of this largely city-dwelling crowd had done, and now Canned Heat would frame the event in the most effective way imaginable.

A special moment occurred during the group's cover of Sam Cooke's "A Change Is Gonna Come." A fan rushed the stage and embraced the Bear before bumming one of his omnipresent Marlboros. But rather than yell for security, Hite incorporated the guy into the performance, gesturing to him as he sang the lyrics, "As long as I got myself a friend / Lord I can't ask for more."

The timing was perfect: Blind Owl stepped forward to take a guitar solo, leaving Hite to deal with the fan and light his cigarette (he left the stage right after). Hite's reaction was one of those small gestures undoubtedly lost in the moment as half a million people grooved to Canned Heat in the fading light, but it was tailor-made for the film. And, though it would not appear in the original theatrical release of *Woodstock*, it clearly resonated with Wadleigh, who saved it for the *Director's Cut* later on.

The band kept things jumping with "Too Many Drivers at the Wheel" and "I Know My Baby." It was 7:56 p.m. when the sun sank below the horizon, but Canned Heat was just getting warmed up. If "Woodstock Boogie" sounds like an impossibly convenient title, that's because the song, from 1968's *Boogie With Canned Heat*, was originally titled "Fried Hockey Boogie." In true blues tradition, this half-hour-long finale provided the musicians an opportunity to solo and strut their stuff. Mole Taylor's bass solo was nothing short of astounding; he played it like a lead instrument. Fito gave Santana drummer Michael Shrieve a serious run for his money when he delivered arguably the most dynamic drum solo of the festival, utilizing every square inch of his double bass kit, and left the audience breathless.

As the last cymbal was silenced, the Bear addressed the crowd. "Thank you very much, everybody, we sure do love ya! And don't y'all forget to boogie. Thank you." John Morris sounded just as enthusiastic. "Ladies and gentlemen, Canned Heat!" There was no doubt in anyone's mind that they would be back for an encore.

With the spotlights blinking to life, Canned Heat delivered "On the Road Again," perhaps the most appropriate title for an encore, ever. With his road-worn Les Paul and that odd falsetto voice, Blind Owl stepped to the mic. In the background, you can clearly hear one of the stage crew say, "Get off the tower, man, I don't want you to kill yourself."

As Blind Owl eased into the tune, the Bear responded with his harp. They were off to the races, laying down that heavy, brooding groove. Mole and Fito were still going strong, nearly an hour into the set, and Snake seemed to have found his comfort zone, trading licks from his Stratocaster with Blind Owl's Les Paul. The encore took on a heavy, almost psychedelic tone as amplifiers buzzed menacingly beneath it all. The Bear's wailing, mournful harp led the band home, and it was over. The festival had hit its stride, and this audience wasn't going *anywhere*.

The Harvest Reaped: Unrelenting Heat

It was business as usual for Canned Heat after the festival. In anticipation of a 1970 European tour, the group entered the recording studio with new guitarist Harvey Mandel. The resulting *Future Blues* sparked some controversy because of its cover art, which shows a smog-encircled planet Earth and satirizes both the moon landing and the flag raising at Iwo Jima in its depiction of astronauts raising an upside-down American flag (military code for "distress") on the surface of the moon. The "distress" in this case was a reflection of Blind Owl's growing environmental activism.

Musically, the album features the band's usual mix of blues covers and originals, with a cover of Wilbert Harrison's "Let's Work Together" the lone hit. During 1970, the Janus label opportunistically released the

band's 1966 Johnny Otis sessions as an album, *Vintage*. The band recorded
shows during its European tour, and cobbled together select tracks to
produce *Canned Heat '70 Concert Live in Europe* later that year.

The band does not appear onscreen during the 1970 theatrical release
of *Woodstock*, but the studio version of "Going Up the Country" provides
the soundtrack for a joyous sequence featuring hippies driving around
and doing what the song suggests, leaving the city and getting back to
nature. The band would later allege on its website that Warner Bros had
made the decision to cut twelve minutes from the original film's running time, eliminating performances by non-Warner acts like Canned
Heat and Jefferson Airplane. Wadleigh felt that "Going Up the Country"
perfectly captured the ethos of Woodstock Nation, so he found a way to
work it into the film.

Canned Heat did appear on the soundtrack albums. *Woodstock: Music
from the Original Soundtrack and More*, released in May 1970, features a

Canned Heat courted controversy with the cover art for this fifth
and final studio release by the original lineup, 1970's *Future Blues*.
Though clearly a riff on both the moon landing and the flag raising
at Iwo Jima, the "distress signal" of the inverted flag was a volatile
visual during the Nixon/Vietnam era.

live version of "Going Up the Country," and *Woodstock 2*, released the following July, features the band's rebranded jam "Woodstock Boogie." But by that time, the band that had created those sounds no longer existed.

Future Blues took on new meaning as Mandel and Taylor split to join up with John Mayall and the Bluesbreakers. Their departure opened the door for Vestine's return; he (and Mandel and Taylor) would come and go from the Canned Heat lineup many times over the years.

On September 3, 1970, in the hills of Topanga Canyon behind the Bear's home, Blind Owl Wilson died of a barbiturate overdose and became a member of the infamous "27 Club." Though his death was officially ruled an accident, he had attempted suicide previously. With the clarity of hindsight, some speculate the quirky introvert may have been on the autism spectrum, and it is clear that he suffered from clinical depression. His parting musical gift to the world was the band's collaborative, Bob Hite–produced double album with idol John Lee Hooker, *Hooker 'n Heat*, released in January 1971.

As far as the legendary Hooker was concerned, Blind Owl was "the greatest harmonica player ever." Without his signature sound, Canned Heat was a different band. The Bear soldiered on until a gig at the Palomino Club in North Hollywood on April 5, 1981. There, during the intermission, he made a fatal error. Mistaking heroin for cocaine, he took a big snort, turned blue, and OD'd, dying later that night of a heart attack.

Yet the band marched on, with Fito de la Parra the only constant member. Canned Heat had become a revolving door, featuring over *thirty* different members who continued to tour and produce new albums, among them eleven studio releases, several collaborations (including with blues legends Clarence "Gatemouth" Brown and Memphis Slim), nine live albums, and twenty compilations. Prodigal "Sunflower" Henry Vestine died from heart failure in Paris on October 20, 1997, following his final stint with the band.

Against all odds, Canned Heat still exists today, if in name only. The current lineup features no original members, but it does reunite some of the classic-era team of Mole Taylor, Snake Mandel, longest-tenured member Fito de al Parra, and vocalist, harmonica player, and guitarist Dale Spalding.

Canned Heat played a number of dates during 2018, including the Flower Power Cruise, a musical boat ride that featured fellow vintage acts including Herman's Hermits, the Turtles (Flo and Eddie), the Guess Who, Felix Cavaliere's Rascals, and the (Sly-less) Family Stone. At press time, Canned Heat had yet to post any tour dates for 2019, but if history is any guide, soon they will be out on the road again.

17

Mountain

The "Cream" of Long Island

We were on Saturday night, right when the lights came on for the first time. 'Cause Friday night it rained, and they just had acoustic acts. Saturday night it was beautiful—we got a great time period. In fact, they made me hide until it got dark because it was a matter of like, "Well, who's ready?" "Who will get on?" 'Cause it was chaos in the beginning.

We flew up in our own helicopter. We were smart. We rented our own. Unfortunately, because I was much heavier at the time, the helicopter pilot did not want to fly one trip. So he took three guys and two. And I remember this distinctly: Bud [Prager]'s wife Gloria gave him six chickens—barbecued chickens—and he didn't want to take them. He said, "They have food there, they have everything—they have for the entertainers—they have bagels."

Well, that was gone in the first hour. Janis Joplin ate everything. And, all of a sudden, about two or three in the morning, after Sly and the Family Stone were on, I think, we were starved. We were sitting behind the stage—there was nothing, and Bud whips out these chickens. And there were people coming up and over, 'cause it smelt pretty damn good at that time. And a—Gloria . . . thank God for you, we fed forty-eight people, I think, that night.

—*Leslie West, Long Island Music Hall of Fame*

As the Seeds Were Sown: A Vagrant from Long Island

It all began when the Beatles played Forest Hills Tennis Stadium on August 29, 1964. Local teenagers Peter Sabatino and Larry Weinstein were inspired by what they witnessed that evening, and resolved that they, too, would start a rock-and-roll band.

Larry's older brother, Leslie, was already an accomplished guitarist, and agreed to join. The next piece of the puzzle was a friend from the neighborhood named Jerry Storch. Storch, a champion-caliber bowler, played piano and fancied himself a songwriter. He had connections at the local bowling alley, which came in handy when the brothers Weinstein got booted from their parents' basement for making too much of a racket with their instruments. Storch talked the bowling alley manager into letting the band set up and rehearse right there in the lobby. Now all they needed was a drummer.

According to legend, the boys' high-school principal called them into his office one day to berate them for their personal grooming habits. Roger Mansour, another "longhair" student, was in the office for the same reason, and just happened to be a drummer. He joined forces with Sabatino and the Weinsteins, and the Vagrants were born.

From the bowling alley to private house parties, the boys graduated to playing clubs, such as Steve Paul's the Scene, on 46th Street in Manhattan. Collectively, they made the decision to drop out of their current school, and drop *in* to Quintano's School for Young Professionals. This led to a record deal with Southern Sound Records.

In July 1965, the group released a single, "Oh Those Eyes" b/w "You're Too Young," but it didn't go anywhere. The Vagrants landed a regular gig in the Hamptons, Long Island's premier summer party destination. There they met another up-and-coming band, the Young Rascals. The Vagrants became enamored of one of the Young Rascals' instruments, the fabled Hammond B-3 organ. One might say that they developed a case of . . . ahem . . . organ envy.

Back in the city, the band began playing at a club called the Rolling Stone, run by an AM disc jockey named Scott Muni. During an autumn residency, the Vagrants made a name for themselves. They were so well received that at one point, one of their wealthy New York fans actually *bought* them the Hammond B-3 organ they had been coveting.

An unusual deal with the folk-oriented Vanguard label in 1966 led to the release of the Vagrants' first single to move a few copies, "I Can't Make a Friend." That single caught the attention of musician and record producer Felix Pappalardi, who got the band a deal with Atco Records. The Atco signing yielded a successful cover of Otis Redding's "Respect," though it was nothing to rival the Aretha Franklin version. Pappalardi had worked with Cream, and with Jesse

The fresh-faced Vagrants, seen here on their 1966 single "I Can't Make a Friend" b/w "Young Blues," were one of the hottest bar bands during their summer residencies out on Long Island, but they couldn't make that jump to the next level of success.

Colin Young's band, the Youngbloods, which piqued Leslie's interest. He was growing impatient with the Vagrants' limited success and yearning for more.

The Vagrants became the house band at a popular Long Beach club called the Action House. They were playing just about every day of the month, and making some decent coin at $1,500 per gig. The lucrative residency allowed the band to begin dabbling in pyrotechnics. An errant pyrotechnic device wound up burning the entire stage—and all of the band's gear—to the ground (including that treasured Hammond B-3).

As NPR's resident music historian Ed Ward once put it on *Fresh Air*, the band was a cash cow, so the booking agency was more than happy to foot the bill for new equipment to keep the gravy train rolling. It wasn't the money that was troubling Leslie, though. He wanted to take the band to a higher level and write hit records. But even with Pappalardi at the helm, a hit record remained elusive.

Pappalardi's collaboration with Gail Collins and Leslie's friend Bert Sommer, "Beside the Sea," failed to chart. The band's lack of commercial success led to a *lot* of squabbling between the brothers, and everybody in the band was messing with drugs. *Something* had to give. Jerry Storch bailed out first, quitting the band in 1968. The champion bowler turned

Released just one month before his band's hot Saturday-evening set at Woodstock, *Mountain* was a Leslie West solo album, the title of which became the new band's name.

rock-and-roller left the business and wound up becoming a rabbi. Larry went into the restaurant business, and Roger went on to become a missionary. Peter hedged his bets, keeping one foot in his catering business and one foot in the world of music, fronting an act called the New Vagrants during the '90s and early 2000s.

And then there was Leslie. He was destined for bigger and better things. In 1969, he decided to change his birth name and go solo. Calling his new act Leslie West Mountain—a tongue-in-cheek reference to his prodigious girth—he assembled a live trio of Norman Landsberg on bass and keys, Ken Janick on drums, and Leslie himself on lead guitar and vocals. They began to play gigs, and Pappalardi expressed an interest in producing an album. Working with Pappalardi, who played the dual role of bassist and producer, Leslie released his solo album, *Mountain*, on the Windfall label in July 1969. Of the eleven tracks, all but one—a cover of Bob Dylan and the Band's "This Wheel's on Fire"—were collaborative originals. Critics likened the sound to a heavier version of Cream, which is exactly what they were aiming for.

In addition to Leslie and Pappalardi, the album lineup features two guys named Norman: Norman "N.D." Smart, formerly of the Remains, on the drums; and Norman Landsberg, helping out part time on the Hammond B-3. Only three of the tracks feature keyboards, so the sound is, in essence, that of a power-trio. Rejuvenated by this new sound, Leslie suggested to Felix that they take the show on the road. Landsberg split to work on another project with Janick, so keyboardist Steve Knight was added to the lineup.

The lineup that would play Woodstock consisted of West, Pappalardi, Smart, and Knight, with the band name shortened to the more egalitarian Mountain. The quartet played just *three* shows as Mountain out on the West Coast before it was time to head east for the festival.

In the Garden: Not Bad for Their *Fourth* Gig

When Mountain took the stage, around 9:00 p.m., it was fully dark. The group's set included the T-Bone Walker classic "Stormy Monday," Jack Bruce's "Theme from an Imaginary Western," and "Long Red," originally written by Leslie and Felix for *Mountain*. Then the group whipped out the first official Mountain original of the evening, "Who Am I but You and the Sun," which would be retitled "For Yasgur's Farm" for the band's debut album, *Climbing!*

Next, Bert Sommer made a spiritual reappearance in the form of "Beside the Sea," the single he co-wrote with Felix and Gail Collins for the Vagrants. The next song, "Waiting to Take You Away," would not appear on an official release until Mountain's 1972 live album *Mountain Live (The Road Goes Ever On)*.

The last tune, "Dreams of Milk and Honey," was another track from Leslie's solo album. The group encored with "Southbound Train," which featured a bit of a misstep, as Leslie flubbed the lyrics. Even so, it was arguably the strongest moment of the set. The audience did not seem to mind one bit, howling in appreciation for the rough and rowdy band, while the Grateful Dead waited in the wings.

The Harvest Reaped: Corky Laing and the Classic Lineup

Mountain underwent some lineup changes after the festival. Most significantly, drummer Norman "N.D." Smart left to join Ian and Sylvia's Great Speckled Bird; Canadian musician Laurence Gordon "Corky" Laing replaced him.

The classic lineup of Mountain was now in place. Corky came on board at the perfect time to enter the studio with his new colleagues to produce Mountain's official debut album, *Climbing!* While officially a "power trio," Mountain's studio sound was bolstered by the contributions of talented musician Steven Knight, who added organ, Mellotron, and percussion to several of tracks.

Perhaps buoyed the power of the muscular "Mississippi Queen," *Climbing!*, released on March 7, 1970, hit #17 on *Billboard*'s Hot 100, instantly surpassing anything Leslie had been able to achieve with the Vagrants. The band enjoyed cross-media exposure when "Mississippi Queen" was featured on the soundtrack of the 1971 Hollywood film *Vanishing Point*.

Leslie was a road warrior by nature, so he wanted to get Mountain out there and gigging. Somehow, the group managed to squeeze in some studio time in the midst of its ambitious touring schedule. The result was the January 1971 release of *Nantucket Sleighride*.

Mountain continued at breakneck pace. Two albums in ten months, even in those days, was a phenomenal achievement. *Nantucket Sleighride* bested *Climbing!* by one point on the *Billboard* Hot 100, clocking in at #16. But, as in the early days of the Vagrants, singles were not one of Mountain's strong suits.

Mountain released a *third* album in November 1971, *Flowers of Evil*. By now, it would be a fair criticism to suggest that the band's ambition was beginning to outpace its creative output. Side one of the album consisted of five new studio tracks, while the other side featured live performances—recorded earlier that year at the Fillmore East—of "Mississippi Queen" and a self-indulgent Leslie West guitar solo titled "Dream Sequence," which lasted nearly half an hour.

In late 1971, Mountain hit the road for a tour of the UK. But fatigue was beginning to take its toll. Felix Pappalardi was suffering from hearing loss, the price of a life lived at high decibels. The group parlayed those UK performances into its first official live album, *Mountain Live: The Road Goes Ever On*. Ironically, by the time the album hit the shelves in April of 1972, Mountain had come to the end of the road. But mountains rise and fall. They would be back.

Felix's health issues were the main reason for the split in 1972. Leslie and Corky, meanwhile, forged ahead, teaming up with Cream bassist Jack Bruce in the short-lived trio West, Bruce, and Laing. The partnership with Bruce fueled a prolific period of creativity. In less than two years' time, the Mountain/Cream supergroup pumped out two studio albums for Columbia Records, 1972's *Why Dontcha* and 1973's *Whatever Turns You On*, as well as a live album, 1974's *Live 'n' Kickin'*. But by then Jack Bruce had pulled the plug on the project, the trio announcing a breakup months before the live album's release.

Leslie and Corky hit the road through the summer of 1973, billing themselves as Leslie West's Wild West Show. By August, Felix was feeling up to working again, so they decided it was time to re-form Mountain, but now Corky was out. The 1973 version of Mountain featured Leslie and Felix, along with Allan Schwartzberg on drums and Bob Mann handling keyboard duties and rhythm guitar. This revamped Mountain hit the road for a tour of Japan, which resulted in a double-live album, *Twin Peaks*, released in February 1974, two months ahead of the West, Bruce, and Laing's *Live 'n' Kickin'*.

Not many people can claim to have released live albums with two different bands within two months of one another. The larger-than-life Leslie West was *everywhere* you looked on record store shelves in those days. But although Mountain finished 1973 and began 1974 with a lot of momentum, the group wouldn't last until the ball drop on New Year's Eve. That night, after a gig at New York City's Felt Forum, Felix called it quits again.

The following year, 1975, dawned on a world without Mountain, as all of the principal members were involved in other projects. It would stay that way until 1981, when Leslie and Corky decided to put the band back together, this time inviting old friend Miller Anderson (of the Woodstock-era Keef Hartley Band) to join the fold and handle bass duties.

Felix Pappalardi was not so fortunate. His wife, Gail Collins Pappalardi, who had been an important part of Mountain's team early on, writing lyrics with Felix and even designing the artwork for several of the albums, shot him in the neck on April 17, 1983, at their Manhattan apartment, killing him almost instantly. No one can say for certain what precipitated this shooting, or whether it really was an accident, as she claimed. The initial charges of second-degree murder and manslaughter were eventually lowered to criminally negligent homicide. Gail served almost two years in prison. She was released on April 30, 1985, and died in 2013.

Meanwhile, the lean and mean early-'80s Mountain soldiered on. It was a foregone conclusion that the restless Anderson would not stick around forever; he lasted three years, before ceding bass duties to

Mark Clarke in 1984. Anderson did stick around to play slide guitar on Mountain's 1984 studio recording *Go for Your Life*, which hit the shelves in March 1985. The album, dedicated to the memory of Pappalardi, failed to chart, and Mountain went on hiatus again, this time for seven years.

Back in the saddle in 1992, Corky and Leslie forged ahead without a permanent bass player. Richie Scarlett and Randy Coven, in turn, handled bass duties through 1994, until Jimi Hendrix Experience alumnus Noel Redding entered the fold, along with Elvin Bishop (an original member of the Paul Butterfield Blues Band) on rhythm guitar. But that revolving door kept on spinning, and soon Mark Clarke was back, and another album, *Man's World*, hit the shelves in 1996. The group's first studio effort in eleven years, it failed to chart, and, once again, Mountain took a sabbatical.

In 2001, Richie Scarlett returned, and Mountain entered the studio to produce *Mystic Fire*, which hit the shelves in 2002. The album features guest vocals by former Rainbow front man Joe Lynn Turner on two tracks. But, once again, the album failed to chart.

The next year, 2003, found Leslie and Corky releasing their joint memoir, a career retrospective titled *Nantucket Sleighride and Other Mountain on-the-Road Stories*. The book did not signal the end of Mountain, though the group's songwriting certainly seemed to have dried up. Following a path well trodden by others, Mountain's 2007 album, *Masters of War*, features a dozen Bob Dylan covers. The group also went the Santana/*Supernatural* route and featured a variety of guest stars, including journeyman Warren Haynes and even Ozzy Osbourne.

Rejuvenated, Mountain hit the road through the end of 2008, this time with Rev Jones on the bass. The group continued to play sporadically until 2010, when Leslie again decided to "go solo." Five years later, Corky got fidgety and started a Mountain side project/tribute band, Corky Laing Plays Mountain, with Joe Venti on the bass and Phil Barker on guitar and lead vocals. Richie Scarlett joined them on the road through 2016, and they have been playing tracks from the full Mountain/Corky catalogue.

Given their history, it would not be at all surprising to see Leslie and Corky reunite for another album and another run of killer live shows.

18

The Grateful Dead

The Shocking Details

Well, we played such a bad set at Woodstock. The weekend was great, but our set was terrible. We were all pretty smashed, and it was at night. Like we knew there were a half-million people out there, but we couldn't see one of them. There were about a hundred people onstage with us, and everyone was scared that it was gonna collapse. On top of that, it was raining or wet, so that every time we touched our guitars, we'd get these electrical shocks. Blue sparks were flying out of our guitars.

—Jerry Garcia to David Bromberg, Jazz and Pop, *February 1971*

As the Seeds Were Sown

The Grateful Dead played its first show at one of Ken Kesey's Acid Tests in San Jose on December 4, 1965. The band formerly known as the Warlocks attracted an enthusiastic and often rowdy following of Hells Angels and hippies, along with colorful characters like early manager Rock Scully and acid chemist, would-be sound engineer, and benefactor Owsley "Bear" Stanley. Local concert hall proprietor and promoter Bill Graham was an early patron, too, and booked them regularly.

After an aborted attempt to record an album in 1966, sessions for Warner Bros in early 1967 led to the release of the group's debut, *The Grateful Dead*, in March of that year. The album features just two originals, "The Golden Road (to Unlimited Devotion)" and "Cream Puff War," and failed to effectively capture the band's dynamic live sound. On

June 18, The Grateful Dead appeared on the third and final night of the Monterey Pop Festival, sandwiched between the Who and Jimi Hendrix. This was not the ideal spot for any band, and the Dead made little if any impact on the audience that night. By September, the group had added second drummer Mickey Hart, while Jerry's old friend and songwriting partner, Robert Hunter, became an official, non-performing member.

The follow up, *Anthem of the Sun*, released in July 1968, blended live recordings with studio recordings, resulting in something that was truer to the band's essential sound. By November, one of the studio musicians, keyboardist Tom Constanten, had become an official member and began touring with the band.

With recording technology evolving to include the 16-track board, the band used it to full advantage on its third album, *Aoxomoxoa*, released on June 20, 1969, following lengthy and expensive studio sessions. There was also a live album in the works, featuring material recorded during shows in early 1969.

The band's reputation as a solid live act was earned primarily on the West Coast. During the twenty-six months leading up to Woodstock, the Grateful Dead played only thirty shows in New York, beginning with a show at Tompkin's Square Park on June 1, 1967. Over the next two years, the group played in venues as diverse as SUNY Stony Brook, the Café Au Go Go, the Fillmore East, Central Park, the Chelsea Hotel, the Playboy Club, the Village Theatre, Palm Gardens, Low Memorial Library (Columbia University), the Electric Circus, and the Pavilion at Flushing Meadows Park.

The Dead began August 1969 with back-to-back shows at the Family Dog in San Francisco on the 2nd and 3rd, and had almost two weeks off before Woodstock. Then it was on to Yasgur's Farm, and everyone was feeling good. What could possibly go wrong?

In the Garden: A Different Type of Buzz

Woodstock would present its own unique set of challenges. The audience was buzzing, following the muscular one-two punch of Canned Heat and Mountain, and hopeful that the Grateful Dead would keep that momentum going. Instead, things came crashing to a halt, and the audience, already more than ten hours into a marathon day, began to grumble.

The Bear, Owsley Stanley, got things off on the wrong foot that night by *crushing* what was supposed to be a revolving stage under the enormous weight of the Dead's sound equipment. The road crew and stagehands had to unload everything from the ruined turntable and reassemble the band's backline by hand. To make matters worse, the stage was flooded with rainwater, and the electrical ground was faulty.

The weather added an ominous layer to the proceedings. Wind filled the Joshua Light Show's underutilized screen like a sail, which, according to eyewitness reports, seemed to *move* the stage forward across the muddy ground.

None of these conditions were ideal for a group of cold, wet, electrically shocked musicians tripping on LSD in the dark. Chip Monck's stage announcement doubled down on the buzz kill: "Those of you who have . . .

Released less than two months before the festival, *Aoxomoxoa* was the third Grateful Dead studio album. The group would go back into the studio to remix it in 1971.

partaken of the green acid, if you would, as soon as convenient, please go to the hospital tent."

The Dead's set was supposed to begin at 10:30 p.m., but the load-in woes continued. The powerful buzz emanating from the P.A. gave a good indication that things were not going to go as planned. Bob Weir sounded worried when he commented, "It's getting zappy up here."

Phil Lesh eloquently describes the nature of the band's troubles in his 2005 memoir, *Searching for the Sound: My Life with the Grateful Dead*. "Back down in the mud, the electrical ground had failed completely, producing in the sound system (and all the band gear and monitors) a sixty-cycle hum the size of New Hampshire. Compared to the background hum you'll hear in any electrified edifice, this was a saber-toothed crotch cricket of a hum: almost obliterating any signal passed into the system. A steel pole fifty feet long was sunk, seeking dry ground. Not a chance."

The lights at the front of the stage that had once shone upon the audience shorted out, leaving the band looking out into total darkness. According to band members' recollections, blue balls of electricity could be seen scuttling across the stage, which continued to creak and shift ominously in the muddy ground. When Phil Lesh plugged into his bass amp, he heard an unusual crackle of static, followed by a voice: "Roger, Charlie Tango, I'm landing now." Somehow or other, the radio signals from the helicopters were channeling through Phil's pickups, and the pilots' transmissions began playing through his amp. Their disembodied voices would remain audible throughout the set.

Finally, the seven-member lineup of Garcia, Weir, McKernan, Lesh, Kreutzmann, Hart, and Constanten was ready. Merry Prankster Ken Babbs grabbed the microphone and addressed the crowd, announcing "one of the best fucking rock groups in the world, the Grateful Dead!"

A "St. Stephen" opener seemed promising, but the band played tentatively, and the song fizzled out after only two verses. They tried to pick up the pace with a cover of Merle Haggard's "Mama Tried." All things considered, this song went off without a hitch, but afterward, as if on cue, all the power to the stage went out, leaving the band standing in the dark, freaking out.

The audience, meanwhile, was growing hostile. On the audiotape, voices can be heard screaming, "Sit *down!*" at those obstructing the view, while those inclined to stand yell back, "Stand *up!*" Meanwhile, other audience members can be heard screaming about the sound. Garcia, who perceived the sound onstage as loud, asks incredulously, "You want it *louder?*" An audience member yells, "We can't hear your voices!" "I don't know, I think somebody's working on it," Jerry muses. Weir chimes in, "It's a sinister plot."

During these delays, Ken Babbs took on the role of spokesperson for the band, and attempted to inject a little levity. Alas, his nervous attempts to humor the audience only seemed to annoy. Perhaps sensing that his fellow San Franciscan was dying up there, Country Joe McDonald walked onstage to try and help him out. Joe spoke for a few minutes, and cautioned the assembled against ingesting the questionable LSD being circulated, while the Grateful Dead scrambled to regroup. Then Babbs continued his acid-addled banter, and the crowd grew increasingly restless. A young lady near the front heckled the baby-faced Weir, "Take your *hair* down," and "Take your hair out of your *shirt!*" A few more minutes of chaos ensued, and then the show began anew.

The band eased into an introspective "Dark Star," which slowly mutated into a more assertive jam. After nearly twenty minutes, for reasons known only to them, instead of launching into the second verse, the musicians segued into "High Time," from the forthcoming album *Workingman's Dead.*

This probably wasn't the best context for an unreleased ballad, and the intermittent interjections from the helicopter pilots made it sound truly bizarre. "High Time" was a low point, yet the band soldiered on. Now it was time for some vintage Pigpen.

The band launched into the grand finale, "Turn on Your Lovelight," its intro accompanied by more of Ken Babbs's lysergic musings, which were becoming disruptive. At one point, Pigpen's mic went dead, rendering his vocals inaudible, but this was soon remedied. The musicians stretched out "Lovelight" for forty-plus minutes, but somewhere along the way made the decision that afterward they would cut and run. John Morris announced, "Ladies and gentlemen, the Grateful Dead," and that was it. There would be no encore.

Audience reactions seemed mixed. While some in the crowd clearly called out "More!," one young lady yelled, "You suck!" Another guy yelled out, "Do you guys know more than two songs?" Even though they only played five songs, between all of the delays and malfunctions the set lasted ninety-five minutes . . . much to the chagrin of Creedence Clearwater Revival's John Fogerty, waiting in the wings, most impatiently.

No less an authority than Tony Sclafani, author of *The Grateful Dead FAQ: All That's Left to Know About the Greatest Jam Band in History*, takes the glass half-full approach, writing, "What's most disappointing about the Dead's Woodstock performance is something that fans and the band have danced around but never quite spoken about. The problem isn't what the Dead did at Woodstock, but what they failed to do. The Dead failed to make like Jimi Hendrix, or Janis Joplin, or Sly and the Family Stone, or the Who. In other words, the Dead failed at being transcendent and at pulling off a career making or career defining performance."

The Harvest Reaped: "The Music Never Stopped"

After Woodstock and the unpleasantness at Altamont Speedway four months later, the Grateful Dead's road stretched out for twenty-six years and a final tally of 2,314 shows.

With the November 1969 release of *Live Dead*, the group began a long-standing tradition of releasing live albums, allowing fans to appreciate the best of its performances from the comfort of home. The Dead's sphere of influence grew beyond the Bay Area to envelop the entire country, Europe, and eventually the world . . . even the pyramids of Giza.

The catalyst for all of the Dead's subsequent success was arguably the 1970 release of two groundbreaking albums, *Workingman's Dead* in June, and *American Beauty* in November. These albums abandoned the amorphous psychedelia of the group's previous efforts in favor of tightly structured songs that earned them some radio play. With the lyrical genius of Robert Hunter and friends like Crosby, Stills, and Nash nudging them to develop their vocal harmonies, the band displayed an affinity for country-tinged folk-rock.

The Dead endured its share of tragedies, and sometimes managed to parlay those tragedies into further triumphs. A set-up drugs bust on the road in New Orleans led to the 1970 single "Truckin'," which features the oft-quoted phrase, "What a long, strange trip it's been." The death of Phil Lesh's father led to the concert favorite "Box of Rain."

When Mickey Hart's father, Lenny, embezzled money from the band, the drummer withdrew from the scene for several years, before returning to the fold in 1974. The biggest tragedy, early on, was the death of Pigpen. The heavy drinker suffered from cirrhosis of the liver, and died of a gastrointestinal hemorrhage on March 8, 1973. He was just twenty-seven.

Pigpen's time in the band overlapped with that of piano player Keith Godchaux, who joined in September 1971 to bolster the lineup. By year's end, his wife, Donna Jean, had joined the mix as a backup vocalist. The couple became swept up in the worlds of booze and heroin but would remain with the band until February 17, 1979, when they decided to strike out on their own with the Heart of Gold Band. Tragically, Keith was killed in an automobile accident the following year, but Donna carried on.

The Godchauxs' departure opened the door for talented keyboardist and vocalist Brent Mydland. Mydland jumped right in on the band's 1980 album *Go to Heaven*, contributing his vocals and songwriting talents. During the seven-year period that followed, he established himself as a force to be reckoned with. But just as Mydland's star was ascendant, Jerry's health began to fail. His old regimen of marijuana and LSD had evolved into snorting cocaine and smoking black-tar heroin. Cocaine and booze were common among the band members, but Garcia's heroin use and underlying health issues made his situation much worse. Rampant drug use and poor eating habits led him to fall into a diabetic coma in July 1986. When he awoke from the coma after five days, he had to relearn his instrument, and the experience frightened him into healthier living habits . . . for a time. The band arrived at a crossroads the following year, with the July 1987 release of *In The Dark*.

The Dead's first studio album in seven years yielded a first Top 10 song, "Touch of Grey," aided, no doubt by MTV's frequent airings of the clever video, which depicted the band members as animated skeletons. Nearly twenty-two years after the Acid Tests—and after eleven studio albums, six live albums, endless touring, and band member side projects too numerous to mention—the Grateful Dead was suddenly the hottest band around, with a double-platinum album.

Ironically, 1989's *Built to Last* would be the final studio album the Grateful Dead ever released. But perhaps the title does resonate, as the surviving former members of the band were all still on the road in 2019.

Multiple dates at hockey arenas could no longer satisfy the demand for tickets; stadium shows became more frequent, and the band employed hundreds of people to make it all happen. Looking back, it seems a cruel irony that, just as Garcia seemed to be firing on all cylinders again, Brent Mydland, a mild-mannered social drinker, got caught up in the trappings and excesses of the rock-and-roll lifestyle. The gifted musician dealt with domestic issues and depression, and eventually succumbed to a "speedball" overdose of morphine and cocaine on July 26, 1990. In yet another of those cruel ironies that seemed to dog the group, his—and the band's—final studio album, released in 1989, was titled *Built to Last*. Mydland wrote and sang lead vocals on four of the nine tracks.

The fact that Mydland was the *third* Grateful Dead keyboard player to die (only Tom Constanten had escaped the reaper) was enough to give some superstitious types pause. Who would be next? His successor was former Tubes member Vince Welnick, who assumed keyboard duties, occasionally aided and abetted on piano by "floating" member Bruce Hornsby, who had a successful career of his own.

The band continued rolling forward after Mydland's death, largely because the operation had grown too big to stop; too many people's livelihoods depended upon the band's endless touring. In many ways, it was no longer fun, particularly for Jerry, who felt the weight of the world on his shoulders. He gained weight, resumed his drug habit, and hid from the eyes of the world in his hotel room.

When the Grateful Dead played an uneven show at Chicago's Soldier Field on July 9, 1995, at the end of a grueling and eventful summer tour, no one had any idea that it would be the last time Jerry Garcia took the stage. He checked himself into rehab at Serenity Knolls in California. There, on August 9, just a week after he turned fifty-three, Garcia passed away.

The Grateful Dead ceased to exist as a touring entity but remained every bit as big and vibrant a business and merchandising entity. Weir actually played a concert the night Garcia died, telling his audience, "If our departed friend taught us anything, it is that music can make sad times seem better."

Over the next twenty years, Weir, Lesh, Kreutzmann, and Hart would play, both solo and together, in a dizzying array of configurations: Phil Lesh and Friends; Ratdog; Weir and Wasserman. After waiting a respectful three years, Weir, Lesh, and Hart formed the Other Ones in 1998, with a revolving cast of likeminded musicians, including Bruce Hornsby, Bill Kreutzmann, Jeff Chimenti, and Susan Tedeschi, releasing an album of Dead covers, unreleased material, and new songs, *The Strange Remain*, in 1999.

By 2003, the group had changed its name to the Dead, and featured the core four of Lesh, Weir, Hart, and Kreutzmann, along with Jimmy Herring, Jeff Chimenti, Rob Barraco, and—for a time—vocalist Joan Osborne. Warren Haynes came on board in 2004, and Herring and Osborne left. After a few years of solo projects, the Dead made another run in 2008–2009, after which the group splintered and mutated once more. Weir and Lesh formed Further with Chimenti, drummer Joe Russo, singer Sunshine Becker, and John Kadlecik (the "Jerry guy" from Grateful Dead tribute band, Dark Star Orchestra). Further proved very popular and enjoyed a five-year run until 2014. Hart and Kreutzmann, meanwhile, had their joint Rhythm Devils project and various side projects to keep them busy.

In 2015, the Core Four reunited for the Fare Thee Well concerts, marking the fifty-year anniversary of the Grateful Dead. Chimenti, Hornsby, and Phish's Trey Anastasio joined them for five sold-out stadium shows. Afterward, Anastasio returned to his own projects, and Lesh returned to California. Weir, Hart, Kreutzmann, and Chimenti got together with former Allman Brother Oteil Burnbridge and guitar wizard John Mayer to form a *new* band, Dead and Company, which has been filling stadiums ever since. At press time, there were Dead and Company shows listed through the summer of 2019. The music never stopped, and the golden road goes ever, ever on.

19

Creedence Clearwater Revival

California Cajuns

> We didn't do very well at Woodstock because of the time segment, and also because we followed the Grateful Dead, therefore everybody was asleep. It seemed like we didn't go on until 2 a.m. The Dead went on and pulled their usual shenanigans. Even though in my mind we made the leap to superstardom that weekend, you'd never know it from the footage. All that does is show us in a poor light at a time when we were the #1 band in the world.
>
> — *John Fogerty, Pete Fornatale Radio Archives, 2009*

As the Seeds Were Sown: Along the Banks of "Green River"

The seeds of Creedence Clearwater Revival were sown at Portola Junior High School in El Cerrito, California. In 1959, classmates Stu Cook, Doug Clifford, and John Fogerty formed a little group called the Blue Velvets. John's big brother Tom, meanwhile, had a band called Spider Webb and the Insects.

Like a lot of groups during the formative years of rock and roll, Spider Webb and the Insects signed a record deal but never actually made any records. Before Tom knew it, the band was no more. Rather than try to reinvent the wheel, he deputized his kid brother's band and had the Blue

Velvets back him. What must have seemed like a purely pragmatic solution would have life-changing consequences for all concerned.

This "backing group" arrangement gave way to Tom becoming an equal member of the Blue Velvets. The band actually lasted for a few years and recorded a couple of singles with Tom singing lead vocals. When the boys changed their name to the Golliwogs, younger brother John began sharing vocal duties with Tom. John's star was on the rise, just as the band found itself mired in controversy.

A "golliwog" was a nineteenth-century construct of children's author Florence Kate Upton, who depicted her golliwog as a goggle-eyed, jet-black ragdoll with a huge afro and large, painted lips. The golliwog found a second life as an *actual* doll, manufactured and marketed to boys as toys until the 1970s. But controversy over the band's name would have to wait, as the Golliwogs hit another bump in the road in 1966, when half the band got drafted.

John Fogerty joined the Army Reserve, and wouldn't be discharged until July of the following year. Doug Clifford, meanwhile, opted for the Coast Guard Reserve. When the two were finished doing their respective hitches, it was back to the music business, full time, as in, no side jobs—just the band, the whole band, and nothing but the band, 24/7.

The Golliwogs landed a recording contract with Fantasy Records in 1967, but the company's concerns over the name being a racist caricature pressured the band into yet another name change. From a name that meant something negative, the four opted for a name that meant . . . well, *nothing*, really, but it *sounded* great: Creedence Clearwater Revival.

The "Creedence" part came from Tom's buddy Credence Newball. They toyed, briefly, with naming the band "Creedence Nuball and the Ruby" in his honor, but after this and a few other offbeat suggestions, cooler heads prevailed. And so, in January 1968, Creedence Clearwater Revival was born.

The "Clearwater" aspect was inspired by the Olympia Brewing Company. The Washington-based brewery made such a big deal about the quality of its water—obtained by drilling down into natural aquifers via "artesian wells"—that it was hard not to notice. This bit of marketing found its way into Olympia Beer's marketing slogan, "It's the Water." *Clear* water, that is.

And "Revival," well, in spite of the religious overtones, in this case it had more to do with the four members' shared sense of renewed commitment to the band. That commitment would prove short-lived, even as the band became successful beyond their wildest dreams. During a whirlwind fifteen months leading up to Woodstock, CCR would, as Fogerty indicated above, go on to become the hottest band in the country.

Debut album *Creedence Clearwater Revival* hit the shelves in May 1968 to mixed reviews. The album opens with a cover of Screaming Jay Hawkins' "I Put a Spell on You," at the vanguard of eight covers, originals, and blasts from the band's past. These include some previously released Golliwogs material, such as John's songwriting breakthrough, "Porterville," and "Walk on the Water," a re-working of the 1966 Fogerty brothers collaboration, "Walking on the Water."

Creedence Clearwater Revival hit the ground running with its May 1968 debut. By the following year, CCR was one of the hottest bands in the land, and the first act to sign on for the Woodstock festival.

The group's first single, an eight-minute-plus cover of Dale Hawkins' "Suzie Q" that spanned *both* sides of a 45, flirted with the Top 10, hitting #11 on the charts, and garnered lots of airplay on AM radio. Momentum was building. The follow-up album, *Bayou Country*, released in January 1969, charted at #7; the single "Proud Mary" b/w "Born on the Bayou" went to #2, beginning a parade of hit singles that made the group a household name—an overnight sensation ten years in the making.

CCR kept the pedal to the metal during 1969, releasing the single "Bad Moon Rising" b/w "Lodi" in April. The single hit #2 and served as the scouting party for the release of the group's third album, *Green River*. On March 9, CCR "arrived" via another medium when they played *The Ed Sullivan Show* for the first time, barreling through "Proud Mary" and "Good Golly Miss Molly." Somehow, you knew they would be back.

The band's rising public profile earned its members a sweet deal with Woodstock Ventures when they agreed to appear at the upcoming festival and do a one-hour set for $10,000, which was about $2,500 more than they'd ever earned for a full two-hour show. Woodstock Ventures was hoping that Creedence—the first band to answer its call—would incentivize other high-profile acts to play the festival.

The festival signing preceded the July release of "Green River" b/w "Commotion," which became CCR's third #2 single of an eventual six. The album of the same name dropped on August 3, less than two weeks before the festival, and hit #1 on the *Billboard* 200. Creedence Clearwater Revival had arrived and was poised for greatness in Bethel.

In the Garden: Will This *Ever* End?

Creedence Clearwater Revival had their work cut out for them when they took the stage around 12:30 a.m. Given the difficult logistics, the load-out/load-in between the Grateful Dead and Creedence Clearwater Revival went as quickly and smoothly as could be expected. Still, the perception of being behind schedule carried over into the set. If the Grateful Dead had turned in a barnburner, hot on the heels of Canned Heat and Mountain, the audience would have been on fire, and it would have been about 11:30 p.m. Saturday.

Instead, CCR took to the stage to find a soggy, exhausted audience, many of whom seemed to be asleep. Like the old saying goes, if you snooze, you lose. John Fogerty was in fine, snarling form as the band opened with "Born on the Bayou," even as the electrical problems that plagued the Dead continued. Bespectacled bassist Stu Cook hung back, half facing the drum kit, while he and burly drummer Doug "Cosmo" Clifford laid down the thunder. As if to emphasize his own lightheartedness, Cosmo wore a bright white T-shirt featuring Mickey Mouse doffing a top hat.

Big brother Tom Fogerty, meanwhile, hung out stage left, dutifully playing rhythm. The rhythm section was characteristically tight, but with his razor sharp vocals, bluesy harp, and crackling guitar leads, John was the focal point. As the opening number ended, he addressed the crowd. "Hi, thank you very much!" But he sounded *really* annoyed when he turned to address the stage crew. "Hey, can you get that thing on? Is it on now? Get it goin'!"

"All right, just to move right along with one of dem shorties, called 'Green River.'" For the non-musician with "untrained ears," it is difficult to discern any sound difficulties in the Woodstock recording of "Green River," John's ode to his favorite childhood soda syrup flavor. This didn't stop him from calling attention to them, however. "Well, we're having a multitude of problems," he said. "I'm sure you don't want to hear about 'em." Turning to the beleaguered crew, he cracked the whip again: "C'mon! C'mon! Forty minutes to get it straight!"

Next up was a cover of Wilson Picket, Eddie Floyd, and Steve Cropper's soulful classic, "Ninety-Nine and a Half (Won't Do)." Fogerty seemed to mellow out a tad after this song, saying only, "Oh, my, thank you!" to the audience. He also seemed to hit a groove on "Bootleg," though there is audible feedback at the song's end, and the band engages in a little fidgety tuning. "Commotion" chugged along at its typically manic pace.

Afterward, sounding subdued yet hopeful, Fogerty asked the crew, "Is it working yet?" He got the reply, "Yeah, right." Next, the band launched into "Bad Moon Rising," which, if anyone actually could have *seen* the moon, might have provided an apt metaphor for that night's technical difficulties. "Proud Mary," the John Fogerty–penned tune that would go on to provide hits and stage material for artists as diverse as Solomon Burke,

Ike and Tina Turner, Elvis Presley, Bruce Springsteen, Johnny Paycheck, George Jones, and—God help us—even *the Osmonds*, followed.

"All right, now we'd like to do an old Screamin' Jay Hawkins tune for ya, 'I Put a Spell on You.'" Turning away from his vocal mic before the word "You" had an opportunity to make it into the P.A., Fogerty can be heard grousing, "Oh, come on."

The incomparable CCR hit parade continued with "Night Time Is the Right Time." When the gospel-flavored tune ended, John began setting the audience up for the kill: "Now we'd like to do a song . . . it's our last number, but I hope you all are doing it, anyway, all day long. It's called 'Keep Ooooon . . . Chooglin'.'" Clocking in at nearly ten minutes, "Chooglin'" was the closest approximation of a long, drawn-out San Francisco–style jam they'd played so far. But even this was a case study in controlled chaos, with the rhythm section of Tom, Doug, and Stu keeping time in the pocket like a metronome, giving John ample room to wail away on his harmonica and guitar. "Goodnight, y'all. Thank ya, we love ya." An encore was a foregone conclusion.

With some in the crowd sounding the familiar plea, "One more song! One more song!" the band tuned up amid the violent buzzing, and prepared to wrap things up. They encored with an almost interminable "Suzie Q," one of the more sinister "love songs" in the rock-and-roll canon. As on "Chooglin'," Tom, Doug, and Stu anchored the song and gave John room to play. That final one-two punch of closing number and encore found the band hitting killer grooves, and really gave the audience a true sense of what Creedence was all about.

Chip Monck seemed pleased as he stepped up for the back-sell, "Ladies and gentlemen, Cree–dence, Clear–wa–ter Re–vi–val," lovingly annunciating each and every syllable as only he could. Tom, Doug, and Stu were also stoked. The only unhappy camper was John. He didn't think things had gone quite so well.

The Harvest Reaped: Put Me In, Coach

The band's experiences at Woodstock caused lead singer John Fogerty to foster an intense dislike for the Grateful Dead and its audience. His frame of mind that night, along with his perfectionism, may also have blinded him to the merits of his own band's set.

There was a chasm of difference between John and his bandmates' perspectives on their performance. John thought the set was below the band's standards; Stu Cook thought they had knocked it out of the park.

Cosmo Clifford and Tom Fogerty were in agreement that the set was pure CCR magic. John's opinion prevailed, however, and CCR wasn't included in the film or on the soundtrack albums . . . much to the chagrin of the others. As a result, many people remain unaware of Creedence's Woodstock performance, though many in attendance remember it as a highlight.

Less than three months after the festival, CCR completed the "hat trick" by releasing its third studio album of 1969, and fourth overall, November 2's *Willie and the Poor Boys*. The album features a rollicking cover of Leadbelly's "Cotton Fields," along with the infectious "Down on the Corner" and the blistering "Fortunate Son," which as a double-sided single hit #3 and #14 on *Billboard*, respectively.

The other standout track on the album is a cover of the traditional tune (another Leadbelly staple), "The Midnight Special." Two weeks later, CCR returned to *The Ed Sullivan Show*, promoting the album with live renditions of "Down on the Corner" and "Fortunate Son," which was about to become a timeless antiwar anthem, though the lyrics never mention Vietnam specifically.

Though Tom, Doug, and Stu had begun to grumble about John's controlling, perfectionist approach, CCR steamrolled into the new decade with another double-sided #2 hit single in January 1970, "Travelin' Band" b/w "Who'll Stop the Rain." Keen-eared listeners figured out fairly quickly that the B-side was, at least in part, a commentary on the band's experiences at Woodstock. The following month found the band gracing the cover of the February 21 issue of *Rolling Stone* magazine, but John was the only member interviewed.

The band was poised to take the show on the road that Spring, across the pond to Europe, but before taking off for the tour, CCR dropped another single, the joyous "Up Around the Bend" b/w "Run Through the Jungle," a foreboding tune with a rather obvious anti-Vietnam sentiment. It was good enough for the #4 spot on

Hot of the presses the first week of August 1969, *Green River* was the second of *three* albums the band would release during 1969. The frantic pace would take a toll on the band members' interpersonal relationships.

Billboard, and provided a teaser for the upcoming album, *Cosmo's Factory*, due out on July 16.

The group released another single to coincide with the album drop: the foot-stomping "Lookin' Out My Back Door" b/w "Long as I Can See the Light," a much more somber, reflective song. The diverse pairing was good enough to earn CCR a sixth #2, though they would never hit that number again.

Cosmo's Factory hit the #1 spot on *Billboard* and would go on to become the band's all-time bestseller. The album approaches jam-band territory with its eleven-minute cover of Marvin Gaye's "I Heard It Through the Grapevine." But the disharmony within the band was rapidly coming to a head. CCR's December 1970 album, aptly titled *Pendulum*, proved to be the breaking point. For all intents and purposes, it may as well have been a John Fogerty solo album, because he wrote all of the songs.

By February 1971, the public learned that the "pendulum" had swung the other way. Tom Fogerty, who had once hired brother John, Stu Cook, and Doug Clifford to be *his* backup band, decided that he'd had enough. He left the group and went solo, leaving CCR as a trio. John was determined to make a go of it, and CCR released the #6 hit "Sweet Hitchhiker" b/w "Door to Door," a tune written by Cook, before taking off on tours of Europe and the United States.

But the Tom Fogerty–less CCR was not long for this world, and any impressions of a more "democratic" approach within the band were largely illusory. Cook and Clifford may have been sharing songwriting, lead vocals, and production duties with John—at John's insistence—but these things were clearly not their strong suit. The two may have been the linchpin of one of the tightest rhythm sections in rock history, but CCR was still John's show.

The group's final album, *Mardi Gras*, hit the shelves in April 1972. The coerced "egalitarian" approach went over with the critics like the proverbial lead balloon. But the album still made money, went gold, and weighed in at #12 on the charts. Notable tracks include "Sweet Hitchhiker," which sounds like classic CCR, and, especially, the group's final single, the beautiful "Someday Never Comes." There's even a playful cover of Ricky Nelson's "Hello Mary Lou," but the writing was already on the wall. The band took the show on the road for a twenty-date tour of the United States, but six months after the album release, CCR called it a career.

In the "Where Are They Now?" category, Tom Fogerty went solo after he left the band, and released several albums, including *Tom Fogerty* (1972), *Excalibur* (1972), *Zephyr National* (1974), and *Myopia* (1974). *Zephyr National* actually features a "reunion" of all four former CCR members on the song "Mystic Isle Avalon," though John recorded his leads separately; this was the last time all four would appear "together" on a song.

After a seven-year gap, Tom returned with *Deal It Out* (1981). After *another* seven-year gap, he recorded *Sidekicks* with Randy Oda, but it wouldn't be released until 1993, capitalizing on CCR's impending induction into the Rock and Roll Hall of Fame. By that point, Tom was gone. In a tragic twist, he had contracted the HIV virus from a blood transfusion during back surgery; the official cause of his passing, on September 6, 1990, was tuberculosis.

Cosmo Clifford and Stu Cook dabbled for a bit as producers in the wake of CCR's breakup, and they also played together in the Don Harrison Band. They didn't really hit a winning formula until 1995, when they swallowed their pride and formed their own CCR tribute band, Creedence Clearwater Revisited. Almost predictably, John Fogerty *sued* them, so they changed their name to Cosmo's Factory, until they were vindicated in a court of law. At press time, Creedence Clearwater Revisited was booked for concerts through March 2019, with more likely to follow.

Last but never least, John Fogerty barely broke stride as he entered 1973 a solo artist, hitting the shelves with *The Blue Ridge Rangers* in April. Unfortunately, the animus he had with his bandmates extended to Fantasy Records. David Geffen bailed him out by buying his contract, but John was still loath to perform any CCR material live. Geffen's intervention led to the 1975 Asylum Records release *John Fogerty*, which featured the bouncy hit single "Rockin All Over the World."

John experienced a rare career misstep with 1976's *Hoodoo*, a subpar album, which Asylum refused to release. He was still embroiled in legal disputes with Fantasy Records, which took a toll on him. The ugly divorce was finalized in 1980, with John getting the short end of the stick, financially. The bitter feud continued for years afterward.

Nevertheless, John bounced back in 1985 with the huge hit *Centerfield* on Warner Bros. The baseball-centric title track became a #4 hit single, and remains a staple at baseball stadiums throughout the country. But "Centerfield" was just one song on an album filled with joyous tracks like "The Old Man Down the Road" and "Rock and Roll Girls."

The 1986 follow-up, *Eye of the Zombie*, fared less well. The people wanted the CCR stuff, and legend has it Bob Dylan convinced John to revisit his storied past. By 1987, he was playing the old CCR catalogue again.

Creedence Clearwater Revival was inducted into the Rock and Roll Hall of Fame in 1993 with a heartfelt speech by long-time fan Bruce Springsteen. In the years since, John Fogerty has released the Grammy Award–winning ("Best Rock Album") *Blue Moon Swamp* (1997), *Déjà Vu All Over Again* (2004), the Grammy-nominated ("Best Rock Album")

Revival (2007), *The Blue Ridge Rangers Rides Again* (2009), and *Wrote a Song for Everyone* (2013), a career retrospective featuring an array of guest stars on classic CCR and Fogerty tracks.

At press time, John Fogerty, still in fine form, was booked for live shows through May 2019, and shows little sign of slowing down anytime soon.

20

Janis Joplin

A Girl Who Sang the Blues

She was wasted. And that is the worst performance I ever saw her do. She was gone . . . she was not so great at Woodstock. She was sloppy. It was sloppy. The audience didn't react badly, but I would say questioningly. I've never heard anyone say that that's one of the greatest performances she ever did.

—*John Morris, Pete Fornatale Radio Archives, 2009*

As the Seeds Were Sown: Port Arthur's Least Likely to Succeed

Janis Lyn Joplin was born January 19, 1943, in the blue-collar oil-boom town of Port Arthur, Texas, the eldest of three children born to Seth Ward Joplin and Dorothy Bonita. Janis was never cut out for life in Port Arthur. By the time she got to Thomas Jefferson High School in 1957, the fourteen-year-old stuck out like a sore thumb among her churchgoing, football-loving, straight-laced classmates.

Janis's teenage social awkwardness was compounded by bad acne and struggles with her weight. In retrospect, it seems almost poetic that she discovered the blues during this period. She was an avid reader who enjoyed painting and other solitary activities, but music would add a dimension to her life like no other.

In spite of her tormentors, Janis persevered with school and graduated in 1960. She forged ahead and enrolled at Lamar State College of Technology in Beaumont, and then at the University of Texas at Austin.

She worked for a time as a waitress at a local bowling alley, but she was destined for bigger things. Whereas her high-school classmates had pretty much *all* treated her cruelly, there were at least some in college who appreciated her uniqueness, like the staff of the school newspaper, the *Daily Texan* (which once did a profile on her), and the crew at the campus humor magazine, the *Texas Ranger*. Janis gravitated toward the artsy, creative set.

Somewhere during her college years, having already absorbed the music of Otis Redding, Bessie Smith, Huddie "Leadbelly" Ledbetter, Ma Rainey, and Willie Mae "Big Momma" Thornton, Janis discovered the music *within*. She began performing live as early as 1962, with a folk trio called the Waller Boys. Given the trajectory of her lifetime, it is almost comical—in the classical sense of the term—that her first known song was a home recording of an original composition titled "What Good Can Drinkin' Do" in December of 1962. A rhetorical question, if ever there was one, from a young woman who fancied herself a beatnik. That song, and other early compositions like "It's Sad to Be Alone," written in the wake of a student write-in campaign to name her Alpha Phi Omega's "Ugliest Man on Campus," offer a great deal of insight into her fragile personality.

Now that Janis had broken the ice on her performing career, she decided to bail out of college and get out of Texas altogether. She arrived in San Francisco in 1963, and made her way from North Beach to the Haight-Ashbury district, where she fell in with fellow future Woodstock performer Jorma Kaukonen. Like Janis, Jorma was all about the blues; the pair recorded several songs. The seven-song 1964 session, which features the sound of Jorma's first wife Margareta typing in the background, would go on to become a popular bootleg known as—what else?—*The Typewriter Tape*.

Janis readily embraced the emerging drug culture. Southern Comfort became her signature drink, but when she started shooting meth and dabbling in heroin, she began to deteriorate before the eyes of her friends. Some of them had the presence of mind to raise funds for a bus ticket, and they sent her packing, back home to Texas. They may have saved her life, if only for the moment.

By May 1965, Janis had decided she was going to turn over a new leaf, to give up the booze and dope and live the straight life. She even went back to college, at Lamar University, where she declared as her major anthropology, of all things. But, all the while, she kept one foot in the music game. She would take the bus to Austin to play weekend gigs as a folk/blues singer, accompanying herself on acoustic guitar in the manner of Leadbelly or Dave Van Ronk. People began to take notice.

During the fall of 1965, Janis got engaged to a man she had met in San Francisco, Peter de Blanc. Perhaps, on some level, this was one last-ditch effort at attaining a normal and stable life, but it was doomed to fail. De Blanc lived in New York and traveled frequently. Even though he was the one who proposed, after doing the old-fashioned "right thing" by traveling to Texas and asking Janis's dad for his blessing, he broke off the engagement. In all likelihood it wouldn't have lasted anyway. As much as Janis loved guys, her libido was all encompassing. She was a committed bisexual who enjoyed the company of women, and *that* would never fly in 1960s Texas.

In 1965, Janis entered the studio for the first time since her San Francisco sessions with Jorma and recorded seven tracks. That material, which included another original tune, "Turtle Blues," wouldn't see the light of day until decades later.

The following year, 1966, proved to be a pivotal one for Janis. Bill Graham's crosstown rival, Chet Helms, owner of the Avalon Ballroom, was managing a band called Big Brother and the Holding Company—an all-boys club consisting of guitarist and vocalist Sam Andrew; James Gurley, a guitarist who also played bass; Peter Albin, a bassist who also played guitar; and Dave Getz, a drummer who also played piano. The consensus on the scene was that the band was *okay*, but nothing special. They needed something more, and Chet had an idea.

Chet knew about Janis from Texas, and in June he decided to play matchmaker by flying her back to San Francisco to join Big Brother as a vocalist. Their first gig together, at Helms' Avalon Ballroom, was well received, and the band's reputation began to grow.

Taking a cue from the Grateful Dead, Big Brother and the Holding Company decided to try the communal-living thing, so they all moved into a big house in Lagunitas, not too far from the Haight. Janis began dating fellow blues and booze enthusiast Pigpen, the *de facto* front man of the Grateful Dead.

Misfortune turned to fortune when Big Brother ran out of funds during a less-than-lucrative run of shows in Chicago, only to have record executive Bob Shad offer the group a deal with his label, Mainstream Records. Even though the first sessions in Chicago didn't pan out so well, Shad stuck with the band through the December recording sessions in San Francisco that led to the release of a self-titled debut album eight months later, in August 1967.

Astute readers will no doubt note that the band's now legendary appearance at the Monterey Pop Festival took place two months *before* the release of its debut. In a power play, Chet Helms wouldn't allow the band's Saturday set to be filmed; he was looking for a payday. The band did its standard set at the time: "Down on Me," "Combination of the Two," "Harry," "Roadblock," and, of course, a cover of Big Mama Thornton's "Ball and Chain." The audience was wowed, prompting Helms to strike a deal with filmmaker D. A. Pennebaker: the band would appear again on Sunday for a brief encore performance of "Combination of the Two," and "Ball and Chain," for potential inclusion in the film.

The good press from the festival brought them to the attention of Albert Grossman, who took over management duties and signed the group to Columbia Records. When the film *Monterey Pop* was released in December 1968, the world got a good look at Big Brother and the Holding Company, but all viewers *really* saw was Janis Joplin, and the gape-mouthed reaction of Mama Cass Elliot, who appears stunned by the Texas Tornado's galvanizing stage presence.

Big Brother didn't rest on their laurels after releasing *Big Brother and the Holding Company*. The album only hit #60; the single "Down on Me" *almost* cracked the Top 40. The group's next album, for Columbia Records, would be a different story. Signing to Columbia changed the band's performance routine; with its promotional muscle, the label took Big Brother out on the road across the country, introducing the group to different audiences along the way. In fact, it was Big Brother and the Holding Company that opened Bill Graham's Fillmore East, on March 8, 1968.

But success has a funny way of fostering stress in a band, particularly when a record label is focusing all of its energy on promoting *one* member, relegating the rest to the role of backup musicians. People like

Albert Grossman began telling Janis that she didn't need those guys; that *she* was the real star.

By this time, the band was already in the studio working on a follow-up album, *Sex, Dope, and Cheap Thrills*, a title the label wisely suggested be shortened to *Cheap Thrills*. Plan A was for it to be a live album, but that wasn't the way it worked out. Instead, the resulting studio album incorporates audience sounds, and ends with a live version of "Ball and Chain" from the Fillmore. Janis was very hands-on in the studio, an active participant in the production. *Cheap Thrills* dropped on August 12 and hit the charts like a fist, spending two solid months at #1.

On September 1, Janis responded to her band's newfound success by announcing her departure. Bill Graham tried to capitalize on this development by booking three Fillmore West shows on September 12, 13, and 14, and marketing them as Janis's *last* go-around with Big Brother. It turned out Bill was only off by thirty-one shows, as Janis stayed on for a

In the wake of their 1967 Monterey Pop festival—or, more importantly, the 1968 film of the festival—Big Brother and the Holding Company moved from Mainstream Records to Columbia House.

cross-country tour with the band through December 1, when they played their final show together at the Family Dog.

Heading into 1969, Janis's new project was called the Kozmic Blues Band. She recruited Big Brother guitarist Sam Andrew and added Brad Campbell on bass, along with session musicians Stephen Ryder on keyboards, and Cornelius Flowers, a.k.a. "Snooky," on the saxophone. There was to be no more psychedelia for Janis—she wanted her new band to have an old-school soul, R&B, and Chicago-blues flavor.

During the latter half of June 1969, Janis, nursing a monstrous heroin habit, hit the studios with members of the Kozmic Blues Band to lay down the tracks for her first solo album, *I've Got Dem Ol' Kozmic Blues Again Mama!* It would not be released until after the Woodstock festival.

In the Garden: A Hardened "Pearl"

Like many of her musical colleagues, Janis had no sense of how big the festival was going to be, and thought of it as just another gig . . . until she took that helicopter ride over the festival site, and got a little nervous.

After hanging out backstage all day Friday, and all day and half the night on Saturday, Janis was not in the best of shape when it came time for her to take the stage at 2:00 a.m. She had been imbibing liberally, and had shot heroin with her friend Peggy Caserta at least once. Some of those who had known her from her earlier days in San Francisco, pre–Columbia Records deal, such as former boyfriend Country Joe McDonald, found her new larger-than-life, rock-star persona a little off-putting.

To make matters worse, people didn't care for her new band very much, and that became a sore spot for the sensitive star. It wasn't that this was a *bad* band, it was just that the Kozmic Blues Band's classic Chicago blues style stood in stark contrast to the more familiar, guitar-based psychedelia of Big Brother and the Holding Company—and that difference was not lost on the more critical members of the Woodstock audience, some of whom could clearly be heard heckling Janis during song breaks.

The Kozmic Blues Band lineup that night featured the horn section of Terry Clements on tenor sax, Cornelius "Snooky" Flowers on baritone sax and vocals, and Luis Garcia on trumpet, along with guitarist John

Till, bassist Brad Campbell, drummer Maury Baker, keyboardist Richard Kermode, and, of course, Janis on lead vocals. Chip Monck gave his usual deadpan introduction: "Please welcome with us . . . Miss Janis Joplin."

Impaired though she was, Janis gave it her all, leading the band through a ten-song, hour-long set that kicked off with a soulful "Raise Your Hand." It began with the crack of the snare drum and an opening salvo from the horn section, which backed off to allow for an extended guitar and bass break, before kicking back in for the final verse.

The Kozmic Blues Band blazed forth with "As Good as You've Been to This World," from the forthcoming album. Janis gave the audience the back-sell, breathlessly announcing, "All right, thank you. That's a tune by Nick Gravenites, very good songwriter, called, 'As Good as You've Been to This World.' That's how good I'm gonna be to you, so you'd better make it good."

It appears that not everybody was pleased with the new material, as just at that moment a voice from the crowd bellowed, "Get off that stage!" Janis stuck to her game plan, continuing with more material from her upcoming solo debut: a soulful cover of the Bee Gees' "To Love Somebody," which, even under these less-than-ideal circumstances, added a dimension of emotion that was lacking in the 1967 pop original. That accursed buzz from the P.A. was still an issue, and most noticeable between songs, but it didn't seem to faze Janis one bit.

After playing two new songs in a row, Janis threw the audience a bone with her Gershwin cover from *Cheap Thrills*, "Summertime." This song was always an audience favorite during the Big Brother era. The horn-led intro was a new touch, but the audience broke out into applause once the familiar eerie, psychedelic guitar and organ began. This may not have been the arrangement they were accustomed to, but the new band definitely added some enjoyable elements. The audience applauded appreciatively.

With the crowd in a good place, it was back to new material for the opening track from the upcoming album. "It's a song called 'Try (Just a Little Bit Harder),'" Janis said. "You know you'd better, baby . . . and you know you gotta." The band hit a groove on this one, complete with backing vocals by Flowers, and provided, arguably, the finest moment of the set. Janis dutifully credited the source. "Okay, that's a song by Jerry

Ragovoy. It's gonna be on our next record, which is called, *I Got Dem Ol'*
Kozmic Blues Again, Mama!" That provided the setup for the title track.
Janis continued, "Talkin' about the Kozmic blues, do you know what I
mean, man? If you don't know what I mean, you will, soon enough," and
then launched into one of her patented cackling laughs.

"Kozmic Blues" has an intro that is at least slightly reminiscent of
"Summertime," but there the similarities end. This is a song full of big
band bombast and Janis's "whoa, yeah" howls. Afterward, she needed a
breather. Enter Flowers.

Breathing heavily and seeming a bit tentative, Janis addressed the
crowd. "All right, thank you. I'd like to introduce somebody from the
band. Gonna do a tune . . . okay? This is . . . [to Snooky] you ready? This is
Snooky . . . Flowers . . . come on. He's gonna do a tune called 'Can't Turn
Ya Loose.' Can't . . . burn yer goose . . . what is that?" And then came that
famous cackling laugh of hers.

Snooky, seeming about at thrilled as the audience, responded to
Janis, "Oh, yeah . . . mercy. You like that, huh?" In a daring move, Snooky
decided to go the old audience participation route. "Mercy, let me hear ya
say, 'Yeah!'" (*"Yeah!"*) "Fuck, no, it ain't nobody. Everybody out in the parking lots, outside in the little tents, you people out in the grass . . . yeah,
grass . . . let me hear everybody say, 'Yeah!'" (*"YEAH!"*) "Shit, no. One more
time, Yeah!" (*"YEAH!!"*)

The band then launched into "I Can't Turn You Loose," a song few in
the audience had ever heard, sung by Flowers, a guy few had ever heard
of. Yet the band did an *excellent* job here, and Flowers, clearly an experienced front man, even got the audience cheering at "Do you wanna hear
the horns blow?"

Janis, meanwhile, was right there, front and center, dancing enthusiastically—if not *gracefully*—with Flowers and without. She got caught up
in the moment and grabbed the microphone to throw in a few shrieking
"whoa, yeah's," before passing it back to Flowers. She stayed right by his
side, smiling from ear-to-ear and dancing maniacally. The applause was
appreciative.

After Snooky's turn at the helm, Janis introduced her closing number,
"Work Me Lord," making sure to talk up Nick Gravenites and his fine
songwriting. She leaped headlong into the song, shrieking, laughing,

snarling, howling, and dancing like a woman possessed. At times, she would turn toward the band and wave her arms like a madwoman orchestra conductor, smiling all the while.

Chip Monck took to the stage to announce her off, and then, just as quickly, back on, for the first encore, "Piece of My Heart," from the beloved *Cheap Thrills* album. This was a more up-tempo version than the studio track. And while Janis could never be accused of "phoning it in," this version did have the feeling of "been there, done that, let's get it over with."

Ever the dutiful MC, Chip jumped up to announce her off, and back on. For her second and final encore, Janis led the band through a shortened version of her signature tune, "Ball and Chain." Had she not set the bar so high at Monterey Pop and venues like the Avalon Ballroom, Winterland, and the Fillmores, this version wouldn't have raised an eyebrow. But she had set a high bar indeed, and this version paled in comparison.

All things considered, between the weather, the hour of night, the sound problems, and Janis's level of intoxication, this was a fairly solid set, though all of those factors did conspire to take a little something off Janis's fastball. Little did she realize, when she walked off that stage, but she only had 414 days to live.

The Harvest Reaped: Get It While You Can

Never one to miss out on a party, Janis hung out for the *rest* of the festival . . . as did her unlikely companion, Friday-night headliner Joan Baez. According to Joan, the two of them spent Monday morning together in Joe Cocker's van, watching Jimi's Hendrix's festival-closing set.

When it came time to review the film footage and audio of her festival performance, Janis was not happy, and would not allow it to be used in the *Woodstock* film or soundtrack albums, though she and Peggy Caserta do briefly appear in a backstage scene. "Work Me Lord," arguably the high point of her set, would later turn up in the *Director's Cut* of the film in 1994.

Janis barreled through 1969 with the September 11 drop of *I Got Dem Ol' Kosmic Blues Again Mama!* The album hit #5 on *Billboard* and went gold, but earned mixed reviews from critics, most of whom couldn't seem to get over the fact that she had left Big Brother and the Holding Company.

Janis celebrated Thanksgiving by doing a duet with Tina Turner, who was opening for the Rolling Stones at the brand new Madison Square Garden that night. Witnesses say it was clear she was "feeling no pain." An erratic Janis played MSG again on December 19 for her final gig of the year, which featured guest appearances by Paul Butterfield and Johnny Winter. This was also the last gig with the Kozmic Blues Band.

Janis lay low as 1970 began, hitting Brazil with Nick Gravenites's wife, Linda, to try and get clean. By April, she was back in the US, back on heroin, and ready to launch a new backing band, Full Tilt Boogie. She and the band played at the Fillmore West on April 4 and then hit the road in mid-May for a US tour.

Beginning on June 27, Janis joined the Band, the Grateful Dead, Sha Na Na, Mountain, and Ten Years After in Toronto as part of an all-star lineup for the Festival Express tour. The party train, loaded with musicians, instruments, and booze, traveled westward from Toronto to Winnipeg to Calgary, playing concerts at every stop until July 4.

Back south of the Canadian border on July 5, Janis hit the West Coast and Hawaii during July, followed by nine East Coast dates, including an appearance at the Festival for Peace on August 6 at New York City's Shea Stadium. Six days later, on August 12, she gave what turned out to be her final performance at Harvard Stadium.

On August 14, Janis fulfilled a goal she had told TV host Dick Cavett about during her appearance on his show on June 25. She went home to Port Arthur, Texas, to attend the ten-year reunion of Thomas Jefferson High School's Class of 1960. Her anticipation reportedly far exceeded the actual event, and the experience bummed her out.

Then it was back to business in California, working with Full Tilt Boogie on her upcoming album, *Pearl*, at Sunset Sound Recorders in Hollywood. At the helm was legendary Doors producer Paul Rothchild, with whom she worked well. She was, once again, very hands-on during

Released in January of 1971, *Pearl* would command the #1 spot on
the *Billboard* 200 for two months. But Janis did not live long enough
to see the album released.

the sessions, and handled all of the arrangements for the nine tracks she
sang lead on.

Then there was the matter of that *tenth* track, "Buried Alive in the
Blues," which appears at the end of side one as an instrumental, though
it was never intended to be. Janis never showed up to lay down her vocal
track for the song on that fateful day, October 4, 1970.

John Cooke, her road manager, went over to the Landmark Motor
Hotel to get her. Upon entering her room, he found her dead on the floor.
Her death was officially listed as resulting from a heroin overdose. Janis
Joplin was just twenty-seven years old.

Her second and final solo album, *Pearl*, was posthumously released
on January 11, 1971. It hit #1 on *Billboard* and would go on to be certified
quadruple platinum; her all-time bestseller. Because of her untimely if not
altogether surprising death, the final track, "Get It While You Can," took
on a whole other level of meaning.

In the decades since her passing, Janis has been honored in books and films, plays and songs; she was inducted into the Rock and Roll Hall of Fame, by Melissa Etheridge, in 1995; earned a Lifetime Achievement award at the 2005 Grammys; was given a star on the Hollywood Walk of Fame in 2013; and got her own US Postal Service stamp in 2014. Her soul and spirit have flown into the mystic, and there she will remain. Forever young, forever a legend, a girl who sang the blues.

21

Sly and the Family Stone

Taking Us Higher

We went on, and you could feel the weight of it. It was heavy. This was the second day, the middle. People were sleeping. It was the middle of the night. It had just rained. Just the experience of getting there for the audience was a major no-one-had-planned thing. They had already been there for twenty-four, maybe thirty-six hours, hearing music, having to find food; standing in line to go to the bathroom. They were spent. It was nighttime. You had been waiting to do your thing for hours now. They were in their sleeping bags, tired, burnt out, hungry, who knows what, asleep. And you went on the stage to make these people get up and going. You could feel it. We started out and did the best we could. You could feel it drag and then, all of a sudden, the third song, I think, you started seeing heads bop up, people starting responding a little bit. Sly could feel it. He had it down by this time. He was great at working an audience in any situation, any diverse situation. He started talking to them. You could feel everybody start to listen to the music, wake up, get up, start dancing. Halfway through the show, the place was rocking. Really incredible experience.

—*Greg Errico (drummer, Sly and the Family Stone) to Joel Selvin,*
Sly and the Family Stone: An Oral History

As the Seeds Were Sown: Everyday People

Loretta, Sylvester, Frederick, Rosemary, and Vaetta Stewart were born in Denton, Texas, and raised in accordance with the teachings of the Church of God in Christ (COGC). The family moved to Vallejo, California, just north of San Francisco, during the 1940s.

Sylvester earned the nickname "Sly" during grade school. He began playing keyboards by age seven, and was a multi-instrumentalist by eleven, skilled on drums, guitar, and bass. Loretta wasn't musical, but the younger children were. Sly, Freddie, Rose, and Vaetta (a.k.a. "Vet") formed a childhood group, the Stewart Four, and recorded and released a religious 78-rpm single, "On the Battlefield of the Lord" b/w "Walking in Jesus' Name," in 1952.

During high school, Sly formed the Webs, who merged with the Viscounts to form a doo-wop group called the Viscaynes. The Viscaynes were a multi-ethnic co-ed band, featuring African American Sly, Filipino Frank Arellano, two white men, and two white women. This integration, unusual at the time, formed the blueprint for Sly and the Family Stone.

Sly sought other outlets for his talents, adopting the name Danny Stewart to pursue solo efforts. He worked as a disc jockey at local soul station KSOL, and later at KDIA. He even worked for a small label, Autumn Records, as a producer.

Freddie, meanwhile, joined forces with Sly to form a duo called the Stewart Brothers. In 1965, he formed a band, Freddie and the Stone Souls, which featured drummer Gregg Errico.

During 1966, Sly formed Sly and the Stoners, billing himself for the first time as "Sly Stone." That group featured Cynthia Robinson on trumpet. During 1967, Sly's saxophonist friend Jerry Martini suggested that Freddie and the Stone Souls merge with Sly and the Stoners. They became Sly Brothers and Sisters, but soon changed their name to Sly and the Family Stone, with the Stewart siblings now all using the surname "Stone." Rosie joined the group on piano and vocals; Sly ceded guitar duties to Freddie, manning the keyboards and harmonica instead.

Vet was with a high-school gospel trio, the Heavenly Tones, but she wanted in on the family band, so Sly deputized her and her bandmates, Mary McCreary and Elva Mouton, as Little Sister, who served as the band's backup singers. The final piece of the puzzle fell into place when Sly hired bass player and vocalist Larry Graham to co-anchor a power-house rhythm section with Gregg Errico.

A regular gig at Winchester Cathedral in Redwood City brought the group to the attention of CBS Records, which signed them to its Epic label. They honed their chops during a grueling, six-day-a-week residency at Las Vegas's Pussycat a Go-Go. There would be no resting on the seventh day for Sly and the Family Stone. They spent their Mondays "off" in the recording studio, laying down tracks for their debut album.

That album, *A Whole New Thing*, dropped in October 1967 to mixed reviews and tepid sales, but the band remained undaunted. CBS honcho Clive Davis encouraged the band to tailor their music to appeal to the masses. The group's sophomore effort, *Dance to the Music*, released just six months later on April 27, 1968, was better received. The single "Dance to the Music" cracked the *Billboard* Top 10 at #8. The album hit #11 on the R&B charts, but struggled on the Pop chart to #142. Either way, it was progress. *Any* crossover appeal during that racially charged era was a

During October 1967, Sly and the Family Stone released their debut, *A Whole New Thing*. They most certainly were.

positive sign. Clive Davis knew what he was talking about. The band members grumbled a bit at his commercial approach, but they heeded his advice.

Epic may have rushed the third studio release a bit. *Life* was another album heralded by the release of its title track as a single. Hitting the shelves in September of '68, just five months after *Dance to the Music*, the album had the dubious distinction of being warmly received by music critics but failing to chart.

The *fourth* time would prove to be the charm. Just two months after *Life* seemed in need of life support, the group rebounded with a hit single. "Everyday People," released in November 1968, was an anthem of inclusion, racial harmony, and diversity. The message resonated; so much so that the song double-teamed the *Billboard* Hot 100 and Soul charts at #1 for a solid month from February 15 to March 14, 1969.

"Everyday People" was merely the opening salvo from *Stand!* When the album dropped on May 3, it hit #13 on the Pop chart and #3 on the R&B chart. To date, the platinum-certified album has moved more than three million copies, and is considered to be one of the greatest albums of all time.

In the Garden: A Funky Wakeup Call

Sly and the Family Stone took to the stage around 3:30 a.m. on Sunday morning, by which time it had become clear that the festival was pulling an "all-nighter." After waiting backstage for what must have seemed an interminable length of time, the musicians not only rose to the occasion, they got the exhausted crowd all revved up and delivered what may just have been *the* definitive performance of the festival.

Like a vision from some outer-space version of the Rose Bowl Parade, on strode Sly (keyboards, harmonica), Freddie (guitar), Rosie (piano), Jerry (saxophone), Cynthia (trumpet), Larry (bass), and Gregg (drums). Little Sister had not come along for this trip, so the Stone siblings supplied all of the vocals, with ad-libs by Cynthia. Leading the parade was Sly, wearing long, white, fringed sleeves with purple accents, his omnipresent choker chain, and a *huge* pair of purple-framed sunglasses that prefigured '70s-era Elton John. The keys on his keyboard were reversed—white for black and black for white—in a visual metaphor of integration.

Freddie wore bright red pants and a vest over a pink shirt. Larry, in a blue silk shirt, wore a large feathered hat straight out of the wardrobe for a *Three Musketeers* movie. Cynthia wore iridescent green from head to toe. Rosie was a vision in her shimmering silver dress and blonde wig. Jerry was clad in modest black, with flower-pattern patches. Gregg, hidden behind the drums, was attired more for comfort than style. But the success of the set that morning went beyond the visual feast and virtuoso musicianship, and entered the realm of the spiritual. From start to finish, this magnificent seven were in perpetual motion, dancing, jumping, clapping, and smiling. When Rosie wasn't tickling the ivories, she wielded a tambourine. Jerry slung a skinless tambourine over his right arm and played it whenever his sax fell silent.

The set began with a spacy keyboard intro, some pulses from the rhythm section, and then "Hey! Hey! Hey!" with a volley from the snare, the group launched into its high-energy opener, "M'Lady." The Stone's signature vocal gymnastics—"Bu-bup-bup-boom, bu-bup-bup-boom, chicka-chacka-boom"—heralded the "beat-box" stylings of the hip-hop world by more than a decade, and the audience was enthralled.

Sly groused a bit about the continuing sound problems, however. "See what, uh, the problem here is that, uh, we've got some equipment . . . wait a minute, man . . . we've got some equipment that is not working properly," he said. "So what we can do is try to hurry up and play to avoid hanging you up, or we can try to wait until the shit works right so that we can play it for you the way we would like to."

The group forged ahead with the deliciously funky "Sing a Simple Song," as more people stirred from their sleeping bags to see what all the fuss was about. By the third song, "You Can Make It if You Try," the crowd was coming alive to the soulfully psychedelic sounds emanating from the P.A.

Now that the band had gotten the audience's attention, it was time to kick this show into high gear—to hit 'em between the eyes with an up-tempo version of "Everyday People," which could very well have been the theme song for the festival.

With momentum building, the band skipped back in time for "Dance to the Music," featuring Cynthia Robinson's command, "Get on up! Dance to the funky music!" The song served as a handy framework to introduce the band members to the audience without breaking stride.

The group then slid seamlessly into "Music Lover/Higher." Sly started rapping to the crowd: "What I'd like you to do is say 'Higher' and throw the peace sign up; it'll do you no harm." Every time Sly sang, "I want to take you higher," the crowd responded, "High-er!" This enthusiastic call-and-response led straight into a full-blown version of "I Want to Take You Higher." The audience was electrified and calling for more.

The encore, "Love City," hit a solid groove, and set "Reverend Sly" up for another audience rap, delivered in the familiar cadences of the preacher. "We're gonna try to spell a four-letter word. We're gonna try to spell a four-letter word. And the word is *love*. It won't do you no harm. We're gonna try to spell love just like this." And when he yelled, "Ell!!" the audience fired back with "ELLL!!" "Say 'Oh!" ("*Oh!!*") "Veee!!" ("*Vee!!!*") "Eee!!" ("*Eeee!!!*")

Released just three months before the Woodstock Festival, *Stand* includes many of the songs the band performed during the wee hours of that fabled Sunday morning.

The band piloted the song on in for a funky landing, with Sly reprising one more round of "I want to take you higher!" When Chip reappeared, the audience begged, "One more! One more!" The second and final encore was the title track from the band's latest album, "Stand!"

The set weighed in at a lean and mean fifty minutes, the unheard exclamation point in the song title "Stand!" a tacit acknowledgment of what many consider to have been the finest moment of the festival. Who could muster the courage to follow such an act? *Who* indeed.

The Harvest Reaped: Old Unreliable

Sly and the Family Stone were at the height of their creative and performance powers. They wasted no time in releasing their next single, "Hot Fun in the Summertime," and watched it climb the charts to #2 by October.

Upon the release of *Woodstock*, the film, the band attempted to capitalize by reissuing previously released singles, only to discover that a rising profile came at a price. The band members found themselves indulging in cocaine and angel dust, fighting among themselves, and fending off political pressure from the likes of the Black Panther Party, which saw Sly, writer of "Don't Call Me Nigger, Whitey," as a potential ally in the Black Power movement.

Epic pressured the band for more commercial material, but amid the competing distractions, production slowed to a trickle as the formerly ambitious septet spiraled downward into drug abuse and infighting. As 1969 drew to a close, the band released the peculiarly titled "Thank You (Falettinme Be Mice Elf Agin)" b/w "Everybody Is a Star." The fact that the B-side made it to the top of both the Soul and Hot 100 charts distracted from the fact that these songs were intended for a full album that never materialized.

Epic bridged the album gap by releasing *Greatest Hits* in November 1970. But the band was in turmoil. Sly had become a paranoid, drug-addicted Panthers associate—a control freak who hired bodyguards, missed concerts, and became isolated from the others. The band could no longer rely on its leader, and that rift led to the departure of Gregg Errico.

After a lengthy dry spell, the band, inspired by Marvin Gaye's *What's Going On* album, responded with *There's a Riot Goin' On*. The album's title was influenced by Leiber and Stoller's tune "Riot in Cell Block #9," but the meaning went deeper than that. Though the packaging lists a title track, the time counter reads "0:00." The only riot going on was inside the band.

The single, "Family Affair," preceded the November 20 album drop by two weeks, and quickly found its way to #1 on the Pop chart. The album debuted at #1, eventually went platinum, and attained critical acclaim, but fans and critics were slow to come around.

That fun, optimistic band of the late '60s was gone. The 1970s incarnation of Sly and the Family Stone was more cynical and pessimistic. Behind the scenes, Sly had essentially taken over the recording process, playing many of the instrumental parts himself, using a drum machine, obsessively overdubbing, bringing in guest stars, and relegating the others to "backup band" status.

The next domino to fall was Larry Graham, who had been feuding with Sly and Freddie for some time. He struck out on his own and formed a band, Graham Central Station. With its killer rhythm section now a thing of the past, Sly's band bore little resemblance to the original seven.

The next two years saw the release of *Fresh* in 1973 and *Small Talk* in 1974. Both of these albums found Sly doubling down on the patterns of behavior he began on *There's a Riot Goin' On*. For all intents and purposes he had become a solo artist with a reluctant and ever-changing band. The hit parade slowed as singles charted lower (if at all), album sales dropped, and reviews grew more mixed. The patterns of drug abuse and absenteeism continued, which had a negative impact on performances.

The band's reputation as a solid live act was shot. Fans, perhaps taking their cue from the band, stopped showing up. Things came to a head following a show at Radio City Music Hall in January 1975. The audience was largely MIA, with the hall filled to only an *eighth* of capacity. The anemic ticket sales weren't enough to make the nut, so the embarrassed group had to borrow money to get back to the West Coast. And that was all she wrote.

Rosie changed her stage name to Rose Banks and embarked on a solo career. Freddie reconciled with Larry and joined Graham Central Station. Vet, too, was out of a job, as Little Sister disbanded. Sly came back in 1975 with *High on You*, followed by *Heard You Missed Me, Well I'm Back* in 1976. The latter of the two is listed as a Sly and the Family Stone album, but for all intents and purposes it is a Sly solo album, and the title is merely wishful thinking. Epic agreed, and dropped the "group" from the label soon thereafter.

Sly returned in 1979 on Warner Bros with yet another wishful-thinking title, *Back on the Right Track*. He wasn't. With his career on life support, Sly latched onto George Clinton and Parliament/Funkadelic, and continued to perform for the next two years. With Clinton's help, Sly began a new album, *Ain't but the One Way*, but bailed out midway through, leaving a producer to complete the project in his absence. He appeared sporadically after that, but the drugs, rehabs, arrests, and other erratic behaviors continued. By 1987, he had become like the Howard Hughes of funk, isolated from public view.

On the day of Sly and the Family Stone's induction into the Rock and Roll Hall of Fame, Sly shocked everyone by showing up unannounced. He took to the stage, gave his thanks, and then disappeared into the night.

Nearly twenty years passed. Then, during the 2006 Grammy Awards, Sly *briefly* took to the stage during an "All-Star Sly and the Family Stone Tribute" and quasi-reunion. He lasted all of three minutes and then was gone again. Such mysterious appearances continued in the years that followed. Sly would appear as a guest with tribute bands, or with George Clinton—if he appeared at *all*, that is. He would perform briefly, and then find some excuse to leave mid-performance.

On August 16, 2011, forty-two years after the legendary Woodstock set, and twenty-nine years since his last album, Sly released *I'm Back! Family and Friends*, which features two originals and a dozen revamped classic with a parade of guest musicians. The album was released to mixed reviews and tepid sales. Though he has continued to appear sporadically in the years since, there is no evidence of new material in the making. As for any chance of a full-fledged Sly and the Family Stone Reunion, that was lost forever when Cynthia Robinson passed away from cancer on November 23, 2015.

22

The Who

America Gone Mad

Ah, the sun coming up to "See Me, Feel Me," was the top. I mean . . .
that was an amazing experience. As soon as the words "See me" came
out of my mouth from the end of *Tommy*, this huge, red, August sun
popped its head out of the horizon, over the crowd. And, that light
show you can't beat. Ah—the smoke, the, ah . . . just the whole event
was something very, very special. And the other thing I remember
most was that I dreamt the whole thing three weeks before it happened. And I thought I was in Vietnam, 'cause I . . . I had this dream
about helicopters and towers and fires and smoke. When I got to
Woodstock, it was Woodstock. That was extraordinary—and that
is true.

—*Roger Daltrey to Pete Fornatale, 1994*

As the Seeds Were Sown: They Are, They Are, They Are the Mods

In February 1964, a band called the Detours—featuring Doug Sandom
on drums, John Entwistle on bass, Roger Daltrey on vocals, and Pete
Townshend on guitar—discovered that there was already another band
using that name, so became the Who, at the suggestion of a friend. The
classic lineup was completed when Keith Moon of the Beachcombers
replaced Sandom on the drum kit. Publicist/manager Peter Meaden
talked the group into renaming itself the High Numbers because, in
Meaden's view, the name had more of a "mod" feel to it. During Meaden's

tenure, the band released its first single, "I Am the Face" backed with "Zoot Suit," but it tanked. Chris Stamp and Kit Lambert took over management of the band, which went back to being the Who.

The Who released its first *official* single, "I Can't Explain," on January 15, 1965, and it hit #8 in England. On January 26, the Who broke into television on the BBC's *Ready Steady Go!*. In September, the band went on its first European tour. But the highlight of 1965 proved to be the Who's third single, "My Generation," released November 29, just ahead of the December release of the group's debut album, *My Generation*, in the UK.

America was beckoning, and in January 1966 the Who appeared on the TV variety program *Shindig!*. The parade of singles continued, while in December, the group's sophomore album, *A Quick One*, was released in the UK. Controversy over the suggestive title led to it being renamed *Happy Jack* for release in "the land of the free." The centerpiece of the

When it hit the shelves on December 3, 1965, *My Generation* took rock 'n' roll to a whole new level. The title track was a war cry for disaffected youth.

album was "A Quick One While He's Away," a nearly ten-minute mini-opera, and a harbinger of Townshend's best work.

Spring 1967 found the Who on its first American tour, opening forty dates for Herman's Hermits. June 18 provided a warm-up for Woodstock, as the Who appeared among an all-star lineup at the three-day Monterey Pop Festival. On September 20, Moon nearly brought down the house on the set of *The Smothers Brothers Comedy Hour* when he used *ten* times his usual amount of explosives to blow up his bass drum during the grand finale. Townshend swears the incident left him deaf in one ear.

The Who had arrived with a literal bang, and America was beginning to take notice. The group rounded out the year on December 15 with the release of *The Who Sell Out*, a concept album that satirized the advertising industry; it was the band's third full-length release and demonstrated that Townshend and his bandmates weren't afraid to experiment.

The Who began 1968 on a disastrous tour of Australia and New Zealand with the Small Faces, during which the group's shows were plagued by poor sound quality and a series of scathing reviews. (The band would not return to Australia until 2004, or New Zealand until 2009.) February proved much more productive, as the band headlined its first US tour. That summer, Pete Townshend became intrigued by the teachings of Meher Baba, an Indian Perfect Spiritual Master. Thereafter, Baba's teachings profoundly influenced his life and writing.

The Who's hard-won reputation as an incendiary, must-see live act in America was its salvation. During the 1968 summer tour, Pete made his first references to a deaf, dumb, and blind boy who would be the protagonist of a future work, *Tommy*. On August 2, during a gig at New York's Singer Bowl, the Who shared the stage with the Doors. On December 11, the Who appeared at—and, some say, stole the show at—*The Rolling Stones' Rock and Roll Circus*, but footage of the intended-for-broadcast show would not be released to the public until 1996.

The Who kicked off 1969 at IBC Studios in London, spending January and February recording *Tommy*, which was released on May 23 and made "rock opera" a part of the musical lexicon. The corresponding US tour in May and June made the band members millionaires. They spent July and the beginning of August touring England, before interrupting that leg to return to the US for a pair of shows. They played at the Tanglewood Music

Shed in Lenox, Massachusetts on August 12, and then had a few days to kill before their appearance at Woodstock.

In the Garden: And Then It Dawned on Them

When they took the stage at 5:00 a.m. on Sunday morning, August 17, the members of the Who were one tired and grumpy bunch. Their festival set was fairly representative of the shows they had been performing during the *Tommy* tour, if a bit shorter: they would start out with some older songs, segue into *Tommy* and play it most of the way through, and then round off the show with some more oldies. They tightened things up a bit for Woodstock by eliminating several *Tommy* tracks.

The group opened with "Heaven and Hell," followed by "I Can't Explain." Then it was *Tommy* time, skipping the "Overture" and launching straight into "It's a Boy," "1921," "Amazing Journey," and "Sparks," followed by Townshend's arrangement of Sonny Boy Williamson's "Eyesight to the Blind" (a.k.a. "The Hawker") and "Christmas." The group skipped "Cousin Kevin," and played fast and loose with the album track order by going into "Tommy Can You Hear Me?" Next they went into "Acid Queen," skipped the lengthy "Underture," and went into "Pinball Wizard."

It was while the band was tuning up after this song that an uninvited visitor took to the stage: Yippie activist Abbie Hoffman. Hoffman grabbed the microphone and yelled, "I think this is a pile of shit, while John Sinclair rots in prison!" (Sinclair, the poet/activist manager of Detroit's MC5, was serving ten years on marijuana charges.) Pete was *not* happy. He dispatched Hoffman from the stage with the butt of a guitar to the back of his head.

Released just three months before the Who's pre-dawn appearance at the Woodstock festival, *Tommy* introduced the term "rock opera" into the lexicon, and became a cultural phenomenon that continues to evolve to this day.

The set resumed with "Do You Think It's Alright," after which a surly

Townshend told the crowd, "The next fuckin' person that walks across this stage is gonna get fuckin' killed!" When the audience responded with enthusiastic cheers, he added, "You can laugh, I mean it!"

The group forged ahead with "Fiddle About," "There's a Doctor," "Go to the Mirror," "Smash the Mirror," "I'm Free," and "Tommy's Holiday Camp" (skipping over "Sensation," "Miracle Cure," "Sally Simpson," and "Welcome"). The emotional climax of the rock opera was the triple threat of "We're Not Gonna Take It," "See Me, Feel Me," and "Listening to You." At 6:05 a.m., the first rays of the new day's sun broke the horizon and shone in Daltrey's eyes, just as he sang the words, "See me, feel me." The crowd went nuts.

The Who finished the set with a couple of classics: covers of Eddie Cochran's "Summertime Blues" and Johnny Kidd and the Pirates' "Shakin' All Over." An encore of "My Generation" segued into an instrumental snippet of "The Naked Eye" and culminated in a patently violent Townshend guitar solo.

The feisty guitarist rewarded the faithful by slamming his Gibson SG on the stage and tossing it over the fence into the crowd (whereupon it was quickly retrieved by a dutiful roadie). Those members of the audience who had remained awake were electrified by the band's performance. Chip Monck sounded like he needed a nap as he said, "Ladies and gentlemen, the Who." It would be nearly two hours before the next act took the stage, but "Saturday" headliner Jefferson Airplane waited in the wings.

The Harvest Reaped: Rock and Roll Immortality

The Who returned to England after that sunrise set and resumed the *Tommy* tour at the Music Hall in Shrewsbury on August 22. The group's next major event was the Isle of Wight Festival, where, on August 30, the boys joined the Band, Richie Havens, and Joe Cocker, among a lineup of twenty-seven artists.

The year ahead proved to be just as eventful. In May 1970, the Who released what is considered by many to be the greatest live album of all time, *Live at Leeds*. The following year got off to a shaky start, as Townshend was having difficulty composing his conceptual follow-up to

Tommy, the fabled *Lifehouse* project. The stress left him on the verge of a nervous breakdown. The band aborted the ambitious project but reimagined some of the material as a regular, single-record release. In July, the band released that inadvertent masterpiece, *Who's Next*, to rave reviews.

In 1973, the Who recorded its second full-fledged rock opera, *Quadrophenia*, at its home studio in London. In October, the band struggled with numerous technical problems while attempting to present *Quadrophenia* on a ten-date UK tour. Townshend opted to use backing tapes instead of a live keyboard player, and consequently there were glitches that triggered fights. Daltrey knocked Townshend out cold during rehearsal one day. Townshend, in turn, gave the soundman a public dressing down at the Newcastle gig, before knocking his amps over in a tantrum. Critics really let the band have it for that one.

Quadrophenia was released in November, and a US tour kicked off on the 20th at the Cow Palace. Keith Moon collapsed onstage from an overdose of pills, which led to one of the more famous incidents in Who history. Pete Townshend asked the audience, "Can anyone play the drums? I mean somebody *good*." A brave nineteen-year-old fan, Scott Halpin, joined the band onstage to complete the final three songs. The rest of the tour continued with more bad behavior, boozing, substance abuse, hotel-room trashings, and arrests. After a four-night stand at Madison Square Garden in 1974, Townshend pulled the plug, suspending touring for the next sixteen months. The Who's September studio release, *Odds and Sods*, a collection of previously unreleased material, was a perfect metaphor for the disjointed state of the band.

The film version of *Tommy* was released amid much fanfare in March 1975, and featured Roger Daltrey in the title role, surrounded by an all-star cast of actors and fellow rock stars. The buzz surrounding the film masked the true state of the band, as evidenced by its gloomy yet brilliant October 18 studio release, *The Who by Numbers*.

The band went out on tour in support of the album during that winter and spring, but problems with Moon continued. During a memorable London performance at Charlton Football Ground, the volume was clocked at 120 decibels 50 meters from the stage, earning the Who a nod in the *Guinness Book of World Records* as "The World's Loudest Band."

The Who's show at Toronto's Maple Leaf Gardens on October 21, 1976, would be the last time Keith Moon performed before a paying audience. On May 25, 1978, he performed his last show *ever*, before an invited audience at Shepperton Studios, an event intended to be a part of the Who's career-spanning documentary, *The Kids Are Alright*.

August 17, 1978, saw the release of the Who's final studio album with Moon, *Who Are You*. On September 8, Moon died of an accidental overdose of the prescription medication Heminevrin, used to treat acute alcohol withdrawal. The remaining members of the band vowed to soldier on without him. They kicked off 1979 by introducing Kenny Jones, formerly of the Faces, as Moon's replacement . . . not that Moon was necessarily replaceable. On June 24, the group released the highly acclaimed career retrospective *The Kids Are Alright*, a film and soundtrack album. This was followed by the August 16 release of the film version of *Quadrophenia*. The year ended in tragedy, however, as eleven fans were trampled to death at a concert in Cincinnati on December 3.

The Who's first studio release without Moon, *Face Dances*, hit the shelves in March 1980, to tepid reviews. The group came to a crossroads in 1982, playing its last UK dates for the next seven years. In September, the band released *It's Hard*, its last studio album until 2005. The band went on a "Farewell Tour," highlighted by two shows at Shea Stadium, featuring the Clash as an opening act.

From 1983 through 1988, the Who regrouped only on two special occasions: the Live Aid Concert for African Famine Relief at Wembley Stadium on July 13, 1985, and the BPI Lifetime Achievement Awards at London's Royal Albert Hall on February 8, 1988, which would mark Kenny Jones's final appearance with the band. It was a performance below the standards of the Who's heyday. The group vowed then and there to never again perform live without proper rehearsal.

With that in mind, the group celebrated its twenty-fifth anniversary in 1989 by reuniting for a forty-three-date tour of the US, augmented by a cast of supporting musicians and backup singers—fifteen people in all. Reviews were mixed. The Who was inducted into the Rock and Roll Hall of Fame in 1990, kicking off its second quarter-century in fine style. Bono of U2 fame did the honors at the podium. The band then marked its thirtieth anniversary with the release of a boxed set, *Thirty Years of Maximum R&B*.

In 1996, the Who revisited *Quadrophenia* live for the Prince's Trust charitable foundation at London's Hyde Park, and then took the show on the road in the US—the group's first tour since 1989. The band toured the US again in 2000, adding Ringo Starr's son Zak Starkey on drums and Pete's brother Simon on rhythm guitar. On November 27 of that year, the group played a benefit at the Royal Albert Hall for Teenage Cancer Trust, with special guests Eddie Vedder, Paul Weller, Bryan Adams, Kelly Jones, Nigel Kennedy, and Noel Gallagher.

In the wake of the terror attacks of September 11, 2001, the Who returned to Madison Square Garden for the benefit Concert for New York on October 20, roaring back to life with fury and energy. John Entwistle passed away from a heart attack at the Hard Rock Hotel in Las Vegas on June 27, 2002, yet the show—and the band, somehow—went on. Pino Palladino took over on bass for the opener of the US leg of the tour at the Hollywood Bowl on July 1.

The Who toured Japan for the first time in 2004, returned to Australia for the first time since '68, and played the newly revamped Isle of Wight festival. July 2005 found the band playing Live 8 and being inducted into the UK Music Hall of Fame. The following year, the Who received the Lifetime Achievement Award at the Vodafone Music Awards. *Endless Wire*, their first studio album in twenty-three years, was released on October 30, 2006, and was very well received.

To support the album, the Who embarked on its most ambitious world tour in decades: 113 shows beginning on June 7, 2006, and wrapping up on December 1, 2007, concentrating on venues and festivals in the US, Canada, UK, and Europe. Along the way, a film, *Amazing Journey: The Story of the Who*, was released in November 2007, introducing the band to yet another generation.

Riding that momentum, the band toured the world *again* in 2008–2009, this time for a thirty-three-date "greatest hits" tour, hitting Japan, Australia, and New Zealand, before returning to the United States. A noteworthy show on that tour was the *VH1 Rock Honors: The Who* event on July 12 at the Pauley Pavilion in Los Angeles. This was a tribute concert featuring performances from such Who disciples as the Foo Fighters,

Pearl Jam, Flaming Lips, and Incubus, highlighted by an eight-song set by the honorees themselves. The honors and accolades kept piling up, as the Who performed the coveted Super Bowl XLIV Halftime Show on February 7, 2010, in Miami.

During 2012–2013, the Who performed a special show at the closing ceremonies of the 2012 Summer Olympics in London before embarking on the fifty-two-date Quadrophenia and More tour of Europe and North America. And when *Rolling Stone* released its "500 Greatest Albums" issue on May 31, 2012, seven of the discs belonged to the Who: *Who's Next* (#28), *Tommy* (#96), *The Who Sell Out* (#113), *Live at Leeds* (#170), *My Generation* (#236), *Quadrophenia* (#266), and *A Quick One (Happy Jack)* (#383).

The Who celebrated its golden anniversary with another tour, The Who Hits 50!, a seventy-date journey that took the group from Abu Dhabi, on November 23, 2014, to Las Vegas, on May 29, 2016. Two of the scheduled shows were canceled so that the band could appear at the 2015 Glastonbury Festival. The tour, which Daltrey referred to as "the long goodbye," was *rumored* to be the band's last. Yet, as we went to press, the Who was booked for live appearances through October 2019. The group may be missing its iconic rhythm section of Keith Moon and John Entwistle, but the Who remains a viable touring entity.

23

Jefferson Airplane

A New Dawn, Believe Me

The story of Woodstock. The first day we are trying to get to the stage which was a hard experience at that point. We rented a station wagon, we all piled in the station wagon, we went down a little quarter of the road—I believe it's a little horse track or something—to get into the middle of the field, and there were cars parked to both sides. The path opened for our station wagon, it was exactly one inch less than our station wagon which we—we mashed the accelerator . . . we went "yahoo" and we went down about, I don't know, a good four hundred cars one inch less than the width of our car and we got to the stage, more or less, then we were trapped there for three days. Yes, and I will never forget going on at sunrise, too. We were in great shape, we looked really fine—we had been up about I don't know how many days—sun streaking into your eyeballs—Paul was trying to tune his twelve string guitar. It was really glorious.

—Jack Casady, Pete Fornatale Radio Archives, 2009

As the Seeds Were Sown: The San Francisco Sound

Marty Balin, born Martyn Jerel Buchwald, had adopted his stage name by age twenty, and became a member of a folk-music quartet called the Town Criers. But he had a vision for something more. With the help of financial backers, he purchased an old pizza parlor on Fillmore Street and converted it into the Matrix Club. His goal was to put together a house band, so he put out feelers in the Haight-Ashbury community. He joined forces with fellow folkie Paul Kantner.

Marty and Paul's first "hire" was female vocalist Signe Toly, a jazz- and folk-inspired twenty-three-year-old from Seattle. Kantner's blues guitarist buddy Jorma Kaukonen soon entered the fold, though he had some reservations about the responsibilities that came with being a member of a band. Up to this point, he had enjoyed the freedom of being a solo artist, playing with friends on and off when the moment was right.

In keeping with the time-honored blues tradition, Jorma's friend Steve Talbot had nicknamed him "Blind Thomas Jefferson Airplane." When the band was looking for a name, Jorma told the others the story. By August, they'd acquired Jerry Peloquin on drums and Bob Harvey on bass. With a name and a rhythm section, this was now a fully functioning band, and thus was the Jefferson Airplane born.

Growing pains ensued. The band launched its live career at Marty's Matrix club on August 13, 1965. Jefferson Airplane was a band of blues and folk enthusiasts influenced by the British Invasion that came up with something unique: the "San Francisco Sound." But Peloquin was a straight-laced sort, and he couldn't take being around people who were so into drugs. He was the first to bail, replaced, temporarily, by Skip Spence. This was puzzling, since Skip wasn't a drummer. A few weeks later, the band decided that Harvey, the *other* half of the rhythm section, was no great shakes, either. Jorma took this opportunity to recruit his bass-playing buddy from back home in Washington, D.C., Jack Casady.

With Jack on board, the Airplane began gigging throughout the Bay Area, crossing paths with promoter Bill Graham, and Grace Slick, lead singer of the Great Society. Positive reviews and advocacy from the *San Francisco Chronicle*'s Ralph J. Gleason helped open doors for the band. RCA Victor Records signed the band to a recording contract. Graham had them open the Fillmore Auditorium, while crosstown rival Chet Helms booked them regularly for the Avalon Ballroom.

Guitarist-turned-drummer Skip Spence stuck around long enough to record the band's aptly named debut, *Jefferson Airplane Takes Off.* The album was very Marty-centric, with Balin acting as principal lead singer and songwriter. The group released a single, "It's No Secret" b/w "Runnin' 'Round This World," a tune Marty co-wrote with Paul. The album garnered mostly positive reviews, but the growing pains . . . and the *birthing* pains . . . continued.

Skip quit the band after completing his studio work, paving the way for classic-era drummer Spencer Dryden. Signe Toly married Merry Prankster Jerry Anderson, became Signe Toly Anderson, and gave birth to a daughter. She wanted out of the band before the debut album even hit the shelves. Bill Graham convinced Signe to stick it out until October. She agreed, and, true to her word, played her final show with the band on October 15.

Signe's replacement, Grace Slick—lured by Casady's virtuosity and Graham's persuasiveness—played her first gig with the band the very next night, October 16. She brought with her experience, swagger, vocal chops, good looks, and two *really* great songs.

No wonder bass master Jack Casady looks tired. The live *Bless Its Pointed Little Head* was a bi-coastal affair, recorded at the Fillmore East *and* Fillmore West.

The classic lineup was now in place, but the group's signature sound remained a work in progress. Before the year was out, the band was featured prominently in the December 1966 issue of *Newsweek*. As 1967 dawned, Bill Graham became the group's manager, staged the Human Be-In at Golden Gate Park, and herded the musicians back into the studio. Grace Slick immediately made her presence felt, contributing "Somebody to Love"—penned for the Great Society as "Someone to Love" by her brother-in-law, Darby Slick—and her own *Alice in Wonderland*–meets-LSD anthem, "White Rabbit."

Both songs were released as A-side singles. "Somebody to Love" b/w Jorma and Marty's "She Has Funny Cars" hit #5 on the *Billboard* Hot 100, while "White Rabbit" b/w "Plastic Fantastic Lover" hit #8. Jorma, meanwhile, announced *his* presence and considerable guitar chops with "Embryonic Journey." According to Jorma, the group's good friend Jerry Garcia served as the album's *de facto* producer, song arranger, and spirit guide. Garcia's offhand remark about the music being "as surrealistic as a pillow" provided the title.

Surrealistic Pillow and the hit singles heralded the Summer of Love and catapulted the Jefferson Airplane to the head of the pack on the Haight-Ashbury scene. Suddenly, the band was doing *The Ed Sullivan Show*, *The Tonight Show Starring Johnny Carson*, and *The Smother's Brothers Comedy Hour*. With its fame spreading beyond the borders of Haight-Ashbury, Jefferson Airplane earned a headlining spot at the Monterey International Pop Festival. Then it was back to the studio for round three.

The result of the mid-1967 sessions was the November release of *After Bathing at Baxter's*. This unusual title was band slang for the aftermath of an LSD trip. The opening track, "The Ballad of You and Me and Pooneil," was the lone single and cracked the *Billboard* Top 50 at #42.

The group was evolving into more of a psychedelic jam band by this point, and Marty wasn't the only one being marginalized by the meteoric success. Grace chafed under Graham's management and demanded his ouster, which led to him being replaced by Bill Thompson, who facilitated the band members' "communal living" years when he set them up at 2400 Fulton Street.

The Jefferson Airplane became the first of the local bands to venture overseas, embarking on an eventful European tour with the Doors late in the summer of '68. Upon returning, the group prepared for another album release. *Crown of Creation*, released in September, took psychedelia to the next level. It easily eclipsed *After Bathing at Baxter's*, hitting #6 on the charts and earning an RIAA gold certification. The album got some modest lead-in sales from the release of the single, "Greasy Heart," *five* months earlier, even though it barely cracked the *Billboard* Hot 100. *Crown of Creation* also features Slick's wistful coming-of-age number, "Lather," penned in honor of Spencer's thirtieth birthday; and "Triad," a tune gifted to the band by the Byrd's David Crosby. The title track single only hit #64.

Given the band's reputation as a live act, the timing was right to kick off 1969 with a live album. *Bless Its Pointed Little Head* cobbled together shows from the Fillmore's East and West and served to showcase the differences between the Jefferson Airplane of the studio and the concert stage. The live sound tended to be heavier, more experimental, and jam-oriented. The nearly twelve-minute finale, "Bear Melt," is a fitting homage to LSD-maker and Grateful Dead benefactor Owsley "Bear" Stanley.

In the spring, the band was back at work on its fifth studio release, *Volunteers*, and upping the ante on its protest and antiwar sentiments. To wit, the original title was to be "Volunteers of Amerika," but RCA balked. The label also took issue with songs like "Uncle Sam's Blues" and "We Can Be Together," which features the lyrics, "Up against the wall, mother-fucker." Clearly, the band was striking some nerves.

While *Volunteers* was in production, the Jefferson Airplane was booked for the coveted Saturday-night headlining slot at the upcoming Woodstock festival. The band pre-gamed for Woodstock by throwing a free concert in Central Park. Then it was time to head up to Bethel.

In the Garden: "Morning Maniac Music"

As Jack would note, once they parked that station wagon, they weren't going *anywhere*. These San Francisco Scene veterans were no strangers to pulling all-nighters or to seeing the sunrise, but ordinarily that would have been *after* the show. In this case, they had to do a show at 8:00 a.m., *after* pulling an all-nighter. Not ideal, by any means, but they muddled through. Even Chip Monck couldn't seem to believe he was introducing another act as he said, "We'll continue, with the Jefferson Airplane."

Grace seized the moment. "All right friends, you have seen the heavy groups, now you will see morning maniac music. Believe me, yeah, it's a new dawn. Yeah, the regular guys . . . and Nicky Hopkins. . . . Good morning, people!"

With that, the band launched into a jammy version of "The Other Side of This Life," a track from the live album. Since former Jeff Beck Group keyboardist Nicky Hopkins had been working on the studio sessions for *Volunteers*, he parlayed the dissolution of his regular gig into a guest appearance with the Jefferson Airplane, making his presence felt on the ivories, stage left. Jorma and Jack, with an assist from Spencer's galloping drumbeat, gave "Somebody to Love" a real Hot-Tuna–esque feel, nothing at all like the album version.

Marty's "3/5 of a Mile in 10 Seconds" was next, with the band hitting a gritty (if a bit sloppy) groove that was met with appreciative applause. Paul's "Won't You Try / Saturday Afternoon," the album closer from *After Bathing at Baxter's*, added the perfect layer of psychedelia to the proceedings, with its vivid imagery of "acid, incense, and balloons." Next, the group previewed Grace and Paul's "Eskimo Blue Day" from the forthcoming *Volunteers*. Grace took the opportunity to reference the acid situation: "Sorry about those who got the green. We've got a *whole* lot of orange, and it was fine . . . it still is fine, everybody is vibrating."

The band continued with "Plastic Fantastic Lover," Marty's closing track from *Surrealistic Pillow*. Next up was "Wooden Ships," the collaborative effort between Paul, David Crosby, and Stephen Stills that had appeared on Crosby, Stills, and Nash's debut album in May, and would later appear on *Volunteers*. Grace gave credit to all of the songwriters during her intro. This deliciously spacey version clocked in at more than twenty-one minutes.

Now it was time for a side dish of tuna . . . Hot Tuna, that is. "Uncle Sam Blues," a traditional blues arranged by Jorma and Jack for the *Volunteers* sessions, would appear instead the following May on *Hot Tuna*, the pair's eponymous debut album. It provided a showcase for Jorma's signature guitar playing and vocal stylings, as well as an opportunity for Grace to hang back and bop her head in time to the music.

With former Great Society vocalist Grace Slick taking over
the microphone stand from Signe Toly Anderson, and Spencer
Dryden now manning the drums, Jefferson Airplane's new
sound was, in the words of Jerry Garcia, "as surrealistic as a
pillow." Arguably, this is the foundational document of psychedelic rock.

The band countered with a preview of "Volunteers," Paul and Marty's
closing track from the forthcoming album. Next up, "The Ballad of You
and Me and Pooneil" illustrated that Melanie wasn't the *only* Woodstock
performer obsessed with A. A. Milne's *Winnie the Pooh* series (see chapter 7). The Paul-penned "Pooneil" is a portmanteau for the titular bear
and local folksinger Fred Neil. The lyrics borrow liberally from Milne's
"Spring Morning," from his children's poetry collection *When We Were
Very Young*. The band had released the song as a single in August 1967,
but it had evolved and mutated over the next three months into the opening track from *After Bathing at Baxter's*. This set-closing festival version
featured some face-melting bass leads by Jack, virtuoso work by Jorma
and the rest, lyrical twists, and even some foreshadowing as Paul sang the
improv lyric, "From the deck of a starship." The group's efforts were met
with cheers and chants of "more" from a clearly appreciative audience.

The first encore, "Come Back Baby" was another traditional blues given the Jorma treatment, but it wouldn't be officially released until years after the festival. Next, the band took the audience through the looking glass with "White Rabbit," which featured spontaneous vocal re-arrangements by Grace. For the final encore, it was up the rabbit hole and back over to the Hundred Acre Wood for Marty and Paul's "The House at Pooneil Corner," Nicky's haunting keyboard work providing the perfect sonic backdrop for the others' psychedelic musings. In true Jefferson Airplane fashion, they were ending this performance—the longest of the weekend so far—on a freaky note.

With the audience yelling for more, John Morris introduced each of the band members by name: "Jack Casady, Spencer Dryden, Paul Kantner . . . I'm sorry, I'm getting tired . . . Marty Balin, Nicky Hopkins played piano with them, Grace Slick . . . God bless you, goodnight from the Jefferson Airplane." He forgot Jorma.

After some further announcements, Morris continued, "We're gonna break for a while, until about one o'clock, give everybody a chance to get a little bit of a catnap. There's plenty of room in the fields. The roads are fairly clear now, so if any of you decided that you've had enough music, and you're getting a little tired . . . yeah, well, there may be one or two, you can get buses out of Monticello . . . everything's cool, everything's very cool all the way around. Thank you all again, it just keeps goin', it's lovely."

The Harvest Reaped: Airplanes, Starships, and a Side of Hot Tuna

Grace and the others stayed to enjoy the festival all the way through to the end of Jimi Hendrix's set. Then they piled into cars and headed down to Manhattan for a taping of *The Dick Cavett Show*, joining Stephen Stills, David Crosby, and a fresh-faced Joni Mitchell. The Jefferson Airplane made history that day by becoming the first to ever sing the words "shit," "fuck," and "motherfucker" on national television, during "We Can Be Together." Oddly enough, the censors didn't seem to notice.

Volunteers hit the shelves in November, earning a respectable #13 on the *Billboard* Pop chart. In addition to "the regular guys and Nicky

Hopkins," old friend Jerry Garcia makes an appearance, along with a pre-CSNY David Crosby and Stephen Stills. This was the last time the original lineup would convene to create a Jefferson Airplane album.

On December 6, a day that will live long in rock-and-roll infamy, the band played at the Rolling Stones' notorious Altamont Speedway concert. During the Jefferson Airplane's set, Marty made the mistake of jumping down from the stage into the fray and mouthing off to one of the Hells Angels on security detail, who then knocked him unconscious. That was pretty much the last straw. Altamont would be the last major event the band played, and as the 1970s dawned, the members of the Jefferson Airplane felt themselves growing further apart.

As the 1970s began, Jefferson Airplane started to mutate as members of the classic lineup went their own ways. Their last hurrah as a unit was the May 1970 single "Mexico" b/w "Have You Seen the Saucers." Spencer, freaked out by his experiences at Altamont, phased himself out of the band at the behest of the others, ceding the drum stool to Joey Covington. This new incarnation of Airplane also featured fiddler Papa John Creach, who would go on to figure heavily in Hot Tuna.

Paul released a solo album, *Blows Against the Empire*, in November 1970. The band played its final shows with Marty on Thanksgiving Day at the Fillmore East. In another sign of impending demise, the group released a highly successful greatest-hits compilation, *The Worst of Jefferson Airplane*, that same month, before ending the year by beginning the sessions for a sixth studio album, *Bark*. Marty did not participate in the sessions, and would officially part ways with the band he founded in March 1971, as he went off in pursuit of a healthier lifestyle.

Grace, pregnant with Paul's child, gave birth to China Wing Kantner on January 25, 1971. The band suffered another setback on May 13 when Grace was injured in a car crash while engaged in a high-speed drag race with Jorma.

In the midst of the delayed *Bark* sessions, Hot Tuna's sophomore effort, *First Pull Up, Then Pull Down* hit the shelves in June. Despite the strikes against it, *Bark*, released in September 1971, hit #11, but apart from a handful of live performances, there was no support tour.

Grace and Paul collaborated to release an album, *Sunfighter*, in November 1971, featuring baby China on the cover. Papa John Creach got in on the act with his December debut, *Papa John Creach*. Hot Tuna's star was in the ascendant as Jorma, Jack, and Papa John began 1972 with their first *true* studio album, *Burgers* (*Hot Tuna* and *First Pull Up, Then Pull Down* had been recorded live).

Jefferson Airplane hit the studio to record its seventh album, *Long John Silver*, in the spring of 1972. The revamped lineup, with John Barbata replacing Covington on drums and Quicksilver Messenger Service's David Frieberg filling Marty's role, then hit the road for two months. Perhaps sensing the end was near, the group recorded shows for a live album, *Thirty Seconds Over Winterland*, which was held back until April 1973. In a fitting coda, Marty returned for the encore at the second Winterland show. And that was all she wrote . . . well, *almost*.

Seventeen years after those Winterland shows, the group reunited (sans Spencer) to record an eighth studio album, 1989's *Jefferson Airplane*. The years in between had been filled with Hot Tuna, Jefferson Starship, the KBC Band (Kantner Balin Casady), and solo projects too numerous to mention.

Following the 1989 reunion tour, Grace Slick announced that she was officially retiring from the music business. On Sunday, October 4 1992, Jorma, Jack, Paul, Marty, and Papa John joined Jefferson Starship's Slick Aguilar onstage in New York's Central Park for the K-Rock Be-In in a partial reunion of Jefferson Airplane/Starship.

In 1996, Jefferson Airplane was inducted into the Rock and Roll Hall of Fame, but Grace was absent for health reasons. Spencer succumbed to colon cancer in 2005. In an eerie coincidence, Paul Kantner and original female lead vocalist Signe Toly Anderson both passed away on the same day, January 28, 2016, taking with them any remaining hopes of a Jefferson Airplane reunion.

24

Joe Cocker

The Grease Band and Himself

We did a very hectic tour, and it was the last gig on the tour. It was just a very strange feeling, you know, hearing all this downwind about this, you know, because we'd played some pretty big places that year. When we got there, it was quite mind-blowing to see . . . to fly over in the helicopter such a mass of people. I mean, we knew it was no . . . I mean that was a . . . still has a big . . . you know, because people have asked me to reflect on it, and it's just that initial jolt of seeing, you know, like Zulu Dawn or something, just coming over the edge and seeing all these people.

—Joe Cocker, WFUV "Oscar Docs" panel discussion, 2006

As the Seeds Were Sown: Born of Sheffield Steel

John Robert Cocker was born on May 20, 1944, in Sheffield, England. Somewhere along the line he acquired the nickname "Joe." The youngest of his family, he had a musical role model in older brother Victor, who performed with a skiffle band. Joe began to idolize Ray Charles and other soul singers. One day in 1956, when Joe was twelve, Victor invited him up onstage to sing with the band, and he caught the performing bug.

By 1960, Joe had formed the Cavaliers, but the group only lasted for a year. He seemed destined for a blue-collar life. He dropped out of school at age fifteen to work for the East Midland Gas Board, but he kept pursuing his musical dreams. The following year, he assumed the stage name Vance Arnold to front the Avengers, a bar band that moved beyond soul to the American blues, which was all the rage among musically inclined British youth. By 1963, this led to an opening slot for an up-and-coming local band called the Rolling Stones.

Joe got his first taste of the recording artist's life during 1964, when he signed on to Decca to record a cover of the Beatles' "I'll Cry Instead" with a little help from his guitarist friends, Jimmy Page and Big Jim Sullivan. When the single failed to chart, the label dropped him, but Joe was undaunted. He returned with the Joe Cocker Blues Band. He was playing the music he loved, but the new band just didn't work out. At this point, he took a year off to regroup and figure out his next move.

In 1966, Joe joined forces with an old friend, Chris Stainton, to form a new group, the Grease Band. "Grease" in this context was intended as a compliment, as in, *that band has a lot of grease.* Early incarnations of the Grease Band featured Joe, Chris, and a revolving cast of musicians playing in the pubs of Sheffield.

Producer Denny Cordell took note of Cocker and Stainton's considerable talents, dragged them out of the Sheffield pub scene, and moved them to London. There, Cordell ushered them into the studio to record "Marjorine," a song co-written by Stainton, which was released as a single in May 1968.

In what would prove to be a life-altering moment, Joe decided to give the Beatles' catalogue another shot and entered the studio to put his own soulful stamp on "With a Little Help from My Friends." Released in October 1968, the single provided Joe with the *perfect* encore song and the perfect title for his upcoming debut album, and gained him the respect and admiration of the Beatles. His version hit #1 on the UK charts.

The success of the single earned Joe and the Grease Band an opening slot on the Who's fall tour of Europe. With the release of a debut album, *With a Little Help from My Friends*, in May, the band hit the road, stopping

Hitting the shelves just three months before the Woodstock festival, Joe Cocker's *With a Little Help from My Friends* heralded the arrival of a formidable new talent.

in California on June 20, in Seattle on the 22nd, and at festivals in Denver on the 27th, Atlanta on the Fourth of July, Atlantic City on August 3, and the Fillmore East on the 8th.

It was there, at the Fillmore, that the band heard about the Woodstock festival for the first time. Denny Cordell wasted no time pitching Artie Kornfeld to book Cocker, and Artie shared a demo tape with Michael Lang and the others. The band signed on for $1,375, which in today's dollars would be around nine grand. Arguably, this was Kornfeld's best signing of the festival, considering the way things worked out in the aftermath.

I'm a Farmer

The four-hour-and-twenty-minute break after Jefferson Airplane left the stage at 9:40 a.m. was filled with activity for those who stayed awake. Hugh Romney and the Hog Farm staged a "Mess Call," complete with a bugler, and then proceeded to introduce Woodstock Nation to the nutritional wonders of granola. And then there was a visit from the "landlord," Max Yasgur.

Yasgur tapped the microphone and asked "Is this thing on?" Then he addressed the crowd:

I'm a farmer. I don't know—I don't know how to speak to twenty people at one time, let alone a crowd like this. But I think you people have proven something to the world. Not only in the town of Bethel or Sullivan County, or New York State. You've proven something to the world. This is the largest group of people ever assembled in one place. We have had no idea that there would be this size group, and because of that, you had quite a few inconveniences as far as water and food and so forth. Your producers have done a mammoth job to see that you're taken care of. They'd enjoy a vote of thanks. But above that, the important thing that you've proven to the world is that half a million kids—and I call you kids because I have children that are older than you are—a half a million young people can get together and have three days of fun and music and have nothing but fun and music. An' I God bless you for it!

In the Garden: With a Little Help from His Friends

At 2:00 p.m., the Grease Band, featuring Chris Stainton on keyboards, Henry McCullough on guitar, Alan Spencer on bass, and Bruce Rowlands on drums, took to the stage . . . *without* Joe Cocker.

The Grease Band warmed the crowd up with instrumental versions of Traffic's "Who Knows What Tomorrow Might Bring" and "(Roamin' Thru the Gloamin' with) 40,000 Headmen." An enthusiastic if not particularly well-rested John Morris then made the introduction: "Ladies and gentleman, Mr. Joe Cocker. Let's go for Sunday!"

Joe Cocker—a stringy-haired, mutton-chop-sideburn'd wild man wearing star-spangled boots and an outrageous long-sleeved tie-dye that rivaled John Sebastian's tie-dyed denim two-piece—was about to blow the Woodstock audience away with his soulful voice and outrageous physicality. He greeted the crowd with a polite, "Yes, yes, well, good afternoon," acknowledged the gathering rain clouds pointed out to him by a fan, and then made certain to dedicate his opening number to Max Yasgur. "We're going to do this little number to start off with, the title suggested by that farming guy who came out; he seemed a nice little bloke. And it's called 'Dear Landlord,' anyway . . ."

Joe quickly worked up a sweat. The audience roared with approval, and they were in for a killer set. The uniqueness of Joe's stage presence was striking, and few in the audience had ever seen anything like him. It was as though his body was plugged directly into the P.A., and it followed wherever the music led. He played air guitar, flapped his hands, pin-wheeled his arms, stamped his feet, rose up on tiptoes while twisting his ankles to odd angles, and rocked violently to and fro, contorting his face and torso as he did so. It was almost as though the spirits of music took possession of him, and the performance clearly drained him.

The band hit a groove on "Something's Comin' On," which Joe introduced as "a balladeering song" that "just about explains the whole situation." Joe seemed keen to introduce every song in his heavy Sheffield accent as helicopters chopped away in the background, making it all but impossible for the audience to understand what he was saying. But his lack of intelligible stage banter mattered little in the face of such a visceral onslaught of sights and sounds. Such was the magnitude of Joe's stage presence.

The set continued in similar fashion with "Do I Still Figure in Your Life," a lovely ballad. Next, after a nearly incomprehensible introduction, came the soulful single "Feeling Alright." The boys in the band were earning their keep, not just with their hot playing but also with their background vocals. Stainton, Spencer, and McCulloch each had a vocal mic, and Stainton punctuated certain songs with falsetto flourishes that cut right through Joe's bluesy growls.

Joe invoked Dylan and the upcoming Isle of Wight Festival before delivering his beautiful cover of "Just Like a Woman." As he finished, he seemed to take a snarky shot at Budweiser beer when he said something that sounded remarkably like, "The only difference between Budweiser and water, let's stick to water."

The set continued with an appropriate "Let's Go Get Stoned," and "I Don't Need a Doctor," before returning to the Dylan well for a breathtaking cover of "I Shall Be Released," which "scooped" the Band's version by several hours. "Hitchcock Railway" and "Something to Say" followed suit.

With thunderheads looming, low and ominous, Joe returned to the stage for his favorite encore and set the crowd up for the kill. "We're gonna leave you with the usual thing. I'd just like to say, as I've said to many people, that this title just about puts it all into focus. Its called 'With a Little Help from Me Friends.' Remember it."

A half-century later, thanks in no small part to the impact of *Woodstock*, the 1970 film, it is clear that we have remembered. Those in attendance as Joe walked off the stage for the final time no doubt carried that song with them for the rest of the weekend. It was the last song they would hear emanating from the P.A. for several hours. With the severity of the approaching thunderstorms, the members of Woodstock Nation would need more than a little help from their friends to get by. But get by they would. Members of Country Joe and the Fish were milling about, not sure whether to start setting up their gear or run for cover.

The Harvest Reaped: De-Greased, Mad Dogs and Englishmen Hit the Road

Back home in England, Joe joined the Who, the Band, and Richie Havens at the Isle of Wight Festival, where they were *all* overshadowed by the return of Bob Dylan.

Joe's parade of singles continued with "Delta Lady" in September, followed by two more Beatles covers: "Something" in November, and "She Came in Through the Bathroom Window" in December. *Joe Cocker!* hit record store shelves in November, and Joe's popularity in the United States exploded.

By the dawn of 1970, Joe had—for lack of a better term—*dissolved* the Grease Band, intending to become a solo artist. Of course, there was still one small matter to contend with. He was already booked for another full

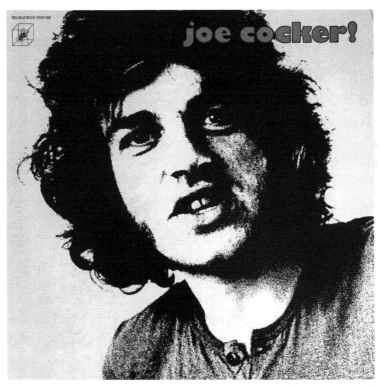

Joe's eponymous, post-festival sophomore effort, *Joe Cocker*, features a cover of the Lovin' Spoonful's "Darling Be Home Soon," a song the group had performed at Woodstock.

concert tour of the United States. He was reluctant to tour, but this was a matter of contractual obligation. On or about March 12, he was informed that if he was to meet his professional obligations, he would need a band, and *fast*.

The Grease Band option was off the table, but with help from Leon Russell, Joe was able to assemble an all-star band in eight days. Made up mainly of session musicians, the group embarked on March 20 for the Mad Dogs and Englishmen tour—one of the more legendary tours in rock-and-roll history. In comparison with the Grease Band, which was a more typical five-piece rock-and-roll band, the Mad Dogs and Englishmen touring band was a bloated monster, co-led in a sort of tacit power struggle by Leon Russell and Joe.

Leon played guitar, tickled the ivories of his boogie-woogie piano, and served as the tour's musical director. Chris Stainton played piano, too, along with the Hammond B-3 organ. If two drummers was good enough for the Grateful Dead, how about *five*, counting percussionists? Manning the skins and banging on various things, in no particular order, were Chuck Blackwell, Jim Keltner, Jim Gordon, Sandy Konikoff, and Bobby Torres. Anchoring that crowded rhythm section was Eric Clapton's well-respected bass player, Carl Radle; Leon Russell's long-time guitar player, Don Preston, was there to lend his axe.

No band of this size would be complete without a horn section, so part-time Rolling Stones sideman Bobby Keys played saxophone, in tandem with fellow veteran sax man Jim Horn. Jim Price rounded out this section on trumpet. Future Grammy winner Rita Coolidge was but one among a parade of backup singers, including "Brown Sugar" herself, Claudia Lennear, along with Pamela Polland, Matthew Moore, Nicole Barclay, Bobby Jones, Donna Washburn, and, last but not least, Denny Cordell . . . yes, Joe's *manager*.

This massive party caravan hit nearly fifty cities, and the tour was captured on film in anticipation of a theatrical release. Likewise, the March 27 and 28 dates at Bill Graham's Fillmore East were recorded and became the *Mad Dogs and Englishmen* live album. Released in August 1970, the album peaked at #2 on *Billboard*, #16 in the UK, and #1 in Australia. It spawned two singles: a cover of the Box Tops' "The Letter" b/w "Space Captain," released in April; and "Cry Me a River," b/w (in *some* cases, depending upon where you bought it) Leon Russell's tour version of "Give Peace a Chance," released in October.

The record company was extremely happy with the whole package. The tour, the album, and the film were all successful, and with the ascendance of Leon Russell's career, the label got even more bang for its buck. But the tour *really* took a toll on Joe's health. Not only were the performances grueling, he was also drinking and partying way too much. He needed a rest. The single "High Time We Went," released in May 1971, hit #22 on the US charts, but we would be waiting a *long* time for the corresponding album to come out.

When Joe returned for a 1972 tour, kicking things off at Madison Square Garden, it was with a more modest ensemble put together by Chris Stainton. The plan was to record the tour for a hybrid album—part live, part studio. Though smaller in scale, this tour was fraught with difficulties. There was the usual excessive drinking and substance abuse, but it was the legal issues—such as members of the entourage getting busted in a barroom brawl in Melbourne, Australia, hot on the heels of their being busted for pot in Adelaide the night *before*—that caused the most headaches. Cocker and the band were invited to leave the country, effective immediately.

These embarrassing international incidents scared Chris into early "retirement," and he became a confirmed studio rat. Denny Cordell, too, parted ways with Joe. Without his two most valued associates, Joe's drinking, drugging, and depression worsened, and production slowed to a crawl. Yes, the album, *Joe Cocker*, came out as planned in November, but the label would be mining it for singles until 1974, even re-releasing "Feeling Alright" to keep up the appearance of productivity.

Joe's 1974 "comeback" album, *I Can Stand a Little Rain*, yielded his most successful single to date, the Billy Preston–Dennis Wilson collaboration "You Are So Beautiful," which hit #5 on *Billboard*. From this point forward, almost all of his material consisted of covers of other artists' songs. His struggles with alcohol had a negative impact on his performances during this period, but in 1976 Michael Lang came back into Joe's life as his manager, and he was determined to get his career back on the right track.

Joe's next career highlight proved to be his most enduring, a duet with Jennifer Warnes on "Up Where We Belong." Released as a single in August 1982 and featured in the film soundtrack of *An Officer and a Gentleman*, it hit #1, was certified platinum, and won the "Best Original Song" award at the 1983 Golden Globes, the Grammys, *and* the BAFTAs (British Academy of Film and Television Arts). Joe and Jennifer also won the Grammy for "Best Pop Performance by a Duo or Group with Vocal." This marked the commercial pinnacle of Joe's career. Though he continued to record and tour for another thirty years, he never attained those heights again.

During the fifty-seven years since he got up to sing with his brother's band, Joe released twenty-two studio albums, sixty-eight singles, nine live albums, fourteen compilations, made thirty guest appearances on others' albums, and released no fewer than seventeen concert films and music video collections on VHS and DVD. In 2012, he released what would prove to be his final studio album, *Fire It Up*. The support tour would take Joe and the band through the United States and Europe during 2012–2013. On September 7, Joe took the stage at Lorely Open Air Theatre in Sankt Goarshausen on the shores of the Rhine for the final show of the tour. It would be the final performance of his storied career.

Soon thereafter, he was diagnosed with lung cancer, to which he succumbed on December 22, 2014. Joe Cocker was seventy years old. Now he truly *is* up where he belongs, in the pantheon of rock and roll, among the greatest blues and soul singers of all time.

25

Country Joe and the Fish

That Guy Looks Familiar

I remember very much the day it rained and when we played, because having battled traffic in and out of there in a limo the day before . . . in and out of the site, I mean . . . it was like, I don't know, it was a twenty mile drive that took two hours. The next day, because we were performing, I knew I had the right to get over there in a helicopter. And I took the helicopter over with Joe Cocker, who . . . and I remember riding . . . I mean I distinctly remember riding above the tree line and seeing how many people were really there. Because the woods were incredibly, fully populated, even before you got to the sort of bowl-shaped arena that was the festival itself . . . that people associate with the festival. I think riding over in the helicopter and riding over the tree line like the pilot let us do showed us how many . . . how very, very many people were really there that you couldn't necessarily see.

— *Barry "The Fish" Melton to Bernard M. Corbett, 2009*

As the Seeds Were Sown: When Joe Met Barry

It was somewhere in the middle of 1965 that "Country" Joe McDonald (see chapter 11) met Brighton Beach, Brooklyn, native Barry Melton. Barry, the son of a working mother and college professor father, moved with his family to the San Fernando Valley when he was a child. He felt the first stirrings of the civil rights movement as a teenager, and with the first stirrings of the war in Vietnam, he began to actively participate in protests. At seventeen, he volunteered with the Congress for Racial

Equality (CORE) to work at the infamous "Freedom Summer," a ten-week voter-registration drive in Mississippi that was plagued by over a thousand arrests, dozens of fire-bombings, more than seventy-five severe beatings, and the murders of at least seven people. It created a groundswell of support that would lead to the Voter Rights Act of 1965.

Following that remarkable experience, Barry hitchhiked around the country and finally wound up in the San Francisco Bay Area, where he fell in with like-minded activists and met Joe McDonald. He became a seventeen-year-old high-school graduate in January 1965 and enrolled immediately for courses as San Francisco State. But this early flirtation with college life proved short-lived, as Barry dropped out after only two months to pursue a career in music. He headed to Berkeley and teamed up with McDonald. Initially, they performed as a duo, but added members as they evolved through a folk and jug-band phase on a collision course with psychedelic rock and roll.

Country Joe and the Fish would feature an added dimension: leftist politics. At the same time he was pursuing music, Joe McDonald was living up to his namesake, Josef Stalin, by becoming a prolific activist and pamphleteer. He put a great deal of time and effort into his underground publication, *Et Tu Brute*, eventually ditching the Shakespearean title for the more musical *Rag Baby*.

At some point during 1965, Joe was looking to take a multimedia approach to his activist magazine, and so the idea was born to turn an issue of *Rag Baby* into a stage production. This necessitated the hiring of additional musicians to form a full band. The inspiration for the band's name (credited to *Rag Baby* co-publisher Ed Denson) came from two sources: Joe's having been named after Stalin, and a quote from Mao Zedong: "The guerilla must move amongst the people as a fish swims in the sea."

Joe and Barry welcomed the vocalist Mike Beardslee, bass player Bill Steele, and, in accordance with their jug-band phase, Carl Schrager, who played the washboard and the kazoo. The first incarnation of Country Joe and the Fish had spawned.

That initial idea for a "play" manifested itself in a self-produced EP, *Rag Baby Talking Issue #1*. This modest debut came in the form of one hundred pressed copies, which were distributed in much the same way as a political pamphlet during student events at Berkeley, and wherever *Rag Baby* was sold. The centerpiece of the four-track EP was the "I-Feel-Like-I'm-Fixin'-to-Die Rag," an anti-Vietnam protest song that quickly became a highlight of the group's live act.

But the extra musicians were only on board to create the EP. Once that was done, it was back to business as usual. Joe and Barry went back to performing as a folk duo, but they had caught the "band bug." Soon thereafter, they began expanding the lineup once more to include Barry's friends Bruce Barthol on bass and Paul Armstrong on guitar, a drummer named John Francis-Gunning, and guitarist/piano player David Bennet Cohen, all of whom had come from a jug-band/bluegrass background.

Joe and Barry found their taste in music evolving beyond the roots music and classic folk of Woody Guthrie to embrace the electric folk-rock sound pioneered by the likes of Bob Dylan. At the same time, their taste in recreational drugs evolved beyond marijuana to an emphasis on more potent psychedelics like LSD. All of these factors influenced the band's sound. Cohen expanded his own musical comfort zone and began playing an electric organ. The band caught on with the locals and quickly outgrew the Jabberwock, the small folk club where Joe and Barry had played many a night, armed only with acoustic instruments. It was there that the folk duo had evolved into a psychedelic sextet. It was home, for a time, but bigger opportunities lay ahead.

The musicians returned to the studio to self-produce an EP more representative of their new sound, the eponymous *Country Joe and the Fish*. They landed on the radars of both Chet Helms and Bill Graham, and the rival venue owners booked them regularly. Major labels came calling, and radio stations from coast to coast introduced listeners to Country Joe and the Fish.

The group landed a deal with Vanguard Records at the end of 1966 and entered the studio early the following year. The studio sessions were marked by lineup changes. Armstrong avoided the draft when he was granted "conscientious objector" status, and was thereby obligated to perform service elsewhere. Gary "Chicken" Hirsh" replaced Francis-Gunning on the drums. The result was *Electric Music for the Mind and Body*, which hit the shelves and cracked the *Billboard* 200 in spring 1967, a pioneering effort on the San Francisco psychedelic scene. One of the songs,

The May 1967 debut by Country Joe and the Fish, *Electric Music for Mind and Body*, helped cement San Francisco's reputation for American psychedelic rock.

"Grace," is an homage to a future icon of psychedelia, Jefferson Airplane's Grace Slick. "Superbird" pokes fun at a popular target of the counterculture, President Lyndon Baines Johnson. But the track that caught everyone's attention was the one that predated the album's release by a full month, "Not So Sweet Martha Lorraine." The single barely cracked the *Billboard* 100, but it remains noteworthy for being the *only* Country Joe and the Fish single ever to reach those heights.

Hot on the heels of the album release, the band played the Monterey Pop Festival, where their set went over really well. They set out for a summer tour, hitting points along the East Coast, and then headed back into the studio to lay down tracks for a follow-up album. *I-Feel-Like-I'm-Fixin'-to-Die*, released in November 1967, featured a psychedelic remix of "The Fish Cheer." The album didn't have the commercial "legs" of the debut, but live audiences were digging the act.

Arriving just seven months after the band's 1967 debut, the title track of their sophomore effort, "I-Feel-Like-I'm-Fixin'-to-Die Rag" became one of the most recognizable protest songs of the Vietnam era, and an audience favorite.

But all was not well. When the band returned to the studio to record a third album, Country Joe went AWOL. The title of that August 1968 release, *Together*, seems ironic, since the musicians were anything *but* together during the recording sessions. Joe did make it back in time to record, and in spite of the turmoil, *Together* proved to be the band's best-selling effort to date, and all of the band members earned songwriting credits. The opening track, "Rock and Soul Music," was a group effort, and became the band's standard opening number.

An infamous moment in New York City's Central Park during the 1968 Schaefer Music Festival garnered Country Joe and the Fish some notoriety. Drummer Gary "Chicken" Hirsch suggested that they change the word "fish" in "The Fish Cheer" to "fuck." The audience, predictably, *loved* the new X-rated version of "The Fish Cheer"; the promoters of the Schaefer Music Festival . . . *not* so much. Schaefer immediately dis-invited the band from any future participation in the popular summer concert series.

Compounding the impact of this "lifetime ban" was the reliably square *Ed Sullivan Show*, which got wind of the incident and canceled the band's scheduled appearance. There was nothing in those days quite like a run-in with Ed Sullivan to gain a band some serious street cred. The revamped "Fish Cheer" became a staple of the band's live performances, consequences be damned. But further changes were in the air.

Bass player Bruce Barthol bailed out after the release of *Together*. During the second week of 1969, Jefferson Airplane's bass master Jack Casady came on board to fill in and helped the band record *Live! Fillmore West 1969*, which would prove to be Country Joe and the Fish's only live album.

Afterward, it was back to the studio, where the Joe and Barry show resumed the helm and all of the songwriting duties. As for "Chicken," he flew the coop to open an art supply store in Oakland. He and multi-instrumentalist David Bennett Cohen appeared on the next studio effort as guest musicians, but they were no longer official members of the band. The album, *Here We Are Again*, was released in July and charted at #48 on the *Billboard* 200, where it would remain for nearly three months. Then it was on to Bethel, with a new lineup.

In the Garden: Back by Popular Demand

The school of "Fish" that swam into Bethel that weekend featured Joe and Barry backed by Mark Kapner on keyboards, Doug Metzner on bass, and Greg "Duke" Dewey on drums—capable musicians all.

The end of Joe Cocker's set just happened to coincide with the opening rumbles of what was shaping up to be a proper summer thunderstorm, so the Woodstock staff focused on battening down the hatches. While John Morris was addressing the crowd and preparing them for the imminent storm, Barry grabbed the microphone and encouraged the audience, "Hey, if you think really hard, maybe we can stop this rain!"

Morris liked that, and momentarily Barry was back, chanting "No RAIN! NO RAIN! NO RAIN!" The audience picked up on the chant and ran with it, but of course the rain didn't stop until it was good and ready, further delaying the festival's schedule . . . such as it was.

From the moment Joe Cocker strode from the stage at 3:25 p.m., it would be three hours and five minutes before another chord was struck. During the rainstorm, a lone girl's voice could be heard yelling, "Hey, Joe Cocker, isn't the rain beautiful?"

No one knew at the time that Barry's impromptu "no rain" cry would become the stuff of legend, just as no one knew they'd be sitting through rain and thunderstorms until 6:30 in the evening with nobody onstage.

But Country Joe and the Fish turned in a performance worth waiting for, delivering fourteen songs in a set that lasted nearly an hour and a half. The opener, "Rock and Soul Music," is immortalized in the film, which prominently features a grinning Barry holding up a joint to the camera. They continued with "(Thing Called) Love," and their lone charting single, "Not So Sweet Martha Lorraine." They followed up with "Sing Sing Sing," "Summer Dresses," "Friend, Lover, Woman, Wife," "Silver and Gold," "Maria," "The Love Machine," and "Ever Since You Told Me That You Love Me (I'm a Nut)." They then broke into a brief instrumental jam, leading into "Crystal Blues."

A reprise of "Rock and Soul Music" followed, and set the table for the inevitable one-two punch encore: "The Fish (Fuck) Cheer" and "I-Feel-Like-I'm-Fixin'-to-Die Rag." The crowd had enjoyed Joe's folk version on Saturday afternoon, but this was the full-band psychedelic treatment, complete with kazoos and ragtime keyboards.

The audience ate it up. Those who stuck around were in for a treat, for waiting in the wings, from across the pond, was Ten Years After.

The Harvest Reaped: A Folk Singer Reborn

Here We Are Again lingered on the *Billboard* charts into fall 1969. By year's end, in a post-Woodstock, post-Altamont world on the brink of a new decade, Country Joe had resumed his folk singing career (see chapter 11). The Woodstock lineup of the band, with Peter Albin back in the fold, returned to the studio in January 1970 to record *CJ Fish*, a collection of tunes penned by Joe and Barry, at least three of which were played at the festival. The album hit the shelves in May 1970, a little more than a month after *Woodstock* hit movie theaters. Vanguard Records attempted to capitalize on the band's Woodstock appearance by ending 1969 with a *Greatest Hits* compilation.

CJ Fish was all she wrote for the band, for the next seven years. Vanguard would return to the well in 1971 for a two-record, career-spanning compilation, *The Life and Times of Country Joe and the Fish*, but there would be no new material until 1977's *Reunion*. The "reunion" alluded to in the title brought Barry and Joe back together with "Chicken" Hirsch, Bruce Barthol, and David Cohen for ten new tracks, most of them written by Joe and Barry, but with Hirsch, Cohen, and Barthol each earning at least one songwriting credit. They also took another shot at their lone charting single, the McDonald-penned "Not So Sweet Martha Lorraine." And that was it for Country Joe and the Fish.

Barry settled down, started a family, and headed back to law school. He passed the bar in 1982 and became a private defense attorney. In 1994, he became the deputy public defender of Mendocino County, California, and eventually of the entire state of California during 1998–1999. The still photograph of him holding the joint onstage at Woodstock came back to haunt him as he pursued his legal career, but it didn't stop him. Barry is still known to pick up a guitar from time to time, playing locally in California with Peter Albin, and making appearances on the summer European festival circuit, but nothing approaching the scale of his "Fish" days.

Joe McDonald wrote the foreword for Pete Fornatale's 2009 book, *Back to the Garden: The Story of Woodstock*. In many ways, he remains the quintessential ambassador for Woodstock Nation, and continues to bring a little bit of that spirit to every live performance.

26

Ten Years After

Fastest Guitar in the West . . . or the East

When we got there, we were supposed to play about three o'clock, as far as I remember. And I got into the gig and I got out of the helicopter and tuned up and I was pretty much ready to go, and the rainstorm broke. Which kind of screwed things up for hours, and I just kind of went out into the audience and joined in, I suppose. And I came back about every hour to see if anything was happening, and it wasn't. And it was much better in the audience than it was backstage, because there wasn't a lot of peace and love backstage. There were a lot of managers!

—*Alvin Lee (Ten Years After), Pete Fornatale Radio Archives, 2009*

As the Seeds Were Sown: Ten Years *Before* . . .

The band that would one day be known as Ten Years After traces its origins to England's Nottinghamshire and Mansfield areas, circa 1960. Like many early British bands, the group was originally named for one of its members, in this case Ivan Joseph Harrison, who went by Ivan Jay, so the band was called Ivan Jay and the Jaycats. After a time, "cats" gave way to "birds," and the group became the Jaybirds. Jaybirds didn't stick, either; the Jaybirds became Ivan Jay and the Jay*men.*

Cats, birds, men, no matter; by 1966, Alvin Lee and Leo Lyons had bid farewell to Ivan Jay altogether, and, taking drummer Rick Lee (no relation) and keyboardist Chick Churchill with them, the four struck out on their own. The newly minted quartet became Blues Trip, then Blues Yard, and finally, in 1966, Ten Years After.

If the band's name begs the question, "Ten years after *what?*" you are not alone. Some have speculated that it refers to the ten years following the onset of Elvis Aaron Presley's recording career in 1956. Others, such as Pete Fornatale, have said that the name refers to ten years since the birth of rock and roll, which seems even more plausible.

Ten Years After followed in the footsteps of the Who and the Rolling Stones by playing at the Marquee Club in London and then signing a contract with Deram Records. In a departure from music business conventions of the time, Ten Years After did not dip its toes in the commercial waters by releasing a single but went directly for a full album release. *Ten Years After* hit the record-store shelves on October 27, 1967. Five of the album's nine tracks are Alvin Lee compositions. Like Cream, the group covered Willie Dixon's "Spoonful," as well as "Help Me" by Dixon, Sonny Boy Williamson, and Ralph Bass; plus Al Kooper's "I Can't Keep from Crying Sometimes," which Kooper had adapted to his keyboard-centric tastes from Blind Willie Johnson's 1928 song "Lord I Just Can't Keep from Crying." The blues being an incestuous—perhaps even *larcenous*—genre by nature, it should come as no surprise that Johnson learned the song from Reverend H. R. Tomlin, who recorded versions of it in 1926 and 1927. And that's about as far back as anyone can trace the thread.

Ten Years After was a solid debut on technical merits, but it failed to chart. Ten Years After earned its reputation the old fashioned way—on the road. The group's gig at London's unusually named Klooks Kleek club on May 14, 1968, was recorded and became the live album *Undead*.

The album hit the shelves in the US exactly one year and one week before Ten Years After's Woodstock festival appearance. The penultimate track on the album is a cover of Gershwin's "Summertime," which scooped Janis Joplin and Big Brother and the Holding Company's version by a mere *two* days. The final track is "I'm Going Home." All told, the five tracks serve as a fitting showcase for Lee's fleet-fingered, six-string virtuosity. The band may not have been at the top of the charts, but this was a solid live act, and the talented guitarist was creating quite a buzz.

Ten Years After kept the momentum going by heading back to Decca's London studios in early September, where, in less than two weeks' time,

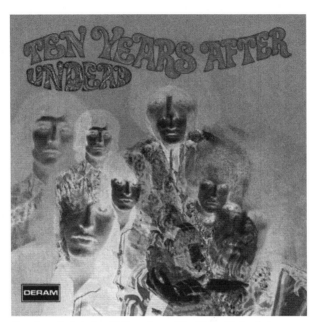

The cleverly titled 1968 live album, *Ten Years Undead*; the cover art also utilizes a photographic negative of the band.

the group laid down the tracks for its sophomore studio effort. This latest platter would feature seven originals by Alvin Lee, with Ric Lee, Chick Churchill, and Leo Lyons each contributing a tune as well. The standout track turned out to be the side-one closer, "Hear Me Calling," but it was the album's title, as much as anything, that would endear the group to the American counterculture. Released on February 22, 1969, *Stonedhenge* featured a psychedelic, Stonehenge-themed album cover. This time the band hit the charts, peaking at #61 on the *Billboard 200*.

During the summer of '69, Ten Years After hit a number of outdoor festivals on the road to Bethel, including a pioneering appearance (for a rock act) at the Newport Jazz Festival, and a set at the Seattle Pop Festival, where Ten Years After joined newcomers Santana among a lineup of twenty-six acts during the weekend of July 25–27.

The band was warmed up, road-tested, and ready to rock—and, thanks to a June recording session at London's Morgan Studios, also had studio album number three in the can and ready to drop in August, perfectly timed to coincide with Woodstock. That album, *Ssssh*, features another lucky seven Alvin Lee compositions, alongside a blistering cover of Sonny

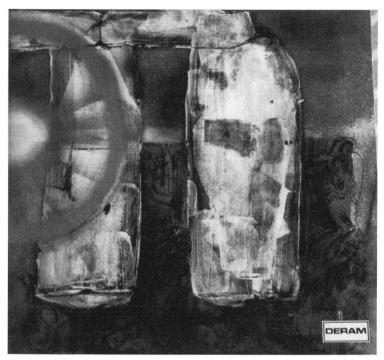

The British album cover for Ten Years After's *Stonedhenge*, released on February 22, 1969; the US cover features a variation on the Stonehenge theme but incorporates the band members' faces.

Boy Williamson's "Good Morning, Little Schoolgirl," which was also a staple of the Grateful Dead's 1960s sets. Ten Years After's chart progress continued as *Ssssh* hit #20 on the *Billboard* 200 and actually cracked the Top 5 back home in England. People were not only taking notice of the band, they were also scooping up the albums. Those hearty souls who chose to remain in Bethel for Sunday night's dance card were in for a real treat.

In the Garden: Show Me the Way to Go Home . . . by Helicopter

Ten Years After, featuring the quartet's original lineup—guitarist-vocalist Alvin Lee, drummer Ric Lee, bassist Leo Lyons, and keyboardist Chick Churchill—strode onto the stage around 8:15 p.m. on Sunday night,

August 17, twenty minutes past sunset, and delivered six songs that electrified the audience.

Whereas the band's albums were trending toward original compositions by this point, its Woodstock set leaned more heavily on covers. The group opened with a one-two punch of classic blues: Willie Dixon's "Spoonful," followed by Sonny Boy Williamson's "Good Morning Little Schoolgirl," then pulled a real rabbit out of the 'ol hat, introducing a J. R. R. Tolkien–inspired number called "The Hobbit," which, for all intents and purposes, was really just a fancy name for an extended Ric Lee drum solo. Next, the band offered its own take on "I Can't Keep from Crying Sometimes," which showcased Alvin's guitar licks more so than Chick's keyboards. The penultimate song of the set was the Sonny Boy Williamson, Willie Dixon, and Ralph Bass collaboration, "Help Me," which is a variation on the theme of "Green Onions," by Booker T. and the M.G.'s.

This amazing jam set the audience up for the kill: the encore, "I'm Going Home," which Alvin introduced by saying, "This is a thing called 'I'm Going Home, by Helicopter.'" For the next eleven heart-stopping minutes, Lee frantically peeled notes from his fretboard like a man possessed, as Ric Lee, Lyons and Churchill laid down a bluesy foundation.

Whether Lee's introductory ad-lib, inspired by the festival's somewhat unusual mode of transportation, was intended to signal a change in the song's title, or if it was merely stage banter with a touch of British humor, it certainly made an impression. In point of fact, the British blues quartet *was* going home . . . or at least back to the hotel . . . by helicopter. But it was the appearance of "I'm Going Home" in the Michael Wadleigh *Woodstock* film the following year that would forever etch that moment into the collective unconscious, with the result that, to this day, many people continue to believe that the addendum, "by helicopter," is a part of the song's title. And few can forget the sight of Alvin, post-set and looking a bit tired, shouldering a large watermelon and striding from the stage in triumph. It was a remarkable performance in every way.

The Harvest Reaped: I'd Love to Change the World, But . . .

The momentum that Ten Years After had been building in the months leading up to Woodstock was only bolstered during the following year by the group's appearance in the film. Suddenly, everybody wanted a piece of them.

The band put in more time at London's Olympic Studios during the waning months of 1969, so as to be ready to greet the new decade with fresh material. *Cricklewood Green* went on sale on April 17, 1970, and received mostly critical acclaim. By this point, Alvin Lee was doing *all* of the songwriting, but no one seemed to mind as long as the band remained successful. The album flirted with the US Top 10, but didn't quite reach that threshold, weighing in at a respectable #14 on the *Billboard* 200. It may have gained a boost from the gimmicky release of the single "Love Like a Man," which earned the band the #10 spot in the UK. The "gimmick" was that the song appeared twice on the release; side A featured the standard three-minute, 45-rpm version; the B-Side was an extended 33-rpm live recording that stretched toward eight minutes. The disc remains something of a collector's item.

The band hit the road for the festival circuit during 1970, joining many Woodstock alumni who had also gotten a boost from the related publicity. Melanie, Mountain, and Sly and the Family Stone were among the twenty-three acts on the bill when Ten Years After hit Toronto's Strawberry Fields Festival on August 10, while the legendary 1970 Isle of Wight festival became a bloated monster, featuring upwards of forty acts over five days, and a crowd estimated to have exceeded six hundred thousand.

The Woodstock model was clearly catching on. Fellow Woodstock alumni joining Ten Years After at the Isle of Wight included, once again, Melanie and Sly and the Family Stone, plus John Sebastian, the Who, Joan Baez, Richie Havens, and Jimi Hendrix. In a humorous twist, all of the Woodstock alums played the last two days of the festival, with Woodstock opener Richie Havens bringing the proceedings to a *close* at the Isle of Wight as Sunday gave way to Monday, August 31.

The band's final act of 1970 was a return to London's Olympic Sound Studios in September, where the members would record their final album for Deram Records, called *Watt*. Music critics began asking the homo-phonic question, "What?" As much as they loved *Cricklewood Green*, they were less enthused by *Watt*.

Perhaps it was the fact that the band chose to end the album with a live recording of Chuck Berry's "Sweet Little Sixteen" from its Isle of Wight set that turned them off. Such tactics can come across as "filler." Was Alvin running out of ideas? Perhaps the formula just needed a shakeup. Ten Years After was still considered a killer live act, and that was the group's bread and butter. Not that the chart numbers were ter-rible. *Watt* hit #21 on *Billboard* and #5 in the UK; even without gimmicky singles, people were still buying the albums.

Despite the tepid response to *Watt*, it had been a *huge* year for Ten Years After, and 1971 was shaping up to be even better. The band moved recording operations from Deram to Columbia Records, which proved to be the creative shot in the arm the group needed. Columbia debut *A Space in Time* found the blues purists trying on a more "classic rock" sound, and featured the group's first bona-fide hit, "I'd Love to Change the World." The album hit #17 stateside, while the single cracked the Top 40 and became a staple of progressive FM radio. The song is wonderfully produced and layered, with a rare Alvin Lee turn on acoustic guitar. The lyrics seem to embrace marginalized groups, albeit by employing termi-nology that would no longer pass muster in our increasingly politically correct society, with its references to "dykes" and "fairies," "freaks" and "hairys."

Herein lies the irony: for all of "I'd Love to Change the World's" posi-tives, the band rarely bothered to play it in concert. Yes, arguably it would have been difficult for the quartet to present the song live without added musicians, but a more likely rationale is that it really wasn't their pre-ferred style of music.

The other single, "Baby Won't You Let Me Rock 'n' Roll You," did not fare as well on the charts, stalling at #61. And while Alvin Lee wrote all ten songs on the album, Chick, Ric, and Leo all get equal co-songwriting credit on the short final track, "Uncle Jam."

The band's 1972 Columbia Records sophomore outing, *Rock and Roll Music to the World*, continued the pattern of Alvin being the lone songwriter, and some have opined that the sound was becoming a bit formulaic. The title track was the single here, and while it was and remains a solid album, there's nothing much remarkable about it.

It was time for a live album to break things up a bit. The double album *Recorded Live* was taped during the last week of January and released in June 1973, just in time for summer. It was a no-frills, warts-and-all, straightforward live album, cobbled together from four shows during the European winter tour. Rather than reinventing the wheel, the track list relied on familiar material like "Good Morning Little Schoolgirl," "Help Me," "Hobbit," "I Can't Keep from Cryin' Sometimes," and "I'm Going Home," mixed in with a few other Alvin Lee originals, but *no* sign of "I'd Love to Change the World."

Ten Years After managed to squeeze in one more studio album for Columbia, the wishfully titled *Positive Vibrations*. It was released in April 1974, whereupon the band broke up. Of the ten tracks, nine were Alvin Lee originals. The lone cover, Little Richard's "Going Back to Birmingham," did little to propel sales, and the album only made #81 on the *Billboard 200*. The band had been on a downward trajectory for a couple of years, so perhaps it was time for a break. It would be fifteen long years before anyone heard from Ten Years After again.

Fifteen years later—you will note that it was 1989, the twentieth anniversary of Woodstock—everyone was talking about that magical weekend in Bethel. *Twenty* years after, Ten Years After, with all original members accounted for, reappeared on Chrysalis Records with the cheekily titled *About Time*. The key difference this time around was that Alvin had found a real songwriting partner in Steve Gould, the bass player from his solo band, and that the group was now employing backup vocalists. Alvin also wrote with another one of his musicians, keyboardist Tim Hinkley. Meanwhile, Leo Lyons had brought in his own bandmates, keyboardist Andy Nye and Tony Crooks. The members may have been branching out musically, and writing songs with other musicians, but none of that mattered much in terms of *About Time*. Time had passed them by.

Over the next fifteen years, there was a steady drip of live albums (*The Friday Rock Show Sessions—Live at Reading 1983*, *Live 1990*, *Live at the Fillmore East 1970*, *One Night Jammed*), and the inevitable compilation releases, the first of which, *Double Deluxe*, dated back to the band's 1970 heyday. It was the first of *twenty-four* such releases. How a band with only nine studio albums can yield more than double that amount of compilation albums remains one of the great mysteries of music marketing.

But we had not yet heard the last of the group. In 2004, Woodstock's thirty-fifth anniversary year, Chick, Rick, and Leo regrouped as Ten Years After . . . *without* Alvin Lee. Not that Alvin left them much choice in the matter; it was his decision to officially leave the band. All of a sudden, the three had discovered their inner songwriters, and, along with Alvin's "replacement," Joe Gooch, they are credited on all nine of the album's original tracks.

Gooch is a fine vocalist, and an excellent guitarist in his own right, and the rhythm section remains in fine form here . . . but it sounds like an entirely different band. This new, three-quarters-full version of Ten Years After had more studio albums in it, including 2008's *Evolution*, which barely made a ripple, commercially speaking. Most recently, (almost) ten years after *Evolution*, 2017's *A Sting in the Tale* hit the shelves.

The group also released a couple of live albums and a live DVD, but it just wasn't the same. The last of these, 2014's *The Name Remains the Same*, hit the shelves just as the band's lineup had become all but unrecognizable. Only Ric Lee and Chick Churchill remained. Mark Bonfanti replaced Goonch, and Leo Lyons yielded his bass slot to Colin Hodgkinson.

Founding member Alvin Lee, considered by many to have been one of the fastest guitarists in history, passed away in Spain on March 6, 2013, due to complications from surgery. He was sixty-eight years old.

27

The Band

Veteran Newcomers

It was funny. You kind of felt you were going to a war. I think we drove down to Stewart Airport, and they helicoptered us into the landing zone and then took us into motor homes to wait for the show. I remember walking around and checking out the thirty-foot stage, elevators in back, immense scaffolding, and an army of muddy people out on the hillside. They were set back about half an acre from the stage. It was the final day of the festival, and they'd run out of fresh food and water. There weren't any dressing rooms because they'd been turned into emergency clinics. There was lots of acid around—they were making announcements about it from the stage—and the audience was immensely under the influence of anything you could think of. This was Sunday, and some of them had been out there four nights already. The crowd was real tired and a little unhealthy.

—*Levon Helm,* This Wheel's On Fire:
Levon Helm and the Story of the Band

As the Seeds Were Sown: Ronnie Hawkins Feathers His Nest

In 1957, Arkansas drummer Levon Helm joined a band called the Hawks, fronted by fellow Arkansan Ronnie Hawkins, a burly and charismatic bandleader, club owner, and talent scout, whose sound was an eclectic blend of rockabilly, bluegrass, country, R&B, and good old-fashioned rock and roll. Hawkins took his act north of the border during

1958, where he found success in Ontario. His *modus operandi* was identifying the best musicians on the scene, and then luring them away to join the Hawks. That keen "hawk eye" landed upon the future members of the Band, and slowly but surely he drew them into his musical aerie.

A local guitar player named Robbie Robertson joined in 1960. During the summer of 1961, a new bass player, Rick Danko, arrived. By fall 1961, the lineup had acquired a talented pianist named Richard Manuel. Before the year was over, the multi-instrumentalist Garth Hudson had become a Hawk, and the five members who would one day become the Band were united within the framework of Ronnie and the Hawks.

As famously recounted in *The Last Waltz*, the arrangement was a tough sell for Hudson. A classically trained musician, he was afraid of disappointing his parents, who had invested heavily in his education. He didn't want to have to tell them that, after all that, he'd gone and joined a rock-and-roll band. So he came up with a clever work-around. The other four members of the band would each pay Hudson a nominal fee to serve as their music teacher.

With varying durations of tenure, the quintet backed Ronnie Hawkins for more than six years, before striking out on its own in 1964, as *Levon and the Hawks*. The musicians also briefly performed as the Canadian Squires, but during the following year, their world would be forever changed when Bob Dylan called them into service to be his backup band.

Levon, unhappy with the folk purists in the audiences booing the new, electric Dylan, bailed out during the first leg of the tour, which featured eight shows between April 30 and May 10, 1965. With Sandy Konikoff (and then Mickey Jones) manning the drum stool, Garth, Robbie, Rick, and Richard joined Dylan for his 1966 World Tour. Between February 4, when they kicked things off in Kentucky at the Convention Center in Louisville, and the finale, a back-to-back at London's Royal Albert Hall on May 26 and 27, the road warriors played a total of forty-four shows throughout the continental United States, Hawaii, Canada, Australia, Europe, and the UK.

Two months after the tour, Dylan had a motorcycle accident while riding his Triumph and disappeared from public view. Bob had been booked for shows that would have taken him and "the band" through the end of 1966. When those remaining performances were canceled, another door opened. It was Dylan, according to legend, who gave the five their name; he always referred to them simply as "the band."

During Dylan's recuperation, they lived communally in a big pink house in Saugerties, making music night and day. Those marathon sessions at *Big Pink* yielded more than a hundred songs, resulting in *The Basement Tapes* for Dylan (not released until 1975) and the Band's 1968 debut, *Music from Big Pink*. During Woodstock weekend, the group was still a month away from the release of its self-titled 1969 follow-up album, *The Band*.

In the Garden: It's 10:00 p.m., Do You Know Where *Dylan* Is?

Faced with the challenge of following Ten Years After, the Band didn't even break a sweat. Robbie Robertson, Rick Danko, Levon Helm, Garth

The Band's 1968 debut album. "Big Pink" refers to a house in Saugerties, New York, where many of these songs first saw the light of day. The house has become a landmark for rock 'n' roll pilgrims who travel from far and wide to pose for photos there .

Hudson, and Richard Manuel may have only had one album under their belts (as the Band), but they had been making music together since 1958.

Chip Monck introduced them: "Ladies and gentleman, please welcome with us, the Band." The haunting organ and percussion intro of "Chest Fever" rolled out across the dark and soggy field. The audience—few of whom had ever seen them perform—responded enthusiastically. The quintet continued with "Don't Do It," which was destined to become a Band classic. Next it was time for a Dylan tune, "Tears of Rage." Richard's mournful yowl more than did the song justice, with Rick kicking in on harmony. At the outset, as if on cue, some yahoo in the audience took the opportunity to yell out, "Where's Dylan?" . . . as if he were hiding under the stage. No Dylan, but no matter. The Band had this.

The set continued with "We Can Talk," "Long Black Veil," and "Don't You Tell Henry." Next up was "Ain't No More Cane on the Brazos," a prison work song that had been preserved by the musical anthropology of Alan Lomax. "This Wheel's on Fire" came next, destined one day to become the theme song for the debauched British sitcom *Absolutely Fabulous*.

As the set moved into the home stretch, it was time to get mellow, so the Band returned to the fount of Dylan for a slow and heartfelt take on "I Shall Be Released," showcasing Richard's mournful falsetto, punctuated by Rick's hound-dog-like howls. They followed up with a really mellow version of "The Weight," which featured Ricky and Levon ad-libbing a little "call-and-response" with the lyrics.

The Band switched gears for the encore, delivering a fun and bouncy cover of the Four Tops' 1966 hit "Loving You Is Sweeter Than Ever," with Rick singing lead. Robbie supplied a stinging guitar solo, punctuated by Garth and Richard's respective ivories. All the while, the Levon and Rick rhythm section laid down the funky foundation.

These guys were obviously seasoned, versatile pros, and theirs would be a tough act to follow. But a couple of bluesy Texas siblings, Johnny and Edgar Winter, were waiting in the wings and ready to give it a shot.

The Harvest Reaped: Waltzing into Tragedy

The Band found itself in the middle of the action for a monumental event at the 1969 Isle of Wight festival: the return of Bob Dylan. The Band "opened" for Dylan that day, August 31, with nine songs; essentially the same as the Woodstock set, with the addition of "To Kingdom Come," a track from *Music from Big Pink*.

After a forty-minute break, the Band returned to the stage in its familiar guise as Dylan's backing group. This was a more robust set of seventeen songs, though not necessarily the ones the audience was hoping for. Dylan was there to showcase his new stuff, from *John Wesley Harding* and *Nashville Skyline*. He was so happy with the set that he included four of the tracks on his next album, *Self-Portrait*.

The members of the Band would forever be associated with Dylan, but they had become a formidable act in their own right. It was time to step out into the spotlight. Their music had already infiltrated the world of film. "The Weight" was included on the soundtrack of *Easy Rider*, packing theaters coast-to-coast since July 1969.

When sophomore album *The Band* hit record store shelves on September 22, it quickly became clear that it was a masterpiece. The two singles, "Rag Mama Rag," and "Up on Cripple Creek" only hit #57 and #25, respectively, but the album as a whole hit #9 on the *Billboard* charts.

With a hit album out, it was a foregone conclusion that the Band would be hitting the road. The realities of touring life during the late '60s and early '70s exacerbated the members' weaknesses for drugs and drink, with Richard, Rick, and Levon being the biggest offenders. When they returned to the studio during May 1970, that road-weariness began to show in the music. The Band recorded in the familiar surroundings of Woodstock, but the themes were anything but comforting.

The title track of the resulting album, "Stage Fright," speaks volumes, as does one of the group's most beloved tunes, "The Shape I'm In." *Stage Fright* was self-produced, mixed by John Simon and the up-and-coming Todd Rundgren. Released August 17, 1970, a full year after Woodstock, the album hit #5, though there were no singles of any consequence; "Time to Kill" only hit #77.

The Band's eponymous post-Woodstock sophomore effort features arguably the most formidable five-piece lineup in rock 'n' roll history.

The Band participated in the party-train ride of the century, the 1970 concert tour of Canada chronicled in the film *Festival Express* (2003). Behind the scenes, Ricky, Levon, and Richard were getting drunk and shooting dope; Garth remained Garth; and Robbie began butting heads with Levon. Those control issues would continue through the 1971 recording sessions for the next album, *Cahoots*. Released in September 1971, *Cahoots* featured the Band's last original material for several years. The festive opening track, "Life Is a Carnival," has Levon, Rick, and Robbie sharing songwriting credit. Robbie collaborated with Irish rocker Van Morrison on "4% Pantomime," and "When I Paint My Masterpiece" is, of course, a Dylan song. Robbie penned the remaining eight tracks.

The Band played four consecutive nights at New York's Academy of Music, and that material formed the basis for a live album. The quintet was bolstered by the genius of New Orleans producer Alan Toussaint, who put together a killer five-man horn section for the shows. Throw in a New Year's Eve cameo by Bob Dylan, and you've got yourself one hell of a live album, no matter the condition of your starting five. Released on August 15, 1972, *Rock of Ages* definitely bought the Band some time.

But the creative well was dry. The next project, *Moondog Matinee*, was a studio album of covers. One of them, Junior Parker and Sam Philips' "Mystery Train," would go on to make the cut at *The Last Waltz*. Clearly the Band needed a change of pace.

On July 28, 1973, the Band joined the Grateful Dead and the Allman Brothers Band for Summer Jam at Watkins Glen. This was an absolutely massive concert, with an estimated six hundred thousand audience members, and it catapulted the Band back into the public consciousness.

Robbie by this time had moved out to Malibu, near Dylan, and there was some talk about the possibly of them doing another album and maybe a tour together. Rick, Levon, Garth, and Richard followed them out there. The resulting album, Bob Dylan's *Planet Waves*, is a masterpiece, featuring not one but two versions of "Forever Young"; a long, mournful take to end side one, followed by a shorter, more up-tempo rendition to begin side two.

The grueling, two-month, twenty-one-city, forty-date North American tour that followed during January and February was Dylan's first full-scale tour since he was last on the road with the Band during 1966. The shows were recorded, yielding the live album *Before the Flood* on June 20. It hit #3 on *Billboard*, and, once again, both Dylan and the Band were relevant. Though in later years both Dylan and members of the Band would downplay the experience—as though they were just going through the motions—the tour got people talking. It also nudged the Band back into the studio.

Recorded during the spring and summer of 1975, *Northern Lights— Southern Cross* hit the shelves on November 1. Once again, Robbie Robertson was the sole songwriter, and several songs, such as "It Makes No Difference," were absolute gems. The critics were complimentary, and the album sold modestly well.

The following year, 1976, saw the release of a greatest hits package, *The Best of the Band*, which sold well. Robbie, though, had had it. He was tired of the road and tired of watching his bandmates deteriorate from substance abuse. The fact that Richard got drunk and nearly broke his neck in a boating accident gave him the opening he needed. He pitched the others on the idea of retiring from the road with a big holiday concert, full of guest stars, to be recorded for release as an album and concert film. That project, dubbed *The Last Waltz*, was the logical outgrowth of the *Rock of Ages* shows. Bill Graham's Winterland Ballroom provided the ideal setting, and Thanksgiving evening was deemed the right holiday. Who else but Bill could pull off a Thanksgiving dinner for five thousand?

Allen Toussaint was back with that killer horn section, and Hollywood heavyweight Martin Scorsese had his team in place to film the whole thing. In addition to the obligatory Dylan appearance, guests included former mentor Ronnie "The Hawk" Hawkins; fellow Canadians Neil Young and Joni Mitchell; Van "The Man" Morrison; Paul Butterfield; New York's own Neil Diamond; British rock royalty Ringo Starr, Eric Clapton, and Ron Wood; and American blues deity Muddy Waters.

The resulting three-record set and film bear witness to what a monumental evening it was. Were it not for the fact that the Band was contractually obligated to Capitol Records for another studio release, that would have been it . . . at least as far as Robbie Robertson was concerned. But Capitol could legally interfere with the plans for *The Last Waltz*'s release on Warner Bros if the group reneged.

The final studio effort by the original lineup of the band, *Islands*, was released in March 1977. Culled together from recordings dating back to 1972, the ten tracks feature a mix of originals and covers, including "Georgia on My Mind," recorded as a favor to Jimmy Carter's presidential campaign. It was met with tepid reviews and mediocre sales. *Anthology*, another greatest-hits package on Capitol, bridged the gap until the 1978 Warner Bros release of *The Last Waltz*. The triple album hit #16, and the film is considered one of the greatest rock documentaries of all time, although a fair criticism is that Scorsese made the film very Robertson-centric. Another problem is that the others hadn't seemed to fully grasp the concept that the event had been marketed as the Band's *last* concert. They assumed they'd be getting back to business as usual. But when Robbie said "Last Waltz," he meant *Last* Waltz.

In 1983, Ricky, Levon, Garth, and Richard went out on the road as the Band, without Robbie. The revamped lineup, rounded out by other former members of the Hawks, never approached the heights of the classic era.

On March 4, 1986, forty-two-year-old Richard Manuel, who had recently fallen off the wagon, took his own life. The remaining three would continue as a unit, while also pursuing solo projects. They recorded three more Band albums without Robbie and Richard. *Jericho* (1993), long delayed because of Richard's suicide, features the ill-fated pianist on a single track, "Country Boy." *High on the Hog*, released in 1996, features only two original compositions. Lastly, 1998's *Jubilation* brought the legendary group's recording career to its conclusion.

In the meantime, Eric Clapton inducted the Band into the Rock and Roll Hall of Fame during the 1994 ceremony, though hard feelings remained. Levon refused to share the stage with Robbie—or show up at *all*—as the three remaining members performed "The Weight" with Clapton and the house band.

Rick Danko, aged fifty-five, passed away in his sleep from heart failure on December 10, 1999. Levon Helm battled cancer, reconciled with Robbie, and passed away on April 19, 2012. He was seventy-one years old.

After *The Last Waltz*, Robbie Robertson dabbled in the film industry for a time, before returning as a solo music artist in 1986. He has since penned three books and released seven albums, including 2011's *How to Become Clairvoyant*.

Garth Hudson, the last man to join the Hawks, appears to be the last man standing . . . on a stage, at least. Garth went solo in 2001, and continues to perform. In 2017, he went out on the road with an all-star lineup for the Last Waltz 40 tour.

28

Johnny (and Edgar) Winter

The Original Blues Brothers

We knew there was a huge crowd. We heard on TV before we even got there that it was huge. We didn't know exactly how many people. We came in, really tired. We had played Detroit and Chicago, and we didn't get much sleep at all. We got Hendrix's spot at 12:30 at night. He didn't want to play then. That was a real good time to play. It was the biggest thing we had ever played. And we had played a lot of big festivals, too. But Woodstock was the biggest. I played my regular songs that I had done on my first album, *The Progressive Blues Experiment*. When we played, the rain had quit. So we went on at a real good time. I think we played a good set.

—Johnny Winter, Archives of the Museum at Bethel Woods

As the Seeds Were Sown: Texas Two-Step

John Dawson Winter III was born to musically inclined parents in Beaumont, Texas, on February 23, 1944, under the sign of Pisces. His Capricorn younger brother Edgar came along almost three years later, on December 28, 1946. Mom played piano, and dad, who worked in the building trades, played banjo and saxophone. John, who went by "Johnny," started out by playing ukulele, the instrument he used during his debut public performance at age ten. He also played clarinet in his school band, and by age twelve, he had picked up the guitar—a Gibson ES-125 that was a gift from his great-grandfather. Edgar, meanwhile, picked up the saxophone from his father, and soon added keyboards to his repertoire, en route to becoming a bona-fide multi-instrumentalist.

Both brothers had "albinism," or a lack of skin pigmentation, a condition that left them with extremely pale complexions, pinkish eyes, and white hair that appeared to glow silver under spotlights, giving them an ethereal, almost supernatural look. The brothers' surname really *is* "Winter"—an odd coincidence. It is a rare occurrence when a performer is born with the perfect stage name, and rarer still when that performer is born for the stage; lightning struck twice in the Winter family.

The brothers' first band, Johnny and the Jammers, landed a record deal in Houston and released a single, "School Day Blues," when they were just fifteen and thirteen. It would be several more years before Johnny landed an album deal, but this was an impressive start.

Texas was and remains one of the focal points of American blues culture, and Johnny was dedicated to the form. He idolized Muddy Waters and B.B. King, just two of the marquee names who often performed in his hometown. Little did Johnny know that one day he would be working with and even *producing* the legendary Muddy Waters. Many would later credit Johnny with revitalizing the blues legend's career, but that is a story for another time.

Although the straightforward rock of "School Day Blues" is "blues" in name only, the brothers would discover the blues *proper* in short order, and it would become an abiding passion. Their new band featured Edgar on piano, Johnny on guitar, David Holliday on drums, Willard Chamberlain on sax, and Dennis Drugan on bass. They soon began sneaking blues numbers into their standard rock-and-roll sets.

One night, seventeen-year-old Johnny went to see B.B. King play at a local Beaumont club, and he nagged the legend until he finally let him up onstage to jam. Johnny launched into "Goin' Down Slow," using B.B.'s beloved "Lucille," of all guitars. When he finished, the mostly black audience rewarded him with a standing ovation. He was hooked.

Johnny's love of the blues led him to Chicago in his early twenties, where he became a student of the game and met all of the major players. The brothers paid their dues on the bar circuit for several years before Sonobeat, a label based in Austin, Texas, offered Johnny his first album deal. Released in 1968, *The Progressive Blues Experiment* features a

Johnny Winter's 1968 debut album features a mix of original material and covers of blues classics; it helped to define the "Texas blues."

number of songs by the likes of Sonny Boy Williamson, B.B. King, and Willie Dixon. Among the ten tracks there were four solid originals. Johnny even took a page out of the old Dylan playbook by writing a song for his idol. Dylan had written "Song to Woody," for Woody Guthrie at a similar age, while Johnny penned "Tribute to Muddy" to honor his own hero and future collaborator, Muddy Waters.

Edgar Winter does *not* appear on Johnny's debut album, though his own turn in the spotlight would come. Accompanying Johnny on the album were bass player Tommy Shannon and drummer "Uncle" John Turner, both of whom would accompany Johnny to the stage in Bethel.

It did not escape the notice of Columbia Records execs that Johnny had won the respect and admiration of many industry heavyweights, including Al Kooper and Mike Bloomfield. When they invited Johnny up onstage to jam, he had the suits in the audience hooked. They ponied up north of half a *million* dollars to land the young Texan—the largest such advance of the period, tripling the $200,000 that Atlantic Records had forwarded Led Zeppelin the previous year. Sonobeat was one thing, but Columbia Records was *big* time, and the label believed in Johnny.

The eponymous *Johnny Winter*, recorded during the winter of 1969, hit the shelves in spring, four months before Woodstock. Of the nine tracks, six were covers of blues classics, and three were original compositions. Edgar was back in the fold, along with Shannon, Turner, and a large roster of session and guest musicians, among them blues legend Willie Dixon.

In 1968, *Rolling Stone*, barely a year old, heralded Johnny Winter as "a cross-eyed albino with long fleecy hair, playing some of the gutsiest fluid blues guitar you've ever heard." The weight of the magazine's endorsement led to Johnny's invitation to play at the 1969 Newport Jazz Festival—where he once again shared the stage with B.B. King—and then to the Woodstock Music and Art Fair.

In the Garden: Sibling Wizardry

After the Band, it was time for a little bit of the Texas blues. Into the spotlight strode twenty-five-year-old Johnny Winter and the rhythm section of Tommy Shannon and "Uncle" John Turner, who had been working with Johnny since his debut album. His twenty-two-year-old kid brother, Edgar, was waiting in the wings, ready to sit in on keyboards for three songs later in the set.

The usually deadpan Chip Monck sounded more enthusiastic than usual as he said, "And welcome with us, please, Johnny Winter." Winter and his band hit the stage just as Sunday morphed into Monday, and the festival officially entered uncharted waters.

Johnny may have appeared exotic and otherworldly while bathed in the glow of the spotlights, but his brand of hard-driving Texas blues was gritty and down-to-earth. To be sure, it had been a long stretch of hard-driving music on Sunday up to this point, but audience members who remained attentive were in for a treat.

Winter opened with a cover of J. B. Lenoir's "Mama, Talk to Your Daughter," and then launched into the snarling, down and dirty "Leland Mississippi Blues," a new song of Johnny's that paid homage to one of his childhood hometowns. While Johnny's guitar solos may not have matched the finger-blurring velocity of Alvin Lee's, they had every bit of Lee's feeling and, arguably, even more tastefulness and power.

Next it was time to offer the audience a music lesson. Johnny addressed the crowd. "This is a bottleneck guitar thing for ya, from uh . . . our first album." That "bottleneck guitar thing" was "Mean Town Blues," and it clocked in at nearly eleven minutes of raunchy, almost menacing blues, played over an oddly simple and repetitive thumping drum beat; just a foot on the bass drum pedal, over and over, for several minutes before the band launches into the explosive finale. Johnny employed an electric twelve-string for most of this song, with a piece of metal conduit serving as a slide.

A cover of B.B. King's "You Done Lost Your Good Thing Now" segued into "Mean Mistreater," an oft-covered blues that dates back to at least 1934, when it was released as "Mean Mistreater Mama" by Leroy Carr and Scrapper Blackwell. The version that appears on Johnny's self-titled sophomore album is credited to James Gordon.

The opening couplet of tunes lasted nearly fifteen minutes. Afterward, Johnny welcomed Edgar to the stage. "I'd like to try something a little different. We just finished cuttin' . . . uh, the next album, in Nashville. My brother Edgar's been working on it. We'd like to try a . . . one of the tunes from the album, and bring out my little brother, Edgar Winter, to do some sax and piano for ya."

Edgar's presence on "I Can't Stand It" gave the band an impressive added dimension of sound. But in spite of this introduction, "I Can't Stand It" would *not* make the final cut for Johnny's third album.

It seemed as though Johnny was in an experimental mood, as he addressed the crowd once more. "Like I said, we just finished this album, and we really haven't been working together with Edgar, so we don't have any material, so we'd like to do a tune we used to do a long time ago . . . kind of a jam thing, featuring Edgar, who's going to sing on this one, 'Tobacco Road.'"

Not only did Edgar sing, and sing *well*, on the John D. Loudermilk song that had already become a blues classic, he also wailed away at different times on both the Hammond B-3 organ and the saxophone during an eleven-minute jam. Edgar's presence onstage coaxed some killer guitar licks from Johnny's fingers. His sibling's piercing blues scream was also well received by the crowd, who clamored for more. "'Rollin' and Tumblin'!" called a voice from the crowd. Instead, Johnny led the band into the Lowman Pauling–penned "Tell the Truth," another song originally intended for his third album that would remain incomplete and unreleased until 2004. The crowd ate it up, and as the musicians put down their instruments and walked from the stage, the audience again yelled for more.

Returning to the stage, Johnny sounded as fresh as he had when he started an hour earlier. He introduced the encore, "Johnny B. Goode," without ever actually mentioning the song by name . . . not that it *needed* any introduction by this point in history. "One of the new little things we've been working on lately," he said, before letting it rip. Edgar took a killer solo on the keyboards to bookend Johnny's stellar fretwork. It was a fun and frenzied finale, well worth the time of those who had decided to stick around. Even as Chip signed them off with "Ladies and gentlemen, Johnny Winter," the crowd continued to call for more.

Johnny's formidable set made him yet another tough act to follow in a weekend *full* of tough acts to follow. But waiting in the wings was one of the biggest and most commercially successful bands of 1969: Blood, Sweat, and Tears.

The Harvest Reaped: Guitar God

On October 27, 1969, *Second Winter* hit the record-store shelves. The album featured two records . . . but only *three* completed sides; side four is actually blank (as many a bewildered stoner discovered when they dropped the needle). The last track on side two is a cover of Dylan's "Highway 61 Revisited." The blues purist was either branching out or looking for material to fill up his records.

Edgar got into the game in 1970 with his own solo debut album, *Entrance*. Many of the tracks were co-written with Johnny, who appears on one track only, "Tobacco Road."

Johnny would remain prolific throughout the '70s and '80s—despite a growing fondness for heroin—though his studio output began to slow down considerably in later years. All told, he released nineteen studio

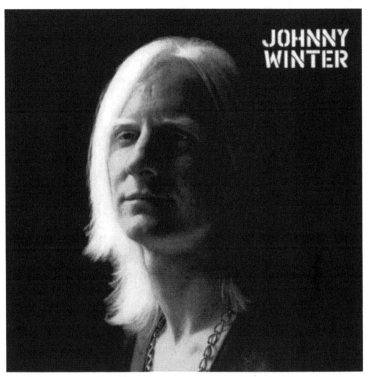

Johnny Winter's sophomore effort was, in a sense, his solo debut, though the album features more studio personnel than his 1968 LP, which he made with a band.

albums, eight live albums (one of which, 2009's *Johnny Winter: The Woodstock Experience*, captured his set at Bethel in all its ragged glory), fifteen compilations, and a series of officially released "bootlegs" titled *Live Bootleg Series*, 2007's Vol. 1 through 2018's Vol. 14, which features the subtitle *It's Johnny's Birthday*.

In addition to his own impressive output, Johnny served as a guest guitarist on eight other albums, beginning in 1975. The majority of these projects paired him with childhood idol Muddy Waters. Others paired him with the likes of Sonny Terry, James Cotton, and his guitar contemporary, Rick Derringer.

A road warrior until the end, Johnny was found dead in a Swiss hotel room on July 16, 2014, just two days after his final concert. He was seventy years old, and, unlike many of his contemporaries, was reported to have died of natural causes, rumored to be pneumonia.

29

Blood, Sweat, and Tears

And All That "Jazz-Rock"

We were playing in Massachusetts the night before, and everyone was saying, "Did you hear? Do you know what's going on?" "What?" "You can't get in; you can't get out! Millions of people! Wow! You have to helicopter." Well, we drove straight in. We played. And we drove straight out. I think I was home in an hour and a half, because everyone was frozen assuming you couldn't get anywhere.

—*Bobby Colomby (drummer, Blood, Sweat, and Tears)*
to Jeremiah Rickert, April 2, 1998

As the Seeds Were Sown: A New "Project" for Al Kooper and Friends

The Monterey Pop Festival was the last hurrah for the Blues Project, an experimental Greenwich Village band; by then, members Steve Katz and Al Kooper, twenty-two and twenty-three, respectively, were looking for something new.

Kooper—an eclectic musical visionary who had played on Dylan's *Highway 61 Revisited* and been a part of his band at the infamous 1965 Newport Folk Festival—found himself getting more and more into jazz. He was fascinated with the Canadian bandleader Maynard Ferguson, and with the concept of "brass rock."

Kooper had a vision for a full-fledged electric rock-and-roll band that would operate like a jazz ensemble and feature a robust horn section. It would be a free-form improvisational mix of rhythm and blues, jazz, pop, and soul, with psychedelic undertones in keeping with the spirit of the times. It would come to be known as "jazz rock," not to be confused with the avant-garde virtuosity of "jazz fusion" (though naturally it often is).

In Kooper's original vision, he saw himself pursuing this new project in London, but when that didn't pan out, he found himself back at his home base in New York City. Steve Katz was on board with the idea, and they soon found a willing rhythm section in drummer Bobby Colomby and bassist Jim Fielder.

From the outset, Kooper let the others know that *he* would be calling the shots. The four started gigging in September 1967. The quartet became a quintet in November with the addition of saxophonist Fred Lipsius, and he in turn brought in trumpeters Randy Brecker and Jerry Weiss, along with trombonist Dick Halligan.

The octet began gigging in mid-November 1967, and New York audiences ate it up. Kooper's reputation as a session musician for the likes of Jimi Hendrix and his affiliation with Dylan were enough to land the group a deal with Columbia Records. All they needed was a name. When Kooper cut his finger and bled all over his keyboards during a gig at Café Au Go Go, he got one: Blood, Sweat, and Tears was born.

The group's first foray into the studio yielded *Child Is Father to the Man*, which hit record-store shelves during the third week of February 1968. The bizarre, conceptual album cover features the band members posing with their own miniature, child-sized selves. The album, produced by the respected John Simon, only hit #48 on the *Billboard* Pop chart, and there were no singles to drive sales. To make matters worse, the band members began fighting among themselves. Kooper, ever the restless spirit, bailed out in March, but stayed on with Columbia Records as a producer. Whether the founder left of his own free will or was ousted in a power play by Colomby and Katz depends on whom you ask. The bottom line is that Kooper was out, and Colomby was now calling the shots. Trumpeters Jerry Weiss and Randy Brecker left soon thereafter to pursue other projects, and Chuck Winfield and Lew Soloff replaced them. Such lineup changes would soon become the norm.

With Colomby and Katz assuming creative control, the group began the search for a new vocalist. Among those considered were a post–Buffalo Springfield, pre-CSN Stephen Stills; Alex Chilton, formerly of the

Led by Al Kooper, the original Blood, Sweat, and Tears made its debut with
Child Is Father to the Man in February 1968. The clever cover art features
the band members holding miniature, child-sized versions of themselves.

Box Tops; and the gifted singer/songwriter Laura Nyro. They were all very
different types of artists, but none of them quite fit the bill. Blood, Sweat,
and Tears' was a big sound, and it required someone with a big voice, and
a swaggering stage presence.

Enter Canadian David Clayton-Thomas, upon the recommendation
of Judy Collins, a woman who knew a thing or two about singing and
performing. Colomby and Katz went to see Clayton-Thomas perform, and
afterward they offered him the job. He accepted.

Clayton-Thomas's big voice was more than replacement enough for
Kooper's *vocal* instrument, but he could not replace Kooper's legendary
keyboards. Halligan stepped up to the plate and made the lateral move,
taking over keyboard duties and bringing in Jerry Hyman as the new
trombonist.

The revamped nine-piece was a force to be reckoned with. The group
was back at its old stomping grounds, Café Au Go Go, in time for summer

1968, right around the time Kooper was putting the finishing touches on *Super Session*, his studio album with Mike Bloomfield and Stephen Stills.

By the fall, the "new" Blood, Sweat, and Tears was road-tested and ready to record. On October 7, the musicians entered the state-of-the-art CBS studios, where they struck gold with the new 16-track recording technology. In just over two weeks, they laid down the tracks for what would prove to be the high-water mark of their career, *Blood, Sweat, and Tears*.

Working with producer James William Guercio—who also produced Blood, Sweat and Tears' Midwestern rivals, the Chicago Transit Authority (later, Chicago)—the group found the perfect sound. The psychedelic undertones and free-form improvisational feel of Kooper's vision were gone as the band took their big sound in a more pop-oriented direction, which paid off in more ways than one.

Released on December 11, 1968, *Blood, Sweat, and Tears* would go on to hold the #1 spot on *Billboard* for nearly two months, making it the biggest album of 1969. And the singles were another success story. Like

This second iteration of Blood, Sweat, and Tears, featuring the swaggering David Clayton-Thomas on lead vocals, bore little resemblance to the original band but was far more commercially viable. The group's self-titled sophomore album hit #1 on the *Billboard* charts.

Creedence Clearwater Revival, the band couldn't seem to get past the #2 spot, but *three* #2 hits from one album is nothing to sneeze at.

The first single, a cover of Brenda Holloway's 1967 hit "You've Made Me So Very Happy" b/w "Blues—Part II" hit #2 on the charts in March 1969, and was all over the radio dial as the festival approached. Likewise "Spinning Wheel," the second single, released in June. An infectious David Clayton-Thomas–penned original, backed with "More and More," it topped out at #2 on the *Billboard* Pop chart, #45 on the US R&B chart, and—for whatever it is worth—#1 on the Easy Listening chart.

As a result of this crossover appeal, the band was all over the AM and FM radio dials heading into the festival, and the album and singles were flying off the shelves. Things were still going the band's way that Sunday night in Bethel. As Bobby Colomby said, they drove right into the site and were ready to play.

In the Garden: Roll 'Em . . . and, Cut!"

Taking the stage at 1:30 a.m., a mere twenty-five minutes after Johnny Winter took his final bow, the nine-member Blood, Sweat, and Tears must have appeared like some sort of giant traveling circus in comparison: Bobby Colomby on drums, Jim Fielder on bass, Steve Katz on guitar, har-monica and backing vocals, Dick Halligan on keyboards, trombone and flute, Jerry Hyman on the trombone, Fred Lipsius on alto sax and piano, Lew Soloff and Chuck Winfield on trumpet and flugelhorn, and, last but not least, David Clayton-Thomas on guitar and lead vocals.

Chip Monck did the honors: "Ladies and gentlemen, please welcome with us, Blood, Sweat and Tears!" The hottest band in the land launched into "More and More" as Wadleigh's cameras were rolling.

Clayton-Thomas was a spectacle to behold, an odd hybrid of 1950s Elvis Presley and 1970s Neil Diamond, in spite of the fact he wore no visible jewelry. He wore black leather pants with two belts—one in the traditional manner, the other slung across his hip at an angle—A fringed, black leather jacket, and a blue satin shirt that reflected every color of the stage lights, appearing by turns to be black, green, purple, and then blue once more. His hair, already receding at twenty-seven, was short by the standards of the time, and he wore thick, full sideburns.

With his burly physique, robust vocals, and exaggerated movements, Clayton-Thomas was a macho, swaggering, larger-than-life stage presence. But with the poor lighting conditions, his eight bandmates were rendered all but invisible. Only Fred Lipsius and David Colomby are fully visible on camera, but only briefly. The others lurk in the shadows, making their presence known only by the sound of their instruments.

There was at least one person present who thought the band should be even *less* visible. Manager Bennett Glotzer, in a fit of shortsightedness, ordered Michael Wadleigh's camera crews to *stop* filming shortly after the band hit the stage. Glotzer was of the mind that the band's appearance fee of $7,500 was not enough for them to "star" in a film. As a result, there is no video—or audio—of the second number, "Just One Smile." Most unfortunate.

The cameras were rolling once more for the third, fourth, and fifth tracks. The band played the fast-paced "Something's Coming On," before slowing things down to evoke the spirit of Al Kooper with the founder's bluesy and soulful "I Love You More Than You'll Ever Know."

With the audience lulled into a bluesy groove, it was time to whip out a hit. "Spinning Wheel" wove its funky magic on the appreciative crowd, the perplexing lyrics evoking, by turns, a carousel, a roulette wheel, a kaleidoscope, and even the paddle wheel of an old steam-powered riverboat. Even Clayton-Thomas couldn't help but chuckle audibly at song's end.

The film crew was hiding toward the back of the stage, behind Colomby's drums, and filming the proceedings through a zoom lens. The visual results are less than stellar. No matter, as it was the last song they filmed. Research suggests that no viable recordings exist of the sixth through tenth songs.

With the cameras off, the group launched in "Sometimes in Winter," a Steve Katz love ballad that featured the co-founder on lead vocals. The song had already been earmarked as the B-side of a forthcoming single. Sticking with the new album, Clayton-Thomas came swaggering back to center stage for the bombastic and funky "Smiling Phases."

Demonstrating a masterful command of pacing, the group switched gears for the slow and bluesy beginning of the 1942 Billie Holiday single, "God Bless the Child." In BST's hands, the song picks up the pace for a jazzy jam halfway through before coming in for a nice, soulful landing; a sexy tune, even with the cryptic biblical references. The soul train rolled on with a cover of Jerry Butler's "I Stand Accused," before BST brought the set to a foot-stomping conclusion with Laura Nyro's oddly upbeat and spiritual "And When I Die."

The encore could only be one song. The group returned to the stage to send the audience off with its smash single version of the Motown classic, "You've Made Me So Very Happy." Someone had the presence of mind to capture the audio of this moment—a fitting end to a perfect one-hour set.

The audience roared its approval as the clock struck 2:30 a.m. They would soon bear witness to one of the defining moments of rock history, as members of three legendary bands joined forces to create something entirely new: Crosby, Stills, Nash, and Young.

The Harvest Reaped: "What Goes Up . . . "

In October, *Blood, Sweat, and Tears* yielded its third and final #2 single, the Laura Nyro–penned "And When I Die" b/w Steve Katz's "Sometimes in Winter." The strength of *Blood, Sweat, and Tears* and its surging singles sustained the band throughout the fall of '69 and the winter of '70.

At the 1970 Grammy Awards on March 11, Blood, Sweat, and Tears' self-titled second album beat out the Beatles' *Abbey Road* for "Album of the Year." It was an intense moment for Bobby Colomby, who recalled to Jeremiah Rickert, "I remember when I got the Grammy, *Abbey Road* was out at the same time, and as soon as I was handed the Grammy, I kept looking. There's got to be a Beatle somewhere I can give this to. I feel guilty. This is ridiculous!"

The momentum the band members had gained was theirs to lose, and lose it they did. What better way to turn off the counterculture than participating in a government sponsored tour? Yet, that's just what BST did when the State Department sponsored the band on a European jaunt during May and June 1970. Whatever street credibility the group had gained by playing Woodstock went right out the window, and album sales began to reflect the change.

That third album featured the Woodstock lineup, Bobby Colomby co-producing with Roy Halee, and bore the bland title *Blood, Sweat, and Tears 3*. The album features just three originals: Clayton-Thomas's almost comically bombastic "Lucretia MacEvil," which only hit #29 on the Pop Singles chart; Halligan and Katz's pseudo-prog-rock snooze "The Battle"; and "Lucretia's Reprise," a funky screamer of a song that sounds like watered down Wilson Picket and is credited to the band as a whole.

The pick of the litter here is the opening track, a soulful cover of Carole King's "Hi-De-Ho," which hit #14 on the *Billboard* Pop Singles chart. The tepid cover of James Taylor's "Fire and Rain" just seems unnecessary. Halligan's arrangement of "Symphony for the Devil / Sympathy for the Devil"—both a reimagining and a classical take on the Rolling Stones song—is certainly ambitious, perhaps even ahead of its time, but it went over the heads of too many listeners.

No matter how clever or complex the group's arrangements may have been, the lack of original songs made *Blood, Sweat, and Tears 3* fair game for criticism. It's an album that lacks a clear sense of identity, and soon enough the band would begin to lose its sense of identity, too. BST played at Caesar's Palace in Las Vegas, and then branched out into film soundtrack work, further eroding its credibility with the counterculture crowd. The band responded to criticism about a lack of original material by releasing *Blood, Sweat, and Tears 4* in June 1971 . . . without Jerry Hyman, who bailed out and was replaced by multi-instrumentalist David Bargeron.

By the end of the year, the band members were hopelessly divided as to their future direction, and as 1972 dawned, the floodgates opened. Clayton-Thomas decided to go solo, and Halligan and Lipsius followed him out the door. Arguably, the band was now Blood, Sweat, and Tears in name only; and so it has remained for the past forty-five years and counting.

To chart the band's history from 1972 forward would require a level of scholarship and detail that would take us far beyond the scope of the current project. Suffice it to say that BST became a revolving door for musicians, and has been home to more than *140* different members to date. Among the boldface names who have played in these configurations of BST are the legendary bassist Jaco Pastorius, Tom "Bones" Malone and "Blue" Lou Marini of *Blues Brothers* fame, as well as the current lead vocalist, Bo Bice . . . yes, the guy who lost out to Carrie Underwood on season four of *American Idol.*

Bobby Colomby retains the rights to the band's name and still calls all the shots, though he hasn't played with BST since 1977. As of press time, Blood, Sweat, and Tears continue to tour, despite not having released any new material since 1980. They are booked through the end of 2019 with shows in Florida, Texas, Oklahoma, and Pennsylvania, Missouri, Indiana, and across the pond in Norway. They have evolved—some might say devolved—into their own tribute band.

30

Crosby, Stills, Nash, and Young

Not Bad for a "Second Gig"

Everyone we respected in the whole goddamn music business was standing in a circle behind us when we went on. Everybody was curious about us. We were the new kid on the block. It was our second public gig. Nobody had ever seen us. Everybody had heard the record. Everybody wondered, "What in the hell are they about?" So when it was rumored that we were about to go on, everybody came. Every band that played there, including all the ones that aren't in the movie, were all standing in an arc behind us, and that was intimidating, to say the least. I'm looking back at Hendrix and Robbie Robertson and Levon Helm and Janis and Sly and Grace and Paul, everybody that I knew and everybody I didn't know. We were so happy it went down well that we could barely handle it.

—*David Crosby,* Long Time Gone

As the Seeds Were Sown: Buffaloes, Byrds, and Hollies

Though many consider Cream to have been the first "supergroup," an argument can be made that Crosby, Stills, Nash, and Young is a better example, because all of the members had been part of high-profile acts before.

Where the Buffalo Springfield Roam

Richie Furay and Stephen Stills were members of a band called the Au Go Go Singers during the mid-'60s. Stills moved on to a band called the Company. During a 1965 tour of Ontario, he met Neil Young, who was with a group called the Squires. The Company went belly up soon thereafter, and Stills returned to California, inviting Richie Furay to join him.

Rick "Super Freak" James was in Canada during 1966, singing lead for a band called the Mynah Birds . . . while AWOL from his post in the United States Navy. The Mynah Birds' bass player, Bruce Palmer, recruited Neil Young to be the lead guitarist. James's presence was enough to land the group a deal with Motown. That deal, in turn, alerted the navy to James's whereabouts, and he was promptly arrested. So much for the Motown deal.

These circumstances put Neil and Bruce on a collision course with Stephen and Richie, as the two Canadians packed their bags for Los Angeles. They were driving along Sunset Boulevard when they spotted someone driving a hearse. There was only *one* guy Stephen had ever known who would drive a hearse for recreational purposes. Sure enough, it was Neil Young, with Bruce Palmer riding shotgun.

The foursome had the makings of a band, but they needed a drummer. At the suggestion of Jim Dickson, the Byrds' manager, they hired Dewey Martin. The band took its name from the Buffalo Springfield Roller Company, which manufactured steamrollers. Why? Evidently there was one parked outside the house where the band convened . . . which is not the worst band-naming story, actually.

The Byrds' Chris Hillman helped land the quartet a regular gig at the Whisky a Go Go, where they debuted on April 11, 1966. Within two months they were road-tested and ready to record. They landed a deal with Atlantic Records.

Buffalo Springfield—a debut so nice they released it *twice*, on December 5, 1966, and March 6, 1967—features the Neil classic "Burned" and Stephen's "Pay the Price." The March 6 version added the band's hit single, "For What It's Worth (Stop, Hey, What's That Sound?)." The album may not have been a smash, but the single hit #7 and put Buffalo Springfield on the map.

Neil Young and Stephen Stills had a history together, as members of the Buffalo Springfield.

Meanwhile, Palmer had been busted for possession of marijuana and deported. Neil and Stephen began butting heads, allowing Richie an opportunity to get a few tracks of his own on the next album. Palmer returned, only to find that *Neil* had left for a spell.

The Byrds' David Crosby pinch-hit for Neil when the Buffalo Springfield played the Monterey Pop Festival on Sunday, June 18, 1967— the first time Crosby and Stills sang together in public. The group's sophomore effort, *Buffalo Springfield Again*, released in November '67 and produced by Ahmet Ertegün, cracked the Top 50 and is considered one of the greatest albums of all time. The most recognizable tracks are the Neil classics, "Mr. Soul," "Expecting to Fly," and "Broken Arrow."

When Palmer was deported *again*, Jim Messina took over on bass. Buffalo Springfield played its final gig at Long Beach Arena on May 5, 1968, and then approached Ertegün to negotiate an amicable divorce. Neil signed with Warner Bros; Stephen and Richie stayed with Atlantic; Jim and Richie then put the finishing touches on *Last Time Around*, which hit the shelves on July 30, 1968.

Once again it was the Neil tracks, "On the Way Home," and "I Am a Child," that stood out. *Last Time Around* hit #42 on *Billboard*—the group's highest chart position ever—but by that point it was over. Richie and Jim formed Poco, while Jim would later join forces with Kenny Loggins as Loggins and Messina.

This Jet Set Is for the Byrds

Chicago native Jim McGuinn was a folk singer, banjo player, and guitarist. He had been a member of the Limeliters, the Chad Mitchell Trio, and Bobby Darin's band, and had also been a session musician. He began covering Beatles tunes in his solo act, which led him to meet and bond with Gene Clark.

Missourian Clark, a veteran of the Surf Riders, joined the New Christy Minstrels in August 1963. When he heard the Beatles, he quit the band, split for Los Angeles, and found himself at the Troubadour club, where he met and formed a duo with McGuinn. One day, Clark and McGuinn met Los Angeles native David Crosby.

Crosby had performed as a folk singer in Greenwich Village, been a part of Les Baxter's Balladeers, and had even recorded studio tracks as early as 1963. Crosby joined forces with McGuinn and Clark to form the Jet Set, and his representative, Jim Dickson, became their manager.

Dickson wanted to cash in on the "British Invasion," so he brought in eighteen-year-old Michael Clarke, a novice drummer who resembled Rolling Stone Brian Jones. But when it came time to record a single, "Please Let Me Love You," he opted to use session musicians. Dickson re-christened them the Beefeaters, evoking images of Britain . . . and gin. No matter. The single went nowhere.

Dickson had a hunch that the three skilled vocalists could do wonders with an unreleased Dylan tune, "Mr. Tambourine Man." With his connections and Dylan's blessing, they came up with a rock-and-roll arrangement. The results delighted Dylan and boosted the band's confidence.

Around this time, McGuinn saw the Beatles movie *A Hard Day's Night*, and his eyes fell upon George Harrison's guitar, the second prototype of the Rickenbacker 360/12. McGuinn was intrigued and acquired the next available model of Rickenbacker twelve-string.

Chris Hillman, the last to join, was a mandolin player with the Scottsville Squirrel Barkers, the Hillmen, and the Green Grass Revival. The nineteen-year-old Hillman joined the Jet Set in October of 1964 as a bass player . . . though he had never played bass before. With Crosby taking over rhythm guitar duties (leaving Clark to play tambourine), all of the pieces were in place.

Dickson, with a verbal assist from Miles Davis, landed the band a deal with Columbia Records in November. The group changed its name to the Byrds, which was similarly flight-related but more organic-sounding than the Jet Set. The Beatles' influence is evident in the alternate spelling—an affectation that would become a rock tradition.

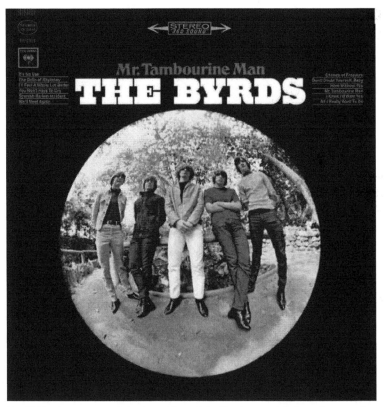

David Crosby was an original member of the Byrds, a multitalented group that also featured Jim "Roger" McGuinn and Gene Clark. In October of 1967, McGuinn fired Crosby, who then bought the *Mayan* and (quite literally) sailed off in a whole new musical direction.

When the Byrds recorded "Mr. Tambourine Man," producer Terry Melcher employed the session musicians who would come to be known as the Wrecking Crew (Leon Russell on keys, Larry Knechtel on bass, Jerry Cole on guitar, and Hal Blaine on the drums) to showcase McGuinn, Clark, and Crosby's vocals, alongside McGuinn's signature guitar. Within a few months, the others improved to the point where Melcher deemed them able to contribute instrumentally to the rest of the album.

By the time "Mr. Tambourine Man" was released, on April 12, 1965, the Byrds enjoyed an enthusiastic following. The single hit #1 just as the album, *Mr. Tambourine Man*, hit the shelves on June 21. The band became a pop phenomenon, with Gene Clark writing the bulk of the original material.

Turn! Turn! Turn! hit the shelves on December 6 and reached #17, with McGuinn and Crosby contributing to the songwriting. The single "Eight Miles High" (March 14, 1966) was banned from some radio stations for its "drug imagery" (though it is really about an airplane ride). In a cruel irony, Clark suffered from an anxiety disorder and was *terrified* of flying, which is mandatory for an international rock star. He quit the band before the single was released and began "flying" solo.

Now a quartet, the Byrds released a third album, *Fifth Dimension*, in July 1966, with Chris picking up some of the vocal slack. One noteworthy track is McGuinn's "Mr. Spaceman," a playful musing about an extraterrestrial "close encounter." The album only hit #24, which some critics blamed on Clark's departure.

With popularity waning and band members butting heads, the Byrds reconvened at year's end to record *Younger Than Yesterday*. Released on February 6, 1967, the album was Chris Hillman's coming-out party as a songwriter and singer. Even with the stellar opener, "So You Want to Be a Rock and Roll Star," it only hit #24, though it has grown in critical stature in the decades since. Jim McGuinn officially changed his name to *Roger* McGuinn that spring (for religious reasons . . . it's a *long* story).

As recording sessions for the Byrds' fifth album began, things turned ugly. Clarke quit. McGuinn and Hillman fired Crosby, and Clark returned . . . for three weeks. When *The Notorious Byrd Brothers* was released on January 15, 1968, Crosby was long gone.

To Crosby's chagrin, McGuinn kept the Byrds going with a revolving lineup, releasing *Sweetheart of the Rodeo* (August 1968), *Dr. Byrds and Mr. Hyde* (March 1969); *Ballad of Easy Rider* (November 1969), *Untitled* (September 1970), *Byrdmaniax* (June 1971), and *Farther Along* (November 1971). McGuinn, Crosby, Clark, Clarke, and Hillman would reunite to record 1973's *Byrds*. Afterward, the Byrds disbanded.

The Hollies

Like many who grew up during the 1950s, English teen Graham Nash was turned on by the harmonies of the Everly Brothers. He and his buddy Alan Clarke began singing, billing themselves as Ricky and Dane Young. They ditched the phony brother routine to join a Manchester band called

The Hollies' 1964 debut, *Stay with the Hollies*. Graham Nash did just that, at least until December 1968, when he left the group with the idea of staying home to be a songwriter. But life had other plans.

the Deltas, and in December 1962 renamed themselves the Hollies, in honor of late legend Buddy Holly . . . *and* the Christmas plant. The original lineup featured Graham and Alan, guitarist Vic Steele, drummer Don Rathbone, and bass player Eric Haydock.

A January 1963 gig at Liverpool's Cavern Club landed the Hollies a deal with Parlophone Records. Steele quit, and multi-instrumentalist Tony Hicks took over. The Hollies' cover of the Coasters' "(Ain't That) Just Like Me" hit #24 on the UK charts. Rathbone was gone by August, and Bobby Elliot took over on drums.

After another Coasters cover, "Searchin'," and a rockin' cover of Maurice Williams and the Zodiacs' "Stay," *Stay with the Hollies* (*Here I Go Again* for the US Imperial Records release) debuted on New Year's Day 1964, and promptly hit #2 in the UK. With its matching suits and hip hairstyles, the group was obviously trying to capture some of that Beatles mojo.

The sophomore album, *In the Hollies Style* (November 1964) featured seven originals credited to a pseudonym, "L. Ransford" (Graham's maternal grandfather). It did not sell well, and was not released in the US. Album three, *Hollies* (*Hear! Hear!* in the US) was a Top 10 hit in the UK, but did not chart in the US, despite the fact that the US version contained Graham Gouldman's "Look Through Any Window," which had cracked the US Top 40 as a single.

The pattern continued with the fourth album, *Would You Believe?* (*Beat Group* in the US). It was a Top 10 hit in the UK but didn't even crack the Top 100 in the US. Around this time, problems arose with Haydock. Bernie Calvert took over bass duties, and the group recorded Gouldman's "Bus Stop," which proved to be a winning formula. The single hit #5 on *both* sides of the pond in June 1966.

The Hollies realized a childhood dream when they got to serve—along with Jimmy Page, John Paul Jones, and Reginald "Elton John" Dwight—as the studio band and principal songwriters (as "L. Ransford") on the Everly Brothers' *Two Yanks in England* (July 1966). They stopped using the pseudonym for album number five, *For Certain Because* (*Stop! Stop! Stop!* in the US, October 1966), which featured originals only.

In May 1967, using singer Marianne Faithfull as a muse, the Hollies released "Carrie Anne," which became a Top 10 single and the opening track on the US version of album number five, *Evolution* (June 1967). The title prophesied Nash's desire to grow and expand as an artist. This led to his sole songwriting credit on "King Midas in Reverse," a single that did *not* have the "golden touch" in terms of sales.

In November 1967, with Graham leading the way, the group released *Butterfly* (*Dear Eloise / King Midas in Reverse* in the US). Conflict ensued, the gist of it that Nash wanted the Hollies to evolve in a more experimental, psychedelic direction, while Clarke and Hicks felt they did better with pop songs. They balked at Nash's next single, "Marrakesh Express," telling him they wanted to do an album of Dylan covers instead. Nash *hated* that idea but contributed vocals to "Blowin' in the Wind."

Nash's final studio work with the band was the single "Listen to Me." Since no one *was* (listening to him, that is), Nash played his final gig with the group at the London Palladium on December 8, 1968. He headed for California, expecting to live out his days as a songwriter. The Hollies, the band he had co-founded, would continue without him.

Crosspollination

One of the first things David Crosby did after being kicked out of the Byrds was to borrow $25,000 from the Monkees' Peter Tork, travel to Fort Lauderdale, Florida, and purchase the *Mayan*, a fifty-nine-foot mahogany schooner built in 1947. He spent most of that year learning to sail it, and eventually sailed home to San Francisco. The *Mayan* would play an important role in many of his future band's greatest hits. Crosby had been hanging out with Stephen Stills since March of '68, when they both attended a party at Mama Cass Elliot's house.

Nash, meanwhile, had met Crosby during the Byrds' 1966 tour of the UK, and the two became friendly. He was still a member of the Hollies in July 1968 when, during a party at folk singer Joni Mitchell's house (or Cass Elliot's house, according to Stills), he joined a jam with Crosby and Stills on Still's song "You Don't Have to Cry." It was not lost upon the three veteran performers that the sound of their voices blended in three-part harmony was magic.

When Nash returned at year's end, the trio reconvened to seek a record deal. The Beatles' Apple Records turned them down, so they turned to

Crosby, Stills, and Nash was released in May of 1969, but because it took so long to get a touring band together, the Woodstock festival wound up becoming the super-group's second-ever live performance; moreover, by that point they had added a *Y*, in the form of Neil Young.

Ahmet Ertügün at Atlantic. As Pete Fornatale described it in *Back to the Garden*:

The very existence of CSN was due, in part, to something akin to a Major League Baseball trade. Crosby was a free agent, thanks to his dismissal from the Byrds. Stills was under contract to Atlantic Records from his time as a member of Buffalo Springfield. And Nash was under contract to Epic Records from his days as a member of the British rock band the Hollies. The question on the table was, "How do you spring Nash from Epic to join Crosby and Stills at Atlantic?" Simple. Fellow Springfield alumnus Richie Furay had already formed his own new band, Poco, and Epic was interested. Solution? Atlantic traded Furay for Nash, and two great new groups put out stunning debut albums in 1969.

Recording sessions took place during February and March 1969, with Stills playing all of the instruments, with the exception of the drums, which were manned by Dallas Taylor. Released on May 29, *Crosby, Stills, and Nash* features Graham's Hollies holdover "Marrakesh Express," and Stills's Judy Collins homage "Suite: Judy Blue Eyes." It proved to be a winning formula. The album would stay on the *Billboard* charts for over three and a half months, peaking at #6, and was eventually certified quadruple platinum.

As an unintended consequence of Stephen's multitasking, Crosby, Stills, and Nash found themselves in need of a band, if they were ever going to take this show on the road. They retained Taylor as drummer, and Stills reached out to Steve Winwood to see if he wanted in as keyboard player. Steve was transitioning from Traffic to Blind Faith, though, so he declined. They gave Buffalo Springfield pal Bruce Palmer a shot as bass player, too, but he didn't work out.

Enter Greg Reeves, a young bassist from Motown, on the recommendation of none other than erstwhile navy deserter Rick James. Though Reeves claimed to be nineteen years old and to have graduated high school in 1968, he carried a phony driver's license (courtesy of James). Though it has never been verified, his birth date is listed in several sources as April 7, 1955, which would make him fourteen at the time of the festival—the youngest musician to perform there by three years and 359 days. Sorry, Henry Gross (see chapter 32).

Ahmet Ertegün had the best suggestion of all. Why not ask Neil Young? *He* played keyboards. Within weeks, Ertegün had structured a deal that would allow Neil the autonomy to pursue solo projects and work with Crazy Horse, while also becoming the official fourth member of the group.

With the stroke of a pen, Crosby, Stills, and Nash became Crosby, Stills, Nash, and Young, and now it was *definitely* time to take this show on the road. Their first gig was at the Auditorium Theatre in Chicago on August 16. The next one was scheduled for some dairy farm in upstate, New York. No pressure.

In the Garden: Acoustic and Electric

At 3:00 a.m., Graham Nash stood at center stage. Stills, seated to his left, and Crosby, to his right, had acoustic guitars and vocal mics. Chip Monck was late to the stage. Amid nervous chuckles, Stills addressed the crowd. "Hey man, I just gotta say that you people have gotta be the strongest bunch of people I ever saw . . . Three days, man! Three days! We just love ya . . . we just love ya. Tell them who we are."

Crosby chimed in, "They'll all know if you just sing. Hello . . . Test . . . forty-nine, sixty-five, hike!"

And then they were off and strumming into the opening bars of "Suite: Judy Blue Eyes." Chip, in the nick of time, made the introduction: "Ladies and gentlemen, please welcome Crosby, Stills, Nash, and Young." With Nash leaning over to share Crosby's vocal mic, they grew stronger and more confident as the song built to a crescendo, and the audience roared its approval. The band seemed relieved.

"Thank you!" said Crosby and Nash in unison. "Thank you, we needed that," said Stills. David added, "This is our second gig." Stephen agreed, "This is the second time we've ever played in front of people, man. We're scared shitless!" A mellow cover of the Beatles' "Blackbird" followed, and unfolded so perfectly that the band could barely contain their joy, with Nash and Stills slapping hands and yelling, "Yeah!" at the end.

Nash introduced the next number. "We'd like to do a Stephen Stills song, one of the best, I think, ever written. It's called 'Helplessly Hoping.'" Stephen, in a playful mood, chimed in, "Helplessly hoping, her helicopter hovers nearby!" But when they got down to business, the song was a thing of beauty.

The set turned serious with David Crosby's solemn and brooding "Guinevere," and nary a peep from the mesmerized audience. Afterward, when the applause subsided, Nash began, "We'd like do a . . . " before being interrupted. "What was that?" he asked. It was one of the crew, asking him to make an announcement: "Get off the projector, whoever's on the projector!" Nash picked up right where he left off. "We'd like to do a medley of our hit . . . " before turning to a yawning Stills. "You all right, lad? It's late at night. You've really been fantastic, waiting for all these people." Then they launched into Graham's "Marrakesh Express." The cheerful tune proved to be a timely change-of-pace.

Stephen was next in the rotation, as Nash announced, "Stephen's going to do a request, a special number for me. This one is a Stephen song. It's going to be on the next album. It's called '4+20.'"

After the tale of loneliness ended, it was the perfect time for Neil. He joined Stephen at center stage for a slow, acoustic jam on his "Mr. Soul," from their Buffalo Springfield days. Sadly, there are no known recordings of the next few songs. Bethel Woods Center for the Arts lists two, "I'm Wonderin'" and "Pre-Road Downs," while other sources list "Wonderin'," a Neil Young song that would not be released until his 1983 "Neil Young and the Shocking Pinks" phase, with the addition of "You Don't Have to Cry," as a lead-in to "Pre-Road Downs," both from *Crosby, Stills, and Nash*.

Tape was rolling again for Crosby's "Long Time Gone." Reeves and Taylor's bottom end, flavored with Neil's keyboards, really rounded out the sound. Stills was so enthusiastic about playing the protest song that he was practically *screaming* the lyrics, and Crosby followed suit. Stills's "Bluebird" came next, but was not recorded. Originally a duet with Richie Furay from *Buffalo Springfield Again*, the song would become a staple of Stills's solo sets.

Tape was rolling again as Nash announced, "We'd like to feature Neil Young now on organ on a song that Neil wrote. It's called 'The Sea of Madness.'" By Neil's often-melancholic standards, "Sea of Madness" is a buoyant, almost cheerful rock-and-roll song, which really allowed the band to let loose as Neil was in fine, strong voice. They closed with "Wooden Ships," a song Crosby had co-written with Stills and Paul Kantner aboard the *Mayan*. It was the second airing of the song that weekend (see chapter 23).

The first encore, the mantra-like "Find the Cost of Freedom," would become the group's go-to encore, but after a pointed "Goodnight" from Nash, a "God bless you" and a "Ladies and gentlemen, Crosby, Stills, Nash, and Young" from Chip, the crowd clamored for more. According to multiple sources, the group delivered. The second encore—though not preserved for posterity on tape—is reported to have been Stills's "49 Bye-Byes," the closing track from the debut album.

It was 4:00 a.m. as CSNY left the stage in triumph. The Paul Butterfield Blues Band waited backstage, but wouldn't take the stage until 6:00 a.m.

The Harvest Reaped: Harmonies Amid Disharmony.

With just two shows under their belts on the first leg of a thirty-nine-date world tour, the *first* order of business for CSNY was watching the rest of the festival, before driving down to New York City for a special Woodstock-themed episode of *The Dick Cavett Show*. Nash wasn't allowed to appear on camera due to visa restrictions, and Neil wanted no part in it, though Stephen and David are featured prominently in the episode. Jefferson Airplane was present and accounted for, and Joni Mitchell, too.

And then there were four. The quartet's debut with Neil Young, *Déjà Vu*, released in March 1970, hit #1 on the *Billboard* chart and #5 in the UK.

Regaling Joni with tales of the festival, David, Stephen, and Graham unwittingly set into motion forces beyond their control, inspiring Joni to write the song "Woodstock." With Geffen and Roberts behind the scenes, it was a foregone conclusion that CSNY would record a rock-and-roll arrangement of the song, which would become the side-one closer of their next album, *Déjà Vu*.

In a stroke of managerial genius, Geffen and Roberts made a deal with Warner Bros to feature the song, and CSNY (or at least *CSN*) prominently in the upcoming *Woodstock* film. Neil refused to appear in the film, and his appearance at Woodstock was essentially edited out of the public record.

The tour continued, taking the band to the Big Sur Folk Festival on September 13 and 14, where CNSY jammed with Dave Mason and Joni Mitchell; and to Altamont on December 6, where CSNY would be the last act to perform before the Rolling Stones. They wrapped up in January 1970 with European shows in London, Stockholm, and Copenhagen.

When *Déjà Vu* dropped in March 1970, it became a monster. The album would remain on the charts for nearly two years, and spawned a slew of hits: "Our House," "Teach Your Children," and, of course, the cover of Joni's "Woodstock," which played over the closing credits of the *Woodstock* film and made CSNY the definitive act of the festival in many people's minds.

But the quarrelsome quartet had already begun sparring, and the hired guns suffered the brunt. Stills fired Reeves, prompting Neil to *hire* the young bassist for his solo album, *After the Gold Rush*. Neil had his own problems with Taylor, and forced the drummer out of the group after the first night of the April tour. At one point, Stills's ego grew so insufferable that the other three even tried to oust *him*. CSNY made it through twenty-three shows and then broke up in July . . . the first of many breakups to come. The tumultuous tour yielded a live album, *4 Way Street*, but there would be no new CSNY activity until 1974.

Elliot Roberts finally corralled all four of them for a thirty-three-date, Bill Graham–led tour in 1974, hitting hockey arenas and stadiums coast-to-coast. The tour sold out, but when it was over, the four of them were as divided as ever. From the band's inception to this day, Crosby, Stills, Nash, and Young have all continued to create music, record albums, tour, and even write books, together and apart, as solos, duets, trios, foursomes, and side projects, circling in and out of one another's orbits as if they were a musical solar system. They have had a star on the Hollywood Walk of Fame since 1978, and were inducted into the Rock and Roll Hall of Fame (as a unit) in 1997. In between, they played at Live Aid, and saw Crosby survive prison time and assorted health issues, including a liver transplant.

After seven studio albums and three live albums as a quartet, they played at Neil Young's 2013 Bridge School Benefit. The 2014 release of the boxed set compilation, *CSNY 1974*, rekindled interest in the group, but true to form they have been at odds with one another ever since. But a thaw may be in the works. As recently as summer 2016, Neil Young and Nash both indicated that they might be open to yet another reunion. Here's to hoping, but not *helplessly*.

In the wake of the 2016 presidential election, murmurs of a reunion began. Young said he'd be open to the idea in January of 2017, and in April of that year, Nash discussed the potential for a reunion based on CSNY's history of sociopolitical activism. Crosby, too, would be open to the idea, though there has been nothing definitive planned as of press time.

31

The Paul Butterfield Blues Band

Harpin' on the Chicago Blues

We had played Chicago the night before. We were supposed to play around ten o'clock at night, so we got to the place around seven or eight and found a sea of bodies and a soup of mud. It turned out we were there all night. So we got to hear a lot of bands. We finally got to go onstage just as the sun was coming up. . . . I believe it was, up to that point, the largest gathering for a music event. I mean, you could see that something enormous was happening.

—*David Sanborn (alto saxophone, the Paul Butterfield Blues Band) to Brian McCoy,* Woodstock at 45

As the Seeds Were Sown: From the Baddest Part of Town

He may not have been born under a *bad* sign, exactly, but future blues legend Paul Vaughn Butterfield *was* born in Hyde Park, on the south side of Chicago, a legendarily rough-and-tumble part of town. Born in 1942, he came of age during the 1950s, a time when music—and the blues in particular—remained highly segregated along racial lines.

The Butterfields were upper-middle class. Paul's dad was an attorney, and his mom a painter. They sent Paul to a fancy prep school, the University of Chicago Laboratory Schools. There he pursued his love of music, and spent seven years studying with Walfrid Kujala, the first flautist of the Chicago Symphony. But all the while the blues kept calling to him.

Paul struck up a friendship with Nick Gravenites, an older musician who would go on to have a powerful influence on Janis Joplin. Paul traded in his flute for a harmonica ... or "harp," in the blues vernacular. A young, white musician crossing over into the historically black world of the Chicago blues, Butterfield, often with Gravenites by his side, found acceptance at many of the smoky clubs on the South Side. There he learned at the feet of a series of boldfaced names like Howlin' Wolf, Otis Rush, Little Walter, Buddy Guy, and even Muddy Waters. Paul and Nick, or "Nick and Paul," in accordance with their billing, landed a residency at a club up north in Old Town called Big John's, and worked all of the coffeehouses on the college circuit.

When Paul graduated prep school in 1960, he came to a life-defining crossroads. Would he follow his parents' wishes and accept that track-and-field scholarship to Brown, or would he walk his own path? A nagging knee injury provided him with the excuse he needed, but he met his folks halfway by enrolling at the University of Chicago. One of his classmates was up-and-coming guitarist Elvin Bishop, and the two bonded over music to the point where their studies fell by the wayside. Like many musicians of the era, they just weren't cut out for college life. Music, they believed, had much more to offer, so they dropped out and formed a band.

Next, Paul struck up a friendship with budding guitar virtuoso Mike Bloomfield and the two began to jam. Clubs like Big John's were the hunting grounds for promoters and talent scouts, and it wasn't long before Paul landed on the radar of another Paul: Paul Rothchild of Elektra Records.

The keen-eared Rothchild signed the Paul Butterfield Blues Band to a record deal. The original 1963 lineup featured Butterfield, Bishop, and two members of Howlin' Wolf's band (drummer Sam Lay and bassist Jerome Arnold), along with the last-minute addition of Mike Bloomfield on guitar and keyboards. It was Rothchild who played matchmaker, persuading Butterfield that Bloomfield should be a part of the band, and he was added to the fold during 1964.

Rothchild had a reputation for being demanding, but he brought out the best in his musicians. He wasn't satisfied with the band's December 1964 studio sessions, nor with subsequent concert recordings at New York's Café Au Go Go, so he pushed the musicians further in the studio until he got the results he wanted. He also booked them for the 1965 Newport Folk Festival, where worlds collided in ways he never envisioned.

Bob Dylan had just released his electric single, "Like a Rolling Stone," featuring Mike Bloomfield on guitar. When Dylan saw Mike with the Paul Butterfield Blues Band delivering an urban blues workshop on Saturday, he was reportedly annoyed by festival honcho Alan Lomax's dismissive attitude toward the band's electric music. In a burst of inspiration, Dylan decided *he* would play electric music that weekend, too. He deputized Mike, Sam, and Jerome from Paul's band to join Al Kooper and Barry Goldberg as his backing band. With just a few hours' rehearsal, Dylan played a short acoustic set, and then returned, wielding a Fender Stratocaster, with the band in tow.

That moment on Sunday night, July 25, 1965, when they launched into "Maggie's Farm," is considered one of the pivotal moments in rock history. Confusion reigned as the band soldiered on through "Like a Rolling Stone" and "Phantom Engineer" (later known as "It Takes a Lot to Laugh, It Takes a Train to Cry"). Though no consensus has ever been reached, it has been said that there were as many cheers as there were boos. Master of ceremonies Peter Yarrow had to coax Dylan back onstage for a two-song acoustic encore, "Mr. Tambourine Man" and "It's All Over Now, Baby Blue." That second encore was a message, as Dylan would not return to Newport for nearly forty years. But the ensuing controversy put the Paul Butterfield Blues Band on the map.

The group added organist Mark Naftalin to the lineup for the sessions that yielded its Mark Abramson/Paul Rothchild–produced debut, *The Paul Butterfield Blues Band* (September 1965). Opening with old pal Nick Gravenites's "Born in Chicago," the album features covers of Elmore James's "Shake Your Money-Maker," Muddy Waters' "Got My Mojo Working," and Junior Parker and Sam Phillips's "Mystery Train," as well as a few tentative originals. Though it only reached #123 on *Billboard*, the album was and remains influential.

Sam Lay took ill and became the first original member of the band to depart, so drummer Billy Davenport took over on skins for album number two. The band moved operations to legendary Chess studios in Chicago, with Rothchild and Abramson behind the boards once more. Released in July 1966, *East-West* outperformed the debut, reaching #65 on the charts. This sophomore effort blended traditional blues with covers of Robert Johnson's "Walkin' Blues," Muddy Waters's "Two Trains Running," Allen Toussaint's "Get Out of My Life Woman," and even an uncredited tune by future Monkee Mike Nesmith called "Mary, Mary." The band's sound was evolving beyond the strict orthodoxies of the Chicago blues to incorporate jazz elements and Eastern influences, as evidenced by the thirteen-minute Bloomfield–Gravenites title track.

Around this time, Bloomfield left, throwing in with Gravenites and Barry Goldberg to form a new group, the Electric Flag. The rhythm section of Jerome Arnold and Billy Davenport followed Bloomfield out the door. Bassist Bugsy Maugh and drummer Phillip Wilson stepped into their shoes, while Bishop became the lead guitarist. The incorporation of David Sanborn and Gene Dinwiddle on alto and tenor saxophones, and Keith Johnson on trumpet, added an intriguing layer as the band gravitated toward a more R&B/soul sound. On Saturday, June 17, 1967, both the Paul Butterfield Blues Band and the Electric Flag played at the Monterey International Pop Festival.

These marked shifts in the Paul Butterfield Blues Band's lineup and sound are inherent in the odd title of album number three, released in December 1967: *The Resurrection of Pigboy Crabshaw*. The album, which peaked at #52, was a step in the right direction commercially.

Adding Al Kooper to the lineup, the group continued in this same musical vein for 1968's *In My Own Dream*, but for whatever reason the album did not fare as well, peaking at #79. More lineup changes followed as Bishop left the band to go solo, followed by Naftalin. By 1969, the only recognizable thing about the Paul Butterfield Blues Band was Butterfield himself. The rest of the lineup had turned over, and the sound was now a heady fusion of jazz, blues, R&B, and soul, punctuated by Paul's signature harmonica stylings.

The title of the now twelve-member band's 1969 release seemed to reflect Paul's ethos: *Keep on Moving*. The album only made #102, but a

Keep on Moving, the Butterfield Blues Band's fifth studio release, hit the shelves in 1969, and provided material for that Monday-morning set list, including "Love March."

last-minute invitation to play the Woodstock festival would gain the band some renewed attention, even as its own lifecycle drew toward a close.

In the Garden: Last Man Standing

With the morning sun still eleven minutes away from the horizon at 6 a.m.,<6:00> a sleepy Chip Monck greeted the crowd. "Good morning. Very shortly we'll continue. Ladies and gentlemen, please warmly greet the Paul Butterfield Blues Band."

The ten-piece incarnation of the band that morning featured lone original member Paul on vocals and harp, twenty-year-old whiz-kid

Buzzy Feiten on guitar, Teddy Harris on piano, Rod Hicks on bass, Phillip Wilson on drums, and a robust horn section: Steve Madalo and Keith Johnson on trumpets, Trevor Lawrence on baritone saxophone, Gene Dinwiddie on tenor sax, and, last but not least, David Sanborn on alto sax.

There is no audio or visual record of the band's opening number, a cover of Booker T. Jones and William Bell's "Born Under a Bad Sign," though the remainder of the forty-five-minute set was captured in one format or another. The second song, "No Amount of Loving," hit the groggy and rapidly dwindling crowd with the force of a Mack truck. It was a big, raunchy, muscular sound. By song's end, the sun had fully cleared the horizon, revealing a grim and overcast Bethel sky.

In spite of Elvin Bishop's absence, the group continued with its own variation of the blues classic "Driftin' Blues," "Driftin' and Driftin'," from *The Resurrection of Pigboy Crabshaw*. The tune chugged along for nine hearty minutes, prominently featuring Paul's harp while making the point that Buzzy was a force to be reckoned with.

Next came the timely and appropriate "Morning Sunrise," a Butterfield original from *Keep on Moving* that would have sounded right at home during Blood, Sweat, and Tears' set. But while David Clayton-Thomas came across as swaggering and over-the-top, Butterfield came across as raw and intense, to the point of being intimidating.

The group stuck with the new album for "All in a Day," which led into the ten-minute-plus finale, "Love March." Paul began to address the crowd, "Hey, maybe we got a . . . *Whoo!*" and then punted to Dinwiddie. "I wanna let Gene tell ya about it, I'm gonna let Gene tell you about it. Go 'head."

Dinwiddie obliged, as he launched into what would prove to be a historic two-minute introductory rap. "Hey . . . hey, I got a little . . . a little somethin' I'd like to lay on you all . . . if you'll bear with me a minute, please. Uh, we gonna do a little march right along through now. It's a love march. We don't carry no guns and things in this army we got, and stuff. Don't nobody have to be worried about keepin' in step; we ain't even got no uniforms to wear; we a poor army and whatnot."

At this point, the audience began to respond with enthusiastic cheers and applause, as Dinwiddie continued, "But we run around . . . thank you . . . in order to keep our heads above the water and whatnot, we sing to one another, and we play to one another. And we try to make each other feel good. Okay, hep, two, three, four . . . ."

Here, Harris's piano and Wilson's drums started easing into a marching tune while Dinwiddie continued, "All of y'all out there, if you wasn't so tired we could all just get up and march 'round this whole area here and be happy and stuff." The horns joined in as he said, "Yeah, you brang little sister with ya, let her march, too. Everybody gonna march and have a good time."

The band was in full swing as the song rose, fell, and rose again in funky ebbs and flows, punctuated by Feiten's mesmerizing guitar, Hicks's pulsating bass, and Dinwiddie's vocals. As the song slowly unwound and came to a stop with a final, lingering note from Buzzy's guitar, Chip announced, "Ladies and gentlemen, the Paul Butterfield Blues Band."

The band gamely returned to the stage for an encore and unleashed a bruising rendition of Little Walter's 1959 hit "Everything's Gonna Be Alright," with Paul's menacing harp leading the way. The next nine minutes featured a full-blown, old school blues jam that gave all of the musicians an opportunity to shine.

It had been a robust forty-five minute set, and the remaining members of the audience were wide-awake and eager for more. But waiting in the wings was an act like unlike any they had ever seen: Sha Na Na.

The Harvest Reaped: Smacked Down

While the Woodstock festival helped launch many careers—particularly for those acts that went on to be featured in the film—it also bore witness to a number of endings. The festival may not have spelled the end of the Paul Butterfield Blues Band, but it arguably coincided with the band's high-water mark.

The first indication that things were winding down came during spring 1970, when the group recorded and released a double live album titled, simply, *Live*. In May, the band's festival performance of "Love March" appeared on side six of the three-record set *Woodstock: Music from the Original Soundtrack and More*.

The end came during 1971, just after the release of *Sometimes I Just Feel Like Smiling*. Elektra tried to cash in with the 1972 release of the obligatory greatest-hits collection: *Golden Butter: The Best of the Paul Butterfield Blues Band*. But by that point, Paul had relocated to Woodstock, and was beginning a new chapter of his life and career.

To trace the trajectory of *all* the band's members going forward would take us beyond the scope of the current project, so a couple of highlights will have to suffice. Alto sax player David Sanborn, an active musician since age fourteen, enjoyed a remarkable career post-Butterfield; with twenty-four albums and six Grammy Awards to his credit, he has played and recorded with dozens of the biggest names in the music business, and continues to tour and record.

The post-PBBB career trajectory of bandleader Paul Butterfield was not quite as glorious. The name of his next band, Better Days, proved to be wishful thinking. The group recorded just two studio albums, *Paul Butterfield's Better Days* and *It All Comes Back*, both for Albert Grossman's Bearsville Records, before breaking up.

In spite of the sunny title, the Butterfield Blues Band disbanded after 1971's *Sometimes I Just Feel Like Smiling*.

Paul's subsequent career consisted mainly of guest appearances with other artists. He was featured in the Band's *The Last Waltz*, and he continued playing with Rick Danko and Richard Manuel in the years after. His health during those years was not good. He suffered from intestinal inflammation (peritonitis), and the painful condition and frequent surgeries led to an overreliance on painkillers—a habit that devolved into full-blown heroin addiction.

The cruel irony is that Paul had never approved of the recreational use of hard drugs, yet he found himself dependent upon them. His final studio album was 1986's *The Legendary Paul Butterfield Rides Again*. But it would prove to be a short ride. Unable to shake his addiction, he overdosed on May 4, 1987, and was found dead in his Los Angeles apartment. He was just forty-four years old.

The Paul Butterfield Blues Band's contributions to Woodstock would be given greater recognition for the festival's fortieth anniversary during 2009, when the group was featured on the resulting CD and DVD releases. "No Amount of Loving," "Love March," and "Everything's Gonna Be Alright" are on the six-CD boxed set *Woodstock: 40 Years On: Back to Yasgur's Farm*, and "Morning Sunrise" is on the four-DVD set *Woodstock: 40th Anniversary Ultimate Collector's Edition*.

In the years since Paul Butterfield's untimely death, there have been a number of tributes, compilations, and posthumous releases, among them a double live album he recorded in 1973 with Better Days, *Live at Winterland Ballroom*. Collectively, these recordings remind us that this complex and often distant man possessed a unique and special talent. A virtuoso on harmonica, Butterfield was a musical pioneer who straddled racial barriers and helped to integrate the world of electric American blues. His harp style, though often imitated, has never been duplicated. His place in the pantheon of music history is secure, as it is unlikely we will see the likes of him again.

32

Sha Na Na

Nostalgic Novelty Act

So between Jimi's hooch and Jerry's hemp, I'm hallucinating so intensely that the rest of the day is this magnificent washing machine of images . . . Joe Cocker's blue boots with the white stars on them, a lake of naked ladies with breasts floating like life boats on a sea of love, Stephen Stills trying to get to the backstage area without a pass—the guard was not impressed—and backstage was an orgy of the most beautiful guitars surrounded by the *Daily News* headline: "Hippies Mired in Sea of Mud." All this and Crosby, Stills, Nash, and Young; Blood, Sweat, and Tears; Johnny Winter; and my buddy Alvin Lee and Ten Years After!

Well, we were waiting to go on . . . let's just say I'm damaged permanently from that afternoon. A buddy of mine who was in my first band in high school was actually a security guard there and he said, "Man, we spent the whole day with Jimi and Jerry hanging out backstage." And I said, "Oh yeah, I remember that." I was gone. I thought we'd never get on. I was a big fan of all those bands—and people started showing up, like Paul Butterfield, unannounced, and they put him right on, and I thought they'd never get to us. Finally, at seven in the morning on Monday morning, we went on.

—*Henry Gross (guitarist, Sha Na Na),*
Pete Fornatale Radio Archives, 2009

As the Seeds Were Sown: Columbia University Students "Get a Job"

In October 1957, a doo-wop group called the Silhouettes walked into Robinson Recording Laboratories in Philadelphia to lay down the tracks for "Get a Job." The quirky lyrics, penned by tenor Richard Lewis, were inspired by his mother's intolerance of his post-military slacker tendencies. She didn't want him lying around the house, so she told him to—you guessed it—"get a job." Decipherable among the song's vocalizations are the oft-repeated and undeniably catchy syllables, "Sha-na-na-na, sha-na-na-na-na."

The single hit the record stores and airwaves in November 1957, and by February it was #1 on *Billboard*'s Pop and R&B singles charts. "Get a Job" would go on to achieve television immortality when the Silhouettes performed it on *American Bandstand* and *The Dick Clark Show*. Later, it would inspire a whole new generation.

Fast-forward to 1969, a time when doo-wop was considered "oldies" music. The folk-music revival had happened, along with the British Invasion, and the birth of folk-rock, country-rock, and psychedelia. In the hallowed halls of Columbia University, a twelve-member choral group began performing, billed as the Kingsmen. The act was the brainchild of graduate student George Leonard, who served as the group's choreographer.

One night, the Kingsmen performed the Diamonds' doo-wop interpretation of the Gladiolas' 1957 R&B hit "Little Darlin'," and the audience went wild. George noted that audiences really seemed to respond to these old doo-wop songs, so that would become the group's focus. And if they were going to *sing* the part, they should also *look* the part. He got the group members to wear dark shades, Elvis Presley–esque gold lamé jumpsuits, and/or muscle shirts and leather jackets, and start greasing their hair back.

When they learned there was already another, more *successful* group called the Kingsmen (see the 1963 cover of Richard Berry's 1955 song "Louie, Louie," immortalized in the 1978 film *Animal House*), they changed their name to Sha Na Na, after the "lyrics" of "Get a Job."

The original Sha Na Na consisted of George's brother Robert A. Leonard (vocals), Alan Cooper (bass vocals), Bruce C. "Bruno" Clarke (bass guitar), David Garrett (vocals), Richard "Joff" Joffe, John "Jocko" Marcellino (drums, vocals), Joe Witkin (piano), Donald "Donny" York (vocals), Frederick "Denny" Greene (vocals), Elliot "Gino" Cahn (rhythm guitar), Scott "Captain Outrageous" or "Tony Santini" Powell (vocals), and, last but not least, freshman Henry Gross (lead guitar).

As the youngest, Henry would go on to embody at least a *partially* correct answer to a recurring Woodstock trivia question: who was the youngest person to perform at the festival? While many persist in the mistaken belief that it was Santana drummer Michael Shrieve—who *appears* to be about sixteen in the film—for many years conventional wisdom has held that Henry Gross, all of eighteen during that memorable Monday morning set, was the youngest. But there is an asterisk. That asterisk refers to Greg Reeves, bass player for CSNY, who claimed to be nineteen-years-old but in reality may have been *considerably* younger (see chapter 30).

It isn't entirely clear how Sha Na Na came to the attention of Woodstock Ventures, but Henry Gross has suggested that both Bill Graham and Jimi Hendrix were aware of the group, and were instrumental in their booking.

In the Garden: Rock and Roll Is Here . . . to *Stay*

Henry Gross and his bandmates spent the entirety of Sunday afternoon through Monday morning on call, hanging around the backstage area, waiting to go on. At last, with just one act remaining in the wings, they got the call.

At 7:30 a.m. Monday morning, those brave souls who remained beheld the bizarre spectacle of Sha Na Na running onto the stage. For most of the audience, this type of music may as well have been from the Paleozoic Era. Their *parents* had danced to this stuff at their high-school proms. Yet the preponderance of audiovisual evidence suggests that Sha Na Na quickly won the crowd over.

In a nod to its namesake, the group opened with the Silhouettes' "Get a Job." Judging by the puzzled expressions on certain faces in the crowd, some were wondering if they'd entered a time warp, or if they were suffering after-effects from the festival's much-maligned LSD. In some cases, the latter may well have been true, but no matter what condition they were in, the audience had just taken their first step on a trip down rock-and-roll memory lane. The remainder of Sha-Na-Na's half-hour set was filled with songs straight out of a late-1950s/early 1960s jukebox, including:

- The Del-Viking's #4 hit from 1957, "Come Go with Me"
- The Rays' 1957 #3 hit "Silhouettes"
- Mark Dinning's macabre 1959 #1 tragedy song "Teen Angel"
- Elvis Presley's (or Leiber and Stoller's) 1957 #1 smash "Jailhouse Rock"
- The Surfaris' 1963 #2 hit "Wipe Out" (a catchy if repetitive surf-music staple that would become a standard first guitar lesson for many a budding rock-and-roller)
- A Marcels-inspired, doo-wop version of Richard Rodgers and Lorenz Hart's 1934 song "Blue Moon" (ancient by pop-music standards, but an undeniable blueprint for 1950s-style rock and roll)
- The Monotones' 1958 #5 hit "(Who Wrote) The Book of Love."
- The Diamonds' #2 hit version of "Little Darlin'" (the song that launched their career)
- Danny and the Juniors' 1958 #1 hit "At the Hop," which would be featured in the *Woodstock* film
- Gene Chandler's 1962 #1 hit "Duke of Earl"
- And, finally, a reprise of "Get a Job," as the group left the stage to enthusiastic cheers and applause.

Each of these songs was delivered with equal parts reverence, skill, and over-the-top bravado and showmanship, and the audience clearly enjoyed it.

After Sha Na Na's set, Henry Gross settled in to watch the final act of the weekend, the guitar god who had—at least according to Henry's recollection—gotten him drunk on Jack Daniels the day before: Jimi Hendrix. As he did so, Henry had an epiphany:

A lot of things went through my mind that I do remember. I just remember being amazed and really feeling that something had gone right finally. But I also do remember, it was a real gut feeling.

It was very strange, watching Jimi play when he went on may have been the moment when I knew I was leaving Sha Na Na. I'm pretty sure of that, because I wanted to do *that* more than I wanted to . . . Sha Na Na was changing, even from the very beginning. You just got the feeling you couldn't really grow with it because it was going to be locked into doing songs you didn't write. It was more like being in a Broadway show . . . you were an actor in a play. Didn't matter that I was in Sha Na Na. The fact that I played well and sang well didn't matter. Anyone could have done it that was a good singer and good guitar player.

The Harvest Reaped: Ready for Prime Time

Henry Gross split from Sha Na Na in 1970 to become a studio musician. Odds are good that you've heard his work. That's Henry playing lead guitar on Jim Croce's celebrated 1973 album *I've Got a Name*. Other examples abound. Henry was right about the band . . . and his premonition about a "Broadway play." His departure set the tone for a revolving roster of Sha Na Na members who were prepared to take the world by storm.

The band participated in 1970's Festival Express train tour of Canada, though its work there wouldn't see the light of day until the film's release in 2003. When *Woodstock* hit theaters, Sha Na Na appeared on screen for less than two minutes, but that was enough to cement the group in the public's consciousness and keep things going. The band's festival and film appearances were the ripple that launched a wave of 1950s nostalgia that led to the play/film *Grease*, the film *American Graffiti*, and the beloved TV series *Happy Days*.

Grease was the first, and most successful, of these nostalgic cultural touchstones. Playwrights Jim Jacobs and Warren Casey first brought 1959 Chicago and the students of Rydell High School to life in a raw-boned and raunchy stage production in the Windy City. Opening off Broadway in a toned-down and sanitized form in February 1972, *Grease* finally landed *on* Broadway, at the Broadhurst Theatre, in June, and then went on to the Royale Theatre and ultimately the Majestic Theatre.

As if on cue, TV honcho Garry Marshall developed a 1950s-themed sitcom, *Happy Days*. The show featured all-American boy Ron Howard, from *The Andy Griffith Show*, and made a star out of Henry Winkler, who played token greaser Arthur "The Fonz" Fonzarelli. But the path to the small screen wasn't that smooth. The pilot for the show was in the can by 1972, and, though it was rejected at the time, it led to the Academy Award–nominated film *American Graffiti*. Due to the blowback effect, the hit film breathed new life into the dormant *Happy Days* project, and the TV show launched into its decade-long, 255-episode run in January 1974, spawning hit spinoffs like *Laverne and Shirley* and *Mork and Mindy*, and lower-quality fare like *Joanie Loves Chachi*.

In the midst of that first historic Broadway run of *Grease*, and the cultural phenomenon of *Happy Days*, Sha Na Na parlayed the wave of 1950s nostalgia the group had helped create into a television variety/

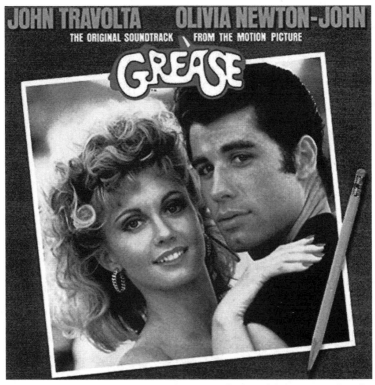

Olivia Newton-John and John Travolta garnered most of the attention, but if it weren't for Sha Na Na, there would have been no *Grease*. The soundtrack album features the band on six tracks.

comedy series of its own. By this point, the band's lineup bore little resemblance to the Woodstock-era Sha Na Na, and it would continue to evolve throughout the show's 1977–1981 run. An outrageous new star, bass vocalist John "Bowser" Bauman, emerged after Woodstock and became a fan favorite. Other TV series originals included Lenny Baker on sax, Danny "Dirty Dan" McBride, Johnny Contardo on vocals, Dave "Chico" Ryan on bass, Frederick "Dennis" Greene, and "Screamin'" Scott Simon on piano. These newer faces joined founding members John "Jocko" Marcellino on drums, Scott "Santini" Powell, and Donald "Donny" York on vocals and keyboards.

A typical episode of *Sha Na Na* featured opening and closing musical numbers, with comedy sketches, satirical songs, and musical guest appearances in between. The most memorable fixture in the supporting cast was the Lady in the Window (Jane Dulo), a disapproving and nosy neighbor who leaned out of her apartment window and hurled sarcastic remarks at the greasers' antics. At the end of each episode, the band would line up onstage. Bowser would say, "Goodnight! Grease for peace," as the group launched into the Spaniels' 1954 hit "Goodnight Sweetheart."

Just as *Sha Na Na* hit the small screen, Sha Na Na was poised to appear on the *big* screen, in the 1978 film adaptation of *Grease*, as—what else—a doo-wop group, Johnny Casino and the Gamblers. In a break with Sha Na Na's traditional practice, the film soundtrack afforded "Screamin'" Scott Simon the opportunity to earn a songwriting credit, for co-writing the original song "Sandy."

Sha Na Na also got to air out its signature song (albeit *without* the original, profane intro, "We just got one thing to say to you fuckin' hippies"), Danny and the Juniors' "Rock and Roll Is Here to Stay," the Imperials' "Tears on My Pillow," Rodgers and Hart's "Blue Moon," and, of course, one by the King himself, Elvis Presley's "Hound Dog."

Inevitably, the Sha Na Na–inspired wave of 1950s nostalgia crested and broke upon the shores of popular culture, but other waves would follow. *Grease* ended its initial Broadway run on April 13, 1980. The curtain fell on *Sha Na Na*, just shy of one hundred episodes, in 1981. *Happy Days* inspired the phrase "jumping the shark," after a September 1977 episode in which a water-skiing and leather-jacketed Fonzie

From the hallowed halls of Columbia University arose the culturally inevitable: the world's first novelty/nostalgia act, Sha Na Na. The title *Rock and Roll Is Here to Stay* has proven oddly prophetic.

jumps—literally—over a penned shark—and was canceled in 1984 after several seasons of declining ratings.

Through it all, Sha Na Na soldiered on. While the nostalgic novelty act boasts an atypical discography, consisting mostly of soundtrack work, compilations, and live recordings, it is a large one, consisting of more than forty releases . . . and even more, if you factor in individual members' solo projects.

Sha Na Na still exists today, though the ever-growing roster of former members (forty-four and counting) is beginning to rival that of Blood, Sweat, and Tears . . . or Columbia University's alumni database. As this book went to press, Sha Na Na was gearing up for its fiftieth anniversary tour in 2019, and will soon be on a stage near you, bidding a whole new generation of doo-wop fans "Goodnight Sweetheart."

33

Jimi Hendrix

Gypsy, Sun, and Rainbows

The non-violence, the very, very good brand of music—I don't mean "good," I mean the very true brand of music. The acceptance of the long-awaited crowd, how they had to sleep in mud and rain and get hassled by this, hassled by that, and still come through, saying that it was a successful festival. That's one of the good things. There's so many stories that you can add up on this thing, if you added them all up, you know, you feel like a king.

—Jimi Hendrix to Mike Eisgrau, onsite reporter for WNEW FM 102.7

As the Seeds Were Sown: From Johnny Allen to James Marshall to Jimi

Johnny Allen Hendrix, a Sagittarius, was born in Seattle on November 27, 1942, to Al and Lucille Hendrix; at age three, his father changed his name to James Marshall Hendrix. Jimmy, as he was known then, walked around playing air guitar and strumming on brooms to the point where people were becoming concerned about him. One day, he found a ukulele in the garbage, and that became his first musical instrument. Lucille would not live to hear her son play professionally. She died at thirty-three from a ruptured spleen, after suffering from cirrhosis of the liver.

Fifteen-year-old Jimmy received an acoustic guitar as a gift from a family friend during his freshman year. He immersed himself in blues records, watched others play, asked questions, and practiced for hours on end. He formed a band called the Velvetones, whereupon he realized his acoustic wouldn't work well in a band context. He needed an electric guitar. Al bought Jimmy a Sopro Ozark 1560 S, which he stored backstage at Birdland, the club where he played with his second band, the Rocking Kings. When the guitar was stolen, Al refused to replace it, so the Rocking Kings chipped in to buy Jimmy a white Silvertone Danelectro. Jimmy painted it red, and would go on to play it with several other bands.

When eighteen-year-old Jimmy got into trouble for joyriding in stolen cars, the judge offered him a choice: join the army or do jail time. He enlisted on May 31, 1961, did his basic training at California's Fort Ord, and was assigned to the 101st Airborne Division at Fort Campbell, Kentucky. Jimmy wrote to his father and asked him to send the guitar. He met a bass-playing fellow soldier named Billy Cox, and the two began jamming with other servicemen as the Casuals. Jimmy made it through paratrooper training, earning his Screaming Eagles patch in January 1962. But, like comic-strip soldier Beetle Bailey, Private Hendrix was unmotivated, a poor shot, often late, and known to sneak off for naps. He was deemed unsuitable for service, and granted an honorable discharge on June 29.

Jimmy regrouped with Cox upon the bass player's discharge in September 1963. They formed the King Kasuals down in Tennessee, and worked a series of clubs known collectively as the Chitlin' Circuit. It was during this period that Jimmy learned tricks like playing guitar with his teeth, and playing behind his head.

Within six years of Woodstock, Jimmy's career trajectory became meteoric. He became a sideman for blues, soul, and R&B legends Solomon Burke, "Wicked" Wilson Picket, Otis Redding, Sam Cooke, Slim Harpo, Jackie Wilson, and the Marvelettes. In early 1964, he made his way to Harlem, where he won an amateur hour at the Apollo Theater. The Isley Brothers hired him to play on their single "Testify," his first recording. By May, he had played on Don Covay's Top 50 hit "Mercy Mercy," and on Rosa Lee Brooks's "My Diary" b/w "Utee," and had hit the road with the Isleys. He stayed with the group for nine months before he grew bored of playing the same songs every night.

Little Richard, in the midst of staging a comeback, hired Jimmy for his backing band, the Upsetters. Jimmy stuck around long enough to play on Richard's 1965 single "I Don't Know What You Got but It's Got Me" and for a TV appearance on Nashville's *Night Train*. In a delicious bit of irony, Richard was "upset" by Hendrix's flamboyant stage antics, and Richard's brother Robert gave Jimmy the boot in late July.

Jimmy rejoined the Isleys to record "Move Over and Let Me Dance," before joining Curtis Knight and the Squires. While with the Squires, Jimmy continued to do session work for the likes of King Curtis, and signed his first recording contract with PPX Studios' Ed Chalpin . . . for one dollar. While playing at the Cheetah Club, Hendrix caught the eye of Keith Richards's girlfriend, Linda Keith.

During the third week of May 1966, Hendrix headed down to Greenwich Village to form his *own* band, Jimmy James and the Blue Flames. After the group landed a residency at Café Wha?, Linda Keith urged Rolling Stones manager Andrew Loog Oldham to represent the guitarist, but he declined. Undaunted, she appealed to the Animals' former bass player, Chas Chandler, who was moving into management and production. Chandler checked out Jimmy James and the Blue Flames at Café' Wha? and was impressed . . . with Hendrix; not so much with the Blue Flames.

Chandler and his partner Michael Jeffery persuaded Hendrix to accompany them to England. They also convinced him to drop "Jimmy James" in favor of the alternate spelling, Jimi Hendrix. Furthermore, they had a band name in mind: the Jimi Hendrix Experience. They recruited bass player Noel Redding and drummer Mitch Mitchell, and brought Hendrix to meet and jam with Cream.

On October 13, 1966, the Jimi Hendrix Experience debuted in France, opening for Johnny Hallyday. Five days later, the band's October 18 performance at Paris's Olympia Theatre was captured on tape. That led to a recording deal with Kit Lambert and Chris Stamp, who had just launched Track Records.

The group's first single, a cover of Billy Roberts's 1962 song "Hey Joe" b/w "Stone Free," hit the shelves and airwaves on October 23, and had peaked at UK #6 by year's end. Jimi was the talk of the town, and members of the Beatles, the Stones, and the Who all came to watch him perform. An interview in London's *Record Mirror* was followed by appearances on the BBC's *Top of the Pops* and *Ready Steady Go!*

When a local journalist made the offhand comment that Hendrix should set his guitar on fire, Chandler sent out for lighter fluid. Hendrix first performed the flaming finale at the London Astoria on March 31, 1967, and the press ate it up. More singles followed: "Purple Haze" in March and "The Wind Cries Mary" in May.

The Chandler-produced album *Are You Experienced* debuted on May 12, 1967, and hit #2 in the UK, second *only* to the Beatles' *Sgt. Pepper's Lonely Hearts Club Band*. It wouldn't be released in the United States until August 23. Meanwhile, on the recommendation of Paul McCartney, the Jimi Hendrix Experience made its American debut on June 18 at the Monterey International Pop Festival, complete with flaming finale. The iconic image of Hendrix on his knees in front of the blazing guitar immortalized one of the defining moments in rock history.

The Experience hit the road, playing legendary California venues like the Whisky a Go Go, the Fillmore, and Golden Gate Park. The Monkees featured Jimi as their opening act, too, but the unusual pairing lasted only six shows.

Chandler wasted no time getting the band back in the studio. *Axis: Bold As Love* debuted on December 1, 1967, and went on to hit #5 in the UK. The 1968 American release fared even better, peaking at #3. Hendrix began to reveal himself as a perfectionist. His demands and obsessiveness in the studio led to conflicts with Chandler and Redding, which would intensify during sessions for the third album.

The *Electric Ladyland* sessions became fragmented. Chandler cut ties with the demanding Hendrix following the July sessions. Redding had one foot out the door already, and formed another band, Fat Mattress. The final sessions lasted from April through August, and the double album was released in October. Among the highlights are the fifteen-minute "Voodoo Chile," featuring Stevie Winwood on organ and Jefferson Airplane's Jack Casady on bass; and Jimi's groundbreaking arrangement of Dylan's "All Along the Watchtower."

Electric Ladyland was the Jimi Hendrix Experience's first—and *last*—#1 album, and though reviews were mixed, it is now considered to be among the greatest of all time. By the summer of 1969, however, the Jimi Hendrix Experience was no more. The group played its final,

The other end of Hendrix's 1967 May–December pair of albums, *Axis: Bold as Love* found him being much more hands-on during studio sessions.

nine-song set at the Denver Pop Festival on Sunday, June 29. The next morning, Redding got on a plane for London.

Jimi had been looking to expand his sound beyond the power-trio format, and the split with Redding afforded the perfect opportunity. He reunited with Billy Cox, and had him reach out to fellow veteran Larry Lee, just back from a tour of duty in Vietnam, to play rhythm guitar. Curiously, instead of adding a keyboardist, Jimi enhanced the rhythm section instead, adding conga players Juma Sultan and Jerry Velez. Jimi's drummer friend Buddy Miles (Wilson Picket's band; The Electric Flag) was available, too, but he decided to stick with Mitchell.

When Jimi learned he'd be headlining the upcoming Woodstock festival, time was of the essence. With just a couple of weeks to spare, Mitch flew back from London. The nameless, experimental lineup convened at Jimi's upstate house to rehearse, though by most accounts the players never really clicked.

Jimi and the band were to be paid $32,000 on the premise that they'd do two sets ($15,000 per set, plus $2,000 for expenses). There *had* been some discussion about Jimi doing an acoustic set on Friday, and then closing out the festival on Sunday at midnight. Neither of those things happened.

Michael Jeffery supposedly *insisted* that Jimi was the headliner, and that Jimi must go on *last*. But John Morris remembers things quite differently, recalling that Jeffery was easy to deal with and very accommodating.

As one reads through all of the conflicting and contradictory accounts of Hendrix at Woodstock, one realizes that what "happened" depends largely upon one's personal perspective. To borrow one of Michael Lang's lines, as immortalized in the *Woodstock* film, "The point is that it happened." The "truth," if ever there were such a thing, has long since been obscured by myth.

In the Garden: No Experience Necessary

By most accounts there were a mere thirty thousand bedraggled, muddy souls in attendance when Jimi took the stage at 9:00 a.m. Monday, and that was just fine with Jimi. He hated large crowds. And, with less than two weeks of rehearsal, the band wasn't quite ready.

Chip Monck announced, "Ladies and gentlemen, the Jimi Hendrix Experience," which was *not* the introduction Hendrix had in mind. The guitarist, who reportedly hadn't slept for three days, spoke next. "I see that we meet again. Yeah, well, well, well." As the crowd erupted, Hendrix attempted to set the record straight:

Dig what I was gonna say. We got tired of the Experience, and every once in a while it was blowin' our minds too much, so we decided to change the whole thing around and call it Gypsy, Sun, and Rainbows. For short, it's nothin' but a Band of Gypsys. We have Billy Cox playing bass. And from Nashville, Tennessee, we have Larry Lee playing guitar over there. Larry Lee. We got Juma playing congas over here. Juma. And we have a heart of . . . Granny Goose . . . excuse me, Mitch Mitchell on drums. And then we got Gerry Velez on congas, too. We got yours truly, healthy, but so what, me worry? . . . Give us about a minute and a half to tune up, okay? Like, we've only had about two rehearsals, so, uh, doing nothing but primary rhythm things, but I mean it's the first ray of the new rising sun, anyways, so it must be starting from the earth, which is rhythm, all right? Can you dig that? When you get your old lady and then you get to a room, and that makes the melody, right?

As the musicians tuned, an audience member offered Jimi some recreational pharmaceuticals: "Jimi! Want some?" Jimi, ever polite, chuckled and said, "I have mine, thank you. I have mine. Thank you very much."

If the audience was expecting a polished run-through of the Jimi Hendrix Experience's hits, they were in for a surprise. What they were about to witness was more of an open-house rehearsal for thirty thousand.

The Band of Gypsys launched into the unreleased "Message to Love," with its life-affirming declaration, "I am what I am. Thank God." The audience greeted the new material enthusiastically, prompting Jimi to say, "Yeah, thanks very much. Overall, that was a thing called 'Message to Universe,' something to get the rats out of your bums . . . and I'd like to go ahead on with another slow thing we'd like to keep on with a little bit of a jam we've been messing around with back at the house. I think I'm gonna call it 'Getting My Heart Back Together Again.' We never stood this far apart from each other. Except when . . . we're gonna do this next song because it's the next one that we know."

By this point, some of the audience members were growing impatient, and they began calling out requests: "Fire!" Hendrix may have been teasing the crowd when he said, "Okay, I think we know about two more songs . . . okay, I think we've got about two more songs that we know . . . we're going to do a slow song, very, very slow and quiet, you know, something to play in the mud with. . . . You want to do that one?"

The band got it together for "Getting My Heart Back Together Again," better known later on as "Hear My Train A-Comin'." Hendrix had been fiddling with this song since 1967 and had recorded it many times, but it was never released during his lifetime. He was never satisfied with it, though the rumbling, bluesy jam laid down by the rhythm section that morning gave him plenty of room to do what he did best: wail away on the guitar.

Afterward, there was a lull in the action. Mitch tapped out a few notes, eager for some momentum. Jimi, rarely a complainer, asked, "Are these microphones all screwed up again, as usual? Yeah? . . . I know what you mean. It's so embarrassing, man. I'm sittin' up here. And people lookin' at me too, man; damn, half a million eyes. Tell somebody to turn off the microphones while we get in tune, all right?"

After a minute or two of tuning, Jimi apologized. "We're very sorry for the delays, but, like, we're tryin' to get things together in between time, because, like I said before, we only jammed a couple of times. But, like I said before, it's the first ray, you know, so there's a whole lot more to go."

The wait was worth it, as the group launched into a nearly ten-minute version of "Spanish Castle Magic," from *Axis: Bold as Love*. The momentum was beginning to build. Next, the band tried something familiar: "Red House," from the UK edition of *Are You Experienced*. Jimi broke his high *E* string, but he didn't miss a beat as he continued playing with five. While Jimi changed strings, Larry Lee—dressed similarly to Hendrix, save for his Gibson Les Paul and the odd green scarf he wore, half-covering his eyes—delivered his unreleased song "Mastermind."

Jimi returned with a playful, flirtatious intro. "Yeah, there's a lot of girlfriends that we love to try to sing about sometimes. We're gonna sing about this one over there in the [unclear] section over there. The one with the yellow underpants on . . . yeah, yeah, you; I remember you last night, there, baby. He he he, ha ha ha. I seen the dirty old man licked your bicycle seat when he was goin' down the street . . . oh, messy, messy."

And, with that, Hendrix's guitar soared into the opening notes of "Foxy Lady," the first track on the UK edition of the debut album, as Billy's bass made its presence known.

When the momentum slipped again, Jimi appeared self-conscious. "Yeah, I know. We're tuning up between every single song, and this is not together and that's not together . . . we all ate in uniform." Jimi mumbled a little, laughed nervously, and said, "You all waited all morning? Golly, I really feel . . . I really hope that, uh, maybe by tomorrow morning we can get *something* together."

More discussion followed. "Yeah, well, like I said before we only ran over a few numbers, so we'd like to try to do this one we was just jammin' at the house. We don't have a name for it, yet. It's just like a instrumental—we'll just float along with it. It goes something like this."

After some fidgety, last-minute tuning, the band dived into the instrumental that came to be known as "Jam Back at the House (Beginnings)." The audience really seemed to get into it, which appeared to bolster Jimi's spirits.

"Before we go any further, we'd like to say, man, y'all had a lot of patience, three days' worth. You've proved to the world what can happen. A little bit of love, and understanding, and *sounnndsss!*" he announced, as he proceeded to make his guitar howl.

Oh, I left my girlfriend at home, I'm sorry. Anyway, we'd like to say we really appreciate you all having patience with us, because this really, really, is nerve-wracking, man—that's why we waited 'til the sunup, and maybe the new day might give us a chance, I don't know, blah-blah, woof-woof. The sky church is still here, as you can see. We'd like to do this song and dedicate it to maybe a soldier in the army singing about his old lady that he dreams about, and humpin' a machine gun instead . . . or it could be a cat, maybe, trying to fall in love with a girl, maybe, but a little bit too scared. That's where the problems come from sometimes, isn't it? I mean, the cat's really insecure a little bit, so they call girls "groupies," and they call girls this, and they call passive people "hippies" and blah-blah, woof-woof on down the line. That's because they fuckin' not in love, man. That's what's happenin'. That's the other half of a man is a woman, and we'd like to play a thing called "Izabella." And don't you ever forget it.

Once again, the transition from preamble to song was fraught with tuning, but the unreleased "Izabella" was well worth the wait.

Speaking of soldiers, next it was time for a double shot from the recently discharged Larry Lee—a soulful break as he played and sang lead on a pair of Curtis Mayfield tunes, "Gypsy Woman" and "Aware of Love."

Jimi returned to *Are You Experienced* for "Fire," and then mixed it up with the unreleased "(Here He Comes) Lover Man," which ended with a flourish. He and the band were about to about to hit their stride. "Thank you very much," he said. "And I would say thank you very much again for all your patience for waiting all these three years to come here and stand a little bit of rain. I'd like to do a thing that . . . a new American anthem until we get another one together. It's called 'Voodoo Child (Slight Return).'"

Jimi's 1967 debut hit the shelves while he and the band were still based in England, but after the Monterey Pop Festival, American audiences embraced their flamboyant native son.

The ensuing, nearly fourteen-minute rendition was appended with a bit of "Stepping Stone," an as-yet-unreleased single. An energized and cheerful Jimi introduced the band again, mid-song, and offered more spacy commentary about the band's name, chuckling as he did so. "And the name of the group is the Southern Rainbows . . . you can call it Band of Gypsys, anything you want to."

The band kept chugging along. Toward the end, Jimi started giving indications (prematurely, as it turned out) that the set was coming to a close. "I'd like to say thank you very much; goodnight. I'd like to say peace, yeah, and happiness. Happiness, yeah." But the band surged forward. "Thank you. You can leave if you want to; we're just jamming, that's all, okay? You can leave or you can hang." But the jam went on, seemingly propelled by a will of its own.

As Jimi plucked the final notes, he pivoted and did something nobody—not even the band—was expecting. With fellow veterans Lee and Cox behind him, he launched into a history-making rendition of "The Star-Spangled Banner," using his guitar virtuosity to recreate the sounds of rockets' red glare and bombs bursting in air. But the set couldn't end there. Next, Jimi forged straight into his hit single "Purple Haze," the opening track on the US edition of *Are You Experienced.*

"Purple Haze" gave way to an extended period of jamming. Later, this portion of the show would be labeled as two distinct pieces, "Woodstock Improvisation" and "Villanova Junction," but at the time Jimi *really* was just making it up as he went along. The bluesy jam came in for a gentle landing, and the exhausted audience erupted into cheers, calling, and then rhythmically *chanting*, for more.

The band returned for an encore, but Jimi didn't seem to know what to play. The audience had *plenty* of suggestions though, screaming out, "Watchtower!" "Stone Free!" and "Wild Thing!" Chuckling nervously, Jimi said, "Yeah, man, absolutely. We're going to try to think of something to play for a second, hold on a second. Wait a minute. Yeah, well we didn't practice any of our own songs, you know—we're just messing around with some other things, because you get kind of tired, you know? Don't you get kind of tired? Anybody get kind of tired?"

Finally, Jimi had an idea. "Okay, now don't laugh at us. We're going to try this one song called 'Valleys of Neptune.' Oh, I don't know, I forgot the words to that one. I can't do that one. What do you want to do then?"

When he was through teasing the audience, Jimi launched into an encore *everyone* knew, "Hey Joe." It would be the final song of the festival, bringing the proceedings to a fitting conclusion. Jimi worked "Goodbye, everybody" into the lyrics, and then brought it on home with a joyful burst of feedback. And, just like that, it was all over.

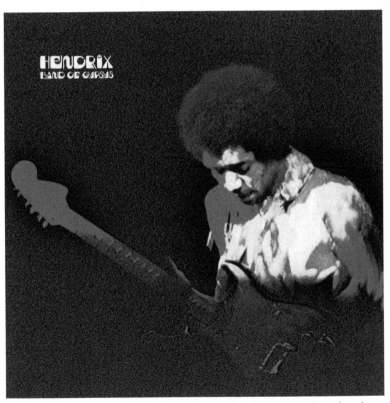

On New Year's Day, 1970, at the dawn of a new decade, Jimi Hendrix played two shows at the Fillmore East with bassist Billy Cox and drummer Buddy Miles. The shows were recorded and yielded this remarkable live album, highlighted by the anti-Vietnam masterpiece "Machine Gun."

The Harvest Reaped: A Bitter Pill to Swallow

Jimi collapsed from exhaustion after the show and slept deeply. He would not be appearing on Dick Cavett's Woodstock-themed show with Crosby, Stills, Joni, and the Jefferson Airplane later that evening. He would only play twice more with Gypsy, Sun, and Rainbows before disbanding the group. He turned up on *The Dick Cavett Show* on September 9 to discuss the festival, and described his version of "The Star-Spangled Banner" as "beautiful," while Cavett took pains to remind his audience that Hendrix was a veteran.

Michael Jeffery longed for a return to form with the Jimi Hendrix Experience, and began plotting Redding's return. Jimi still had a contractual obligation to Ed Chalpin, so he grabbed Billy and drummer Buddy Miles to ring in the New Year with four shows over two days at the Fillmore East. The shows were recorded for a live album.

When the Band of Gypsys performed at a January 28 benefit at Madison Square Garden for the Moratorium Committee (an anti–Vietnam War organization), there were bad vibes. Someone dosed Jimi with acid, and the set fell apart when he walked off in the middle of the opening song, "Earth Blues." Jeffery fired Buddy Miles, and Billy quit in protest.

In spite of Jeffery's maneuvering, and the public's perception of a reunion, Jimi had no intention of working with Redding again. When Redding showed up for rehearsals, Jimi made a power play and told him that he was out and Cox was in.

The Fillmore East New Year's shows were released as *Band of Gypsys* on March 25, to mixed reviews. The centerpiece is the nearly thirteen-minute "Machine Gun," a brooding and haunting antiwar song that many consider to be Hendrix's magnum opus. But the road beckoned.

The American leg of the Cry of Love tour consisted of thirty-two shows from coast to coast, and wrapped up in Honolulu on August 1. The new lineup was billed as the New Jimi Hendrix Experience, or the Cry of Love Band. Jimi played the Atlanta International Pop Festival on the Fourth of July, when the audience peaked at an estimated five hundred thousand.

While the group toured, work continued on Jimi's pet project, Electric Lady Studios in Greenwich Village. He'd barely had an opportunity to use it since it became functional, and the European leg of the tour was imminent. They cut the ribbon for a grand opening celebration on August 25–26, before jetting off for the Isle of Wight Festival.

Jimi's headlining performance in the wee hours of August 31 had echoes of the Grateful Dead's at Woodstock: his amp was picking up the security guards' walkie-talkies and broadcasting their transmissions, which made for an eerie rendition of "Machine Gun." But the tour was not going well. Jimi was depressed, unhappy with his management, and showing the wear and tear of too much LSD, speed, pot, booze, and hash. He wanted nothing more than to be back in New York enjoying his new studio, and his performances became erratic. He bailed out in the middle of a gig in Denmark, offering the cryptic remark, "I've been dead a long time now."

Mercifully, the tour came to an end after a disastrous performance at Germany's Isle of Fehmarn Festival on September 6. The band flew back to London, where Jimi continued to exhibit signs of depression. Billy, meanwhile, suffered a bad acid trip and split for home. Jimi got up to jam with Eric Burdon and War at a club on September 16, but he was clearly not himself.

Jimi spent his last night on this earth with his girlfriend, Monika Dannemann, at the Smarkand Hotel. At some point during an evening spent eating and drinking and visiting a friend's party, he'd taken nine of Dannemann's prescription sleeping pills. When she awoke at 11:00 a.m. on September 18, Jimi was unresponsive. Nearly twenty minutes elapsed before she called for an ambulance, and another nine before paramedics arrived. Jimi was rushed to St. Mary Abbot's Hospital, where he was pronounced dead at 12:45 p.m. The official cause of death was asphyxia. The barbiturates in his system were the culprit. He was twenty-seven years old. His body was laid to rest near his mother, Lucille, at Greenwood Cemetery in Renton, a suburb outside of Seattle, on October 1.

With a wealth of recorded material in the vault, it wasn't long before the parade of posthumous album releases began. *Cry of Love* and *Rainbow Bridge* hit the shelves in 1971, followed by *War Heroes* (1972), *Loose Ends* (1974), *Crash Landing* and *Midnight Lightning* (1975), *Nine to the Universe* (1980), *First Rays of the New Rising Sun* and *South Southern Delta* (1997), *Valleys of Neptune* (2010), *People, Hell and Angels* (2013), and *Both*

Sides of the Sky (2018). And this was just the studio material. Beginning with *Woodstock II* (1971), Hendrix was captured live, in concert, on twenty-seven different live album releases, most recently *Machine Gun: The Fillmore East First Show* (2016). Additionally, his music appears on two film soundtrack albums, nineteen anthologies, and there have been twenty-eight two-sided singles released . . . so far.

Jimi's legacy has attained almost mythological proportions since his untimely demise. One might even say that Hendrix has achieved a type of immortality as he continues to astound and influence new generations of guitarists, none of whom—thus far—has been his equal.

34

As Ye Sow, So Shall Ye Reap

The Legacy of Woodstock

Ladies and gentlemen, thank you so very much. We've got one little last trip we'd like to lay on you, if it's at all possible. There's a couple of packages of garbage bags here. If, on your way out, you wouldn't mind taking one, filling it up, and leaving it where you fill it, that certainly would be appreciated. Anything you can do to give us a hand to leave this area somewhat the way we found it . . . I don't think it will ever be quite the same . . . but somewhat the way we found it, it certainly would be appreciated. It's been a delight seeing you. May we wish you anything that the person next to you wishes for you; good wishes, good day, and a good life. Thank you.

—*Chip Monck, in his farewell address to the dregs of the Woodstock festival audience on Monday morning*

Cleaned Up and Cleaned Out

Max Yasgur's alfalfa field took quite a beating during the festival. It took dozens of volunteers several days using bulldozers and a fire pit to get rid of all the trash.

The financial mess took a little longer to resolve. Woodstock Ventures' plan to build a recording studio with the "profits" from the festival would have to wait. They had gone over budget by at least 300 percent. They were forced to refund up to eighteen thousand ticket fees to people who

The iconic dove-and-guitar imagery of the classic festival
poster was reimagined for this *Woodstock* movie poster—one
of several different designs—and it is beautiful in its simplicity. Note that "love" has now been added on to the old "3 Days
of Peace & Music" subtitle.

were unable to get to the festival site. They were $1.4 million in debt, and
had to spend months settling roughly eighty lawsuits from neighboring
property owners.

Artie Kornfeld and Michael Lang sold their stock in Woodstock
Ventures back to Roberts and Rosenman for $31,750 apiece. It would take
some time, but with the success of the film, the investors eventually broke
even and turned a profit. They are earning residuals to this day.

There was some talk—mostly idle—about doing it all over again in
1970, but that wasn't in Max Yasgur's plans. As far as he was concerned,
it was back to the dairy business as usual. Sadly, it would not be for long.

Max suffered a heart attack and passed away in 1973, aged fifty-three, leaving his land to an uncertain future.

As the years passed, Yasgur's estate began selling off parcels of land. A Brooklyn auto-glass shop owner, Louis Nicky, purchased 37.5 acres in 1981—a parcel that included the stage area. Three years later, Wayne Saward built the concrete-and-cast-iron monument that stands there to this day. Nicky passed away just before the festival's twentieth anniversary in 1989, and bequeathed the land to June Gelish, who had little interest in the festival's legacy. She would spend the next seven years doing everything in her power to keep curiosity seekers away from the site, and acquiring more and more of the surrounding land.

On July 30, 1996, Gelish sold out to Allan Gerry, who paid her $1 million for 1,400 acres, including the festival site and much of the surrounding area.

Bethel Woods Center for the Arts and the Museum at Bethel Woods

Gerry was much more sensitive to the historical significance of the site, and to the idea of hosting live shows. The Gerry Foundation, with a $15 million contribution from New York State, set about the $40 million development project that, on July 1, 2006, would open to the public as the Bethel Woods Center for the Arts.

Six weeks later, on August 13, Crosby, Stills, Nash, and Young performed there for sixteen thousand fans—a much more modest crowd than the one that had greeted them thirty-seven years earlier. The project was fully realized on June 2, 2008, when the Museum at Bethel Woods opened its doors.

Michael Wadleigh's *Woodstock*: The Medium and the Message

Michael Wadleigh faced a daunting task, post-festival: culling through 120 miles of film on a thousand reels to come up with a reasonable-length theatrical release. The resulting three-hour-and-five-minute film arrived in theaters on March 26, 1970. It would go on to win "Best Documentary" at the 1971 Academy Awards.

With a budget of just $600,000, Woodstock grossed $50,000,000 in the United States alone. This film, more so than anything else, became the defining source document of the festival. Judging by many of the performers' accounts of Woodstock, the film shaped, codified, and in some cases severely distorted their recollections of that fabled weekend.

Of the thirty-two acts that performed at the Woodstock Music and Art Fair, only seventeen appear in the film, leaving fifteen on the cutting room floor. Among the film's absentees are Sweetwater, Bert Sommer, the Incredible String Band, Tim Hardin, Ravi Shankar, Melanie, Quill, Keef Hartley, Mountain, the Grateful Dead, Creedence Clearwater Revival, the Band, Blood, Sweat and Tears, Johnny (and Edgar) Winter, and the Paul Butterfield Blues Band.

For all intents and purposes, you can include Canned Heat in the omission file. Though "Going Up the Country" does appear on the original theatrical release's soundtrack, it is a studio recording, not the version the band played at the festival. Additionally, apart from depicting Richie Havens as the festival opener, and Jimi Hendrix as the closer, the film plays fast and loose with the order of the performances.

In 1994, a twenty-fifth-anniversary Directors' Cut was released on VHS and DVD. This iteration padded the running time by forty minutes, with more footage of Jimi Hendrix and Jefferson Airplane, as well as footage of Canned Heat and Janis Joplin.

The ante was upped fifteen years later with the 2009 40th Anniversary Edition. This was made available on DVD and Blu-Ray in two versions, a "Special Edition" (two discs) and an "Ultimate Collector's Edition" (three discs). The larger of the two added two more hours of performances, bringing fans their first view of sets by the Paul Butterfield Blues Band, the Grateful Dead, Mountain, Creedence Clearwater Revival, and Johnny Winter. It also featured additional footage of Joan Baez, Canned Heat, Joe Cocker, the Who, Jefferson Airplane, Country Joe McDonald, and Santana.

When Woodstock: 3 Days of Peace and Music: The Director's Cut, 40th Anniversary Revisited was released in 2014, it was essentially the same as the 2009 release, but with more HD and Blu-Ray bonus tracks.

Enterprising motel magnate Eliot Tiber returned to the headlines in 2009 when his version of the Woodstock events was chronicled in the Ang Lee film *Taking Woodstock*. The film is based on Tiber's 2007 memoir *Taking Woodstock: A True Story of a Riot, a Concert, and a Life*.

Shortly after ringing in 2019, Michael Lang, once again a partner in Woodstock Ventures, announced plans for Woodstock 50, to be held at Watkins Glen on August 16, 17, and 18. Carlos Santana was the first to announce his participation, and approximately forty acts will be on the bill. Meanwhile, the Bethel Woods Center for the Arts announced plans for a fiftieth anniversary concert on the site of the original festival. Officially named the Bethel Woods Music and Culture Festival, it too will take place from August 16 through 18. No lineup has been announced at press time, but reportedly some of the biggest acts in the world have been approached. Suffice it to say that these competing festivals will be stories for another time.

For the Record: *Woodstock: Music from the Original Soundtrack and More* . . . and Still More

Hot on the heels of the hit film came the three-record set *Woodstock: Music from the Original Soundtrack and More*. Like the film, the album, released on May 11, 1970, plays fast and loose with the festival's running order. Side one kicks off with John Sebastian's "I Had a Dream," and the set goes on to feature performances by Canned Heat, Richie Havens, Country Joe and the Fish, Arlo Guthrie, Sha Na Na, Country Joe McDonald, Joan

The *Woodstock* soundtrack album; like the film, the three-record set plays fast and loose with the order of performances, yet manages to become a work of art unto itself.

Baez, CSN (and CSNY), the Who, Joe Cocker, Santana, Ten Years After, Jefferson Airplane, Sly and the Family Stone, the Paul Butterfield Blues Band, and Jimi Hendrix. The version of CSNY's "Sea of Madness" heard here isn't even from Woodstock, but is taken from a Fillmore East show a month later.

The following year, on July 12, 1971, Melanie and Mountain were added to the mix for a double album, *Woodstock Two*. The twenty-fifth anniversary year, 1994, saw several releases, including a twelve-track single-CD compilation, *The Best of Woodstock*. A more complete picture of the festival began to take shape with *Woodstock: Three Days of Peace and Music*, a four-CD set that blends selections from both original albums with additional tracks and stage announcements. This was concurrent with the release of the fourteen-track *Woodstock Diary*.

The fortieth anniversary saw the release of the six-CD set *Woodstock: 40 Years On: Back to Yasgur's Farm*, which contains even more

Released about a year after the first *Woodstock* album, *Woodstock 2* features performances from the festival that did *not* make it into the 1970 film.

performances and stage announcements. Every artist who performed at the festival is represented here, with three notable exceptions: the Band, Ten Years After, and the Keef Hartley Band. (None of Keef's set has ever seen the light of day on an official release.) The most ambitious release that year had to be *The Woodstock Experience*, a ten-CD set that features festival performances and studio material by five Woodstock alumni: Santana, Janis Joplin, Sly and the Family Stone, Jefferson Airplane, and Johnny Winter.

Getting Back to the Garden: Woodstock Revivals, Big and Small

Max Yasgur may or may not have been open to the idea of renting out his land for another go-around in 1970, but the point became moot on Election Day 1969, when the town of Bethel gave its supervisor the boot.

Later, the town and New York State enacted legislation against mass gatherings, in hopes of avoiding future festivals. The ominous vibrations and fallout from the Altamont Speedway Free Festival on December 6 served to quell talk of large outdoor music festivals . . . but only for a while.

Woodstock 1979: Ten Years After, As It Were

On the occasion of Woodstock's tenth anniversary, festival alumni descended upon a different kind of garden, Madison Square Garden. There, fans watched Richie Havens, Canned Heat, Country Joe and the Fish, and Paul Butterfield, playing with Rick Danko of the Band. Twelve years later, the event would be packaged for video release as *The Celebration Continues: Woodstock '79*.

Woodstock Reunion 1979: Parr Meadows

The following month, on Saturday, September 8, several of the acts from the MSG show—Danko and Butterfield, Canned Heat, Richie Havens, and Country Joe McDonald—joined fellow Woodstock alums Stephen Stills,

Mountain's Leslie West, Santana's Michael Shrieve, Jefferson Airplane alumnus Jorma Kaukonen, Johnny Winter, and John Sebastian to perform at the Parr Meadows racetrack in Long Island for a crowd estimated at up to forty thousand. There was no official recording released, though bootlegs are out there.

Woodstock 1989: The Forgotten Woodstock

This twentieth-anniversary event just sort of *happened*. It's true. Legend has it that one guy, folk singer Rich Pell, showed up at the original festival site in Bethel with a guitar and started playing. Pell was not trespassing. He had obtained permission from June Gelish, and personally took care of all the staging details. It snowballed from there. Volunteers brought in sound equipment, lights, and staging, and the whole affair wound up looking and sounding very professional.

Woodstock alumnus Melanie Safka and Savoy Brown were the biggest names on the bill; the rest of the lineup featured local acts. Wavy Gravy (formerly Hugh Romney) and Merry Prankster/author Ken Kesey made the scene, along with a sea of music fans, including Jimi Hendrix's dad, Al.

The impromptu jams lasted for seven straight days. Local newspaper the *Sullivan County Democrat* covered the event and estimated that 150,000 people attended the festival. Spontaneous or not, the festival was recorded by a man named Barry Benson and packaged for release as *20th Anniversary Festival: A Musical Documentary of Woodstock '89*.

Philly Folly

While all of this was happening in Bethel, an event billed as "Remember Woodstock" was staged at the Imperial Hotel in Swan Lake by Philadelphia based Banner Productions. Melanie played this event, too, along with John Sebastian, but it was a disaster. Only about four hundred people showed up.

Woodstock 1994: 2 More Days of Peace and Music vs. Bethel '94 and Bernstein

The poster for Woodstock 1994, advertising "2 more days of peace and music," got it slightly wrong. It actually turned out to be three days, but they were peaceful, despite the large Saugerties crowd of 350,000.

The original idea, hatched by Woodstock Ventures in 1993, was to hold the twenty-fifth-anniversary festival in Bethel. But despite the town of Bethel's approval, Sullivan County pulled the plug on the plan, fearing the area was still ill equipped to handle a projected crowd of a quarter-million.

Concurrently, the current owner of the festival site, June Gelish, partnered with Robert Gersch on a plan to stage a festival of their own, but they faced some savvy competition. New York–based promoter Sid Bernstein—who told anyone who would listen that he was the man who brought the Beatles to America (which *is* partially true)—filed a proposal, and the Bethel Town Board gave him the nod. Unfortunately, Bernstein dropped the ball. He lacked sufficient funding to stage the event, and his outside investors bailed out when they saw that ticket sales were slow. The show *would* have featured Mountain, Richie Havens, and the omnipresent Melanie.

Meanwhile, Gersch and Gelish's event, billed as Bethel '94, went on as planned, with original festival alums Richie Havens, Melanie, Country Joe McDonald, Mountain, John Sebastian, Blood, Sweat, and Tears, Canned Heat, Sha Na Na, and Iron Butterfly (they made it *this* time), joining such noteworthy acts as the Chambers Brothers, Tom Paxton, Judy Collins, Leon Russell, and Fleetwood Mac.

Ultimately, Woodstock Ventures' forward-thinking, multi-generational Saugerties plan was the one that proved most successful. The lineup for Woodstock 1994: 2 More Days of Peace and Music featured the perfect blend of original festival alumni such as Santana, CSN, Joe Cocker, Country Joe McDonald, the Band (featuring Bob Weir of the Grateful Dead), plus veteran acts like Bob Dylan, Johnny Cash, Traffic, the Allman Brothers Band, Todd Rundgren, Peter Gabriel, and Aerosmith, along with more contemporary acts like Blind Melon, Blues Traveler, Collective Soul, Arrested Development, Cypress Hill, Green Day, the

Rollins Band, the Red Hot Chili Peppers, Primus, Youssou N'Dour, the Violent Femmes, Melissa Etheridge, the Spin Doctors, Salt 'N Pepa, Sheryl Crow, Orleans, Nine Inch Nails, and Metallica.

Przystanek Woodstock: Let's Take This Show on the Road

Imitation is the sincerest form of flattery. The free, annual Przystanek Woodstock, in Kustrin, Poland, with its theme of "Love, Friendship, and Music," first staged on July 15–16, 1995, has become in recent years *the* largest outdoor music festival in all of Europe, averaging around 625,000 concertgoers, down from a record-high of 750,000 in 2014.

A Day in the Garden 1998: Gerry Tests the Waters

After purchasing the 1,400 acres from Gelish, Allen Gerry decided to test the waters with a three-day-concert on August 14–16, on the twenty-ninth anniversary of the festival. This event featured Pete Townshend, Joni Mitchell, Don Henley, Stevie Nicks, and the Goo Goo Dolls. The festival went smoothly, but Gerry had bigger plans in mind (see Bethel Woods Center for the Arts and the Museum at Bethel Woods).

Woodstock 1999: When in Rome . . .

At certain times, Woodstock 1999, or Woodstock '99, was more reminiscent of the Rolling Stones' infamous Altamont Speedway concert than it was the original Woodstock. Things got just a little out of control in the oppressive hundred-degree July heat. There were fights, overdoses, bonfires, and at least one reported rape.

This *enormous* event, held two hundred miles further upstate from Bethel in Rome, New York, took place from July 22 through 25, at the decommissioned Griffiss Air Force Base. Unlike earlier iterations of Woodstock, Woodstock 1999 featured multiple stages—the West Stage, the East Stage, and the Emerging Artists Stage—and hosted *110* different acts, far too many to list. *None* of the acts from the original festival performed, though a few members of those original acts did, such as Mickey Hart of the Grateful Dead and John Entwistle of the Who. More than five hundred state troopers moonlighted as security at the site, and an estimated four hundred thousand people attended. Despite what the late Hunter S. Thompson might have called the "ominous vibrations," the festival was recorded, and a thirty-two-song sample was released as the two-disc set, *Woodstock 1999*.

Woodstock 2009: The Heroes of Woodstock Tour

Yes, *tour*. To celebrate the fortieth anniversary of the Woodstock Music and Art Fair, organizers tried a new approach. Rather than the traditional format in which musical pilgrims came to the mountain, they would bring the mountain to the pilgrims, in the form of a sixteen-date tour of North America, with stops in Michigan, Illinois, Ohio, Pennsylvania, New York (including an August 15 anniversary date at the Bethel Woods Center for the Arts), Connecticut, Massachusetts, Maine, Texas, Washington, and California.

Many familiar names and faces appeared along the way, including Canned Heat, Ten Years After, John Sebastian, Melanie, Mountain, and Country Joe McDonald, who performed at all of the shows and served as master of ceremonies. Other performers included former Grateful Dead member Tom Constanten, Jefferson Starship, the Levon Helm Band, Quicksilver Messenger Service, and Janis Joplin's former band, Big Brother and the Holding Company.

Thus far, there have been no official album or video releases from the Heroes of Woodstock tour, though ticket-holders were entitled to download MP3 soundboards of the concert(s) they attended.

Woodstock 2019: Reflections on Half a Century of Peace and Music

In 2009, Michael Lang (with Holly George Warren) published a memoir, *The Road to Woodstock*, while Artie Kornfeld published *The Pied Piper of Woodstock*, billing himself as the "Creator of Woodstock 1969." Earlier on, in 1979, Michael (and Jean Young) had published *Woodstock Festival Remembered*. But their former Woodstock Ventures partners Joel

Rosenman and John Roberts beat both of them to the bookstore shelves with their co-authored 1974 venture, *Young Men with Unlimited Capital.*

To the surprise of no one, the four have very different perspectives on their history-making 1969 concert, and relationships between them have been strained at times. By the time you read these words, fifty years—a half-century—will have passed since Artie Kornfeld and Michael Lang met with John Roberts and Joel Rosenman to begin the conversations that led to the Woodstock Music and Art Fair.

The festival, immortalized by various recording devices, remains as vibrant today as it did the day Richie Havens strode onto that Bethel stage, but the members of Woodstock Nation who made it all possible have begun to fade. From the time these words were written to the moment you opened this book, we are likely to have lost several more.

How best to preserve their legacy? How best to honor their memory? By planting gardens of our own, as Arlo Guthrie might say, inch-by-inch and row-by-row. All we need, as Country Joe once told us, is "good vibes, nice music, outdoors, and some snacks. It don't get better than that."

Joni was right, too. We *are* stardust. We are golden. And we've definitely got to get ourselves back to the garden. Let's roll up our sleeves and get a move on; there's work to be done. If you close your eyes, you can almost hear the helicopters in the distance.

Selected Bibliography

"13 Things You Didn't Know About Woodstock." *Huffington Post.* November 25, 2013.

Aaron, Peter. *The Band FAQ: All That's Left to Know About the Fathers of Americana.* Montclair: Backbeat Books. 2016.

Anderson, Miller. *Let It Rock.* DME (Dmitry M. Epstein) Interview with Miller Anderson. March 2008. www.dmme.net/interviews/mander.html

"Arlo Guthrie's 'Alice' Is Alive, Glad to Be Here." *Pittsburgh Post-Gazette.* November 22, 2026.

Baez, Joan. *And a Voice to Sing With.* New York: Summit. 1987.

Bethel Woods Center for the Arts. www.bethelwoodscenter.org.

Belmont, Bill. "Country Joe McDonald, Biography." www.countryjoe.com

Bowman, Rob. "Life Is a Carnival." *Goldmine.* 26 July 1991.

Boyd, Glen. *Neil Young FAQ: Everything Left to Know About the Iconic and Mercurial Rocker.* Montclair: Backbeat Books. 2012.

Bromberg, David N. "Jerry Garcia Interview." *Jazz and Pop.* February 1971.

Brown, Mick. "In Truth, Ravi Shankar Couldn't Stand the Hippies." *Telegraph.* December 12, 2012.

Corbett, Bernard M. Interview with Barry "The Fish" Melton. 2009.

Crosby, David, and Gottlieb, Carl. *Long Time Gone: The Autobiography of David Crosby.* New York: Doubleday, 1988.

Draper, Robert. "O Janis." *Texas Monthly.* October 1992.

Eder, Bruce. "Bert Sommer." www.allmusic.com

Eder, Bruce. "Blood, Sweat and Tears." www.allmusic.com

Eisgrau, Mike. Onsite Jimi Hendrix interview. WNEW FM 102.7. 1969.

Eskridge, Larry. "Woodstock Aftermath: Mud, Money, Memories." *Daily Ledger.* August 22, 2009.

Fornatale, Pete. *Back to the Garden: The Story of Woodstock.* New York: Touchstone, 2009

Fornatale, Pete. Pete Fornatale Radio Archives. 2009.

Harris, Will. "Michael McKean Sets the Record Straight on the Left Banke." *News, Reviews, and Interviews*. May 19, 2013.

Helm, Levon, and Steven Davis. *This Wheel's On Fire: Levon Helm and the Story of the Band*. New York: William Morrow and Company, Inc. 1993.

Hill, Michael. "50 Years Later, Dylan's Motorcycle Crash Remains Mysterious." Associated Press. July 28, 2016.

Jucha, Gary J. *Jimi Hendrix FAQ: All That's Left to Know About the Voodoo Child*. Montclair: Backbeat Books. 2013.

Lambo, John. *Melanie: The First Lady of Woodstock*. CreateSpace Independent Publishing Platform. December 15, 2011.

Lavezzoli, Peter. *The Dawn of Indian Music in the West* New York: Continuum Books. 2006.

Lesh, Phil. *Searching for the Sound: My Life With the Grateful Dead*. New York: Little, Brown, and Company. 2005

McCoy, Brian. "Woodstock at 45: David Sanborn Remembers." *Yeah Stub*. August 14, 2014.

Rickert, Jeremiah. "Interview with Bobby Columby." www.rdrop.com/users/rickert/bobby.html. April 2, 1998.

Rulmann, William. "Woody Guthrie. www.allmusic.com

Santana, Carlos. *The Universal Tone: Bringing My Story to Light*. New York: Little, Brown and Company. 2014.

Sclafani, Tony. *The Grateful Dead FAQ: All That's Left to Know About the Greatest Jam Band in History*. Montclair: Backbeat Books. 2013.

Scully, Rock, with David Dalton. *Living with the Dead: Twenty Years on the Bus with Garcia and the Grateful Dead*. New York: Little, Brown and Company. 1996.

Segretto, Mike. *The Who FAQ: All That's Left to Know About Fifty Years of Maximum R&B*. Montclair: Backbeat Books. 2014.

Selvin, Joel. *Sly and the Family Stone: An Oral History*. New York: Avon Books. 1998.

Setlist.fm.

Shankar, Anoushka. *Bapi: Love of My Life*. New Delhi: Lustre Press, Roli Books. 2002. New York: Little, Brown, and Company. 1996.

Shankar, Ravi. *My Music, My Life*. New York: Simon and Schuster Adult Publishing Group. 1968.

—. *Learning Indian Music: A Systematic Approach.* Fort Lauderdale: Onomatopoeia. 1979.

—, Harrison, George (ed.). *Raga Mala.* London: Genesis Publications. 1997.

Shepard, Richard F. "Pop Rock Festival Finds New Home." *New York Times.* July 23, 1969.

Sly and the Family Stone. www.slystonemusic.com/biography/

Stafford, James. "The (Kind of) Complete Woodstock: Paul Butterfield Blues Band." *Why It Matters: Music, Memoir, More.* March 15, 2013.

Sunrise Sunset. Sunrise and Sunset Times Calendar: August 1969, Bethel, New York, United States. www.sunrisesunset.com.

Thomsom, Graeme. "Tim Hardin: Remembering the Lost Genius of His Music." *Telegraph.* January 19, 2013.

Traguardo, Tony. "Catching Up with Melanie—Eurodisc Agenda 1994 Cover Story." *Tony Traguardo's Website . . . and Why Not. But More Importantly . . . Why?* March 2, 1994.

Tritt, Annie. "David Crosby's Schooner Muse." *Wall Street Journal.* 2012.

Van Stijgeren, Dolf. "4WaySite Catches Up with Greg Reeves." www.4WaySite.com. 2014.

Ward, Ed. "The Vagrants: A Hot '60s Band, for Exactly Four Years." *Fresh Air.* March 29, 2011.

Whitaker, Adrian. *Be Glad: An Incredible String Band Compendium.* London: Helter Skelter Publishing. 2013.

Woodstock Project, The. Woodstock Complete 2012. www.sahr.com/woodstockproject/woodstockcomplete2012/

Woodstock Timeline. *Times Herald Record.* www.recordonline.com. April 23, 2016.

World History Project: Woodstock Music and Art Fair 1969. www.worldhistoryproject.org

Index